Signifiers and Acts

SUNY series, Insinuations:
Philosophy, Psychoanalysis, Literature
Charles Shepherdson, editor

Signifiers and Acts

Freedom in Lacan's Theory of the Subject

ED PLUTH

State University of New York Press

Published by
State University of New York Press, Albany

Printed in the United States of America

For information, contact State University of New York Press, Albany, NY
www.sunypress.edu

Production by Diane Ganeles
Marketing by Anne M. Valentine

Library of Congress Cataloging-in-Publication Data

Pluth, Ed.
Signifiers and acts : freedom in Lacan's theory of the subject / Ed Pluth.
p. cm. — (SUNY series, insinuations : philosophy, psychoanalysis, literature)
Includes bibliographical references and index.
ISBN 978-0-7914-7243-9 (hardcover : alk. paper)
ISBN 978-0-7914-7244-6 (pbk. : alk. paper)
1. Lacan, Jacques, 1901–1981. 2. Psychoanalysis. 3. Psychoanalysis and philosophy. 4. Phenomenology. 5. Psycholinguistics. I. Title.

BF109.L23P58 2007
150.19′5092—dc22

2006101105

10 9 8 7 6 5 4 3 2 1

To An

Contents

Acknowledgments

An earlier version of part of chapter 4 was published as "*A Chè Vuoi?* Stage: Lacan's Theory of Subject Formation" in *ERR: The Journal of Affiliated Psychoanalytic Workgroups* 1:2 (2002): 25–32.

A modified version of chapter 1 was previously published as "Lacan's Subversion of the Subject" in Continental Philosophy Review. 39:3. July 2006. 293–312.

Chapter 6 is based on "How Acts Use Signifiers," previously published in *Journal for Lacanian Studies* 2:1 (2004): 18–33.

I would like to thank the many people who have been of help to me throughout the creation of this book. Fred Evans and Bruce Fink were fantastic mentors during its production, and their comments have made this work immeasurably better. Ed Casey, Dany Nobus, and Wilhelm Wurzer also made very helpful comments on an early draft. David Blomme, Dominiek Hoens, Sigi Jöttkandt, and Marc de Kesel were significant interlocutors during a very important part of this book's gestation period, and the group of researchers at the Cesuur study center in Ghent, Belgium, provided years of intellectual stimulation and conversation. Finally, enormous thanks are due to An Bulkens for constant support and insight. Dedicating this book to her is hardly enough, but it is a start.

Introduction

I had probably come across the phrase "philosophical anthropology" before, but I first really noticed it in a 1997 course guide for the philosophy department at the Catholic University of Leuven, Belgium. I was immediately struck by two things: what I thought was the datedness of the phrase, and the virtual nonexistence of it in the United States. This led me to wonder whether it was only in Belgium (or at least Belgian English) that people still talked about things such as philosophical anthropology. I was, of course, wrong. (I should add that the course was very interesting, and it was actually on the subject and trauma.)

A few years later the term came up again when I was trying to find a way to explain to myself something that was going on in Lacan's work. Although Lacan was primarily concerned with training analysts and developing a way in which he could teach the art (or science?) of psychoanalysis, he does make claims that go beyond the clinic. My concern was with describing the nature of these claims, and no other term came to mind but philosophical anthropology. Why was I not happy with this? Philosophical anthropology, I suppose, is an attempt to say something about what it is to be human in general. It is not simply philosophy, since it is not speaking about the nature of things in general, and it is not simply anthropology, since it is doing more than describing particular cultures. It is trying to describe what it means to be human—as such. And right away, one can guess why the phrase had a filthy aura about it for someone versed in contemporary continental philosophy. Could Lacan be anything other than ahistorical, Eurocentric, and imperialist in his attempt to say something about "the human" (man!) as such? And apart from the ethical and political objections one can make, there are serious epistemological problems too:

Can we possibly know what it is to be human in general, in all possible conditions? Do we have an experience of such a thing, or is this not just a silly invention of pure reason?

Lacan does seem to think that there are at least two cross-cultural and transhistorical factors involved in being human: No one is born speaking, and sexuality is initially experienced by each individual as a kind of trauma. But what is important is what occurs in the interaction of these two facts. Because of this, Lacan's work is not imperiously ahistorical. Although Lacan does seem to engage in a minimal amount of philosophical anthropology with some aspects of his ideas about language and sexuality, he avoids being imperialistic and ahistorical by granting importance to the specific historical and cultural configurations in which sexuality and language interact, in different ways.

I have absolutely no interest in rehabilitating a phrase such as philosophical anthropology, and certainly no interest in rehabilitating a discipline such as philosophical anthropology under a new name. But I am interested in addressing issues surrounding agency and subjectivity, and this is why I think Lacan's work is extremely useful and important. Instead of saying that Lacan is doing philosophical anthropology when his generalizations take him outside of the clinic, I would say that what he is doing is subject theory. This line of inquiry would be different from philosophical anthropology because its object is not "man" as such but something that may or may not be a feature of human life somewhere, sometimes—indicating how contingent the object of Lacan's study is. Philosophical anthropology would be concerned with articulating universal and necessary truths about "man." Subjects, although human, do not always occur when there is a human being, and this indicates already one of the major ways in which Lacan's use of the term *subject* differs from its traditional use. "Subjects," according to Lacan, are contingent products of a particular configuration of language and sexuality.

This could make Lacan sound like a typical poststructuralist antihumanist, perhaps eagerly awaiting the famous Foucauldian death of man. To an extent he may be, but he differs from most poststructuralists, precisely because he continues thinking about the subject. He formulates his project in exactly these terms:

> Psychoanalysis is neither a Weltanschauung, nor a philosophy that claims to provide the key to the universe. It is governed by a particular aim, which is historically defined by the elaboration of the notion of the subject. It poses this notion in a new way, by leading the subject back to its signifying dependence. (XI, 77/90)

While much of Lacan's work was concerned with unearthing this subject's dependence on signifiers, I will be arguing that this is only part of his approach. Even though the subject depends on signifiers, Lacan is far from holding that the subject is a mere plaything of structures, or that it is reducible to language.

How does the topic of the subject tend to be treated today, when it is preserved? Many contemporary theories, when they consider the topic at all, tend to focus on the subjected nature of the subject. Subjects are thought of in terms of being subject to things such as language, history, power, being, the given, the world, genetics, or the body. In line with this is the idea that agency, if it exists, is also to be situated outside of the conscious subject's domain. Agency is not located in a conscious act of decision but must be looked for in the various structures to which subjects are subjected: perhaps history and its deep structures determine the possibilities for our actions; perhaps it is the unconscious that acts and decides for us; perhaps being turns toward us or away from us; perhaps power relations determine our actions and possible revolts; perhaps genes make us what we are. If it can be said that a theory of the subject is preserved by these perspectives, then this subject tends to be dissolved into what determines it. In other words, the subject posited by these schools of thought tends to be a subject immanent in its structures.

The most common alternative to this view would be a kind of classically humanistic voluntarism, and it seems that we are then left with two possible views of the subject: either the subject is determined and possibly created by its structures, or the subject is free and voluntaristic. But I wish to say that a rejection of voluntarism does not commit one to determinism, and, after establishing the general framework for Lacan's theory of the subject, this is precisely the ground that I will be arguing Lacan's theory of the act stakes out. My guiding concern in this work is to use Lacan's theory to show how the subject and freedom can be reconnected without giving too much to the subject (as a transcendental approach would do) and without giving too much to freedom either (as a voluntarist approach would do). What will the term *subject* mean, then, if it is not something attributed to consciousness and is not a voluntaristic agent either? Clearly this notion of the subject will have little in common with the traditional view, although it will share one of that view's most important traits. "Subject" will still have something to do with freedom, but this is not a freedom that can be considered a possession or a metaphysical attribute of the subject. This kind of freedom is not at all a condition for action but would serve as a name for a particular type of action.

Lacan considers the subject as an effect or a function of the interaction of two things, which I will for now very roughly summarize under the headings of language and sexuality. Saying that the subject is a function or an effect means that this subject is neither the transcendental, constitutive subject of phenomenology and Kant, nor is it the immanent subject of many poststructuralist theories. This take on the subject can be understood as a permutation of Althusser's notion of history as a process without a subject, only the Lacanian view would add that such a "process without a [classical] subject" is just what should be called "subject," and that such a process is found not only in history but in the biography of the individual as well. Both the transcendental and Lacanian views on the subject theorize agency, and they are right to do so, while both the immanent and Lacanian views emphasize nonconscious structures, and they are also right to do so. My claim is that Lacan's theory embraces the best of each approach.

THE LACANIAN ACT

Describing Lacan's theory of the subject as, at least in part, a theory of freedom is not without problems, especially given some of Lacan's views on freedom. Consider the following, from a talk given in 1960:

> Freud's thinking is not humanist and nothing allows this term to be applied to him. It has, however, a, let's say, humanitarian temperance and temperament, despite the bad odor this word has in our time. But the curious thing is that it is not progressivist. It has no faith in an immanent movement of freedom: neither of consciousness, nor of the masses. Oddly. And this is why it surpasses the bourgeois milieu of ethics, against which it would otherwise not be able to protest, not any more than it would against everything that is happening in our day: including the ethic that reigns in the East—an ethic which, like any other, is an ethic of moral order and the service of the State. (Lacan 1986, 175)

This passage, along with many others that could have been given, is part of the cautionary tale Lacan usually tells about our belief in freedom. In an interview for a Belgian television station in 1972, the interviewer, Françoise Wolff, was led to ask Lacan: "So, in a psychoanalysis there is not a repression of freedom?" Lacan replied: "Yes...these terms, the term, makes me laugh, yes. I never talk about freedom" (Lacan 1972). This is not exactly true—freedom does come up for discussion sometimes in Lacan's work. But it is never really a lively concept for him, and when he did discuss it, it was usually in derogatory terms, often with a disparaging reference to existentialism. So, effectively, he never talked about freedom. For example, in "Propos sur la causalité psychique," Lacan wrote that "in this movement which leads man to a more and more adequate consciousness of himself, his freedom merges with the development of his servitude" (Lacan 1966, 182). And elsewhere, "existentialism can be judged on the basis of the justifications it provides for the subjective impasses that do, indeed, result therefrom: a freedom that is never so authentically affirmed as when it is within the walls of a prison" (Lacan 1966, 99/Lacan 2002, 8). Finally, and most strikingly, in his third seminar he compares the "discourse of freedom" to psychosis:

> I tried last time to show you that the ego, whatever we make of its function, and I shall go no further than to give it the function of a discourse of reality, always implies as a correlate a discourse that has nothing to do with reality. With the impertinence that, as everyone knows, is characteristic of me I designated this the discourse of freedom, essential to modern man insofar as he is structured by a certain conception of his own autonomy. I pointed out its fundamentally biased and incomplete, inexpressible, fragmentary, differentiated, and profoundly delusional nature. I set out from this general parallel to point out to you what, in relation to the ego, is apt, in the subject fallen prey to psychosis, to proliferate into a delusion. I'm not saying it's the same thing. I'm saying it's in the same place. (III, 144–145/165)

Clearly Lacan was not in agreement with the sometimes euphoric pronouncements about being free to which Sartre's work, and the works of others, could lead. By calling this "discourse on freedom" a delusion, Lacan is pointing out that a belief in one's radical freedom is often an alibi for avoiding an acknowledgment of one's determination (by the unconscious, in particular). We want nothing more than to believe we are free. Because of this, Lacan was more inclined to argue against freedom and for determination.

Nevertheless, my thesis here is that there is a theory of freedom in Lacan's work, particularly in his theory of the act. Lacan's critiques of freedom need to be read as critiques of philosophical doctrines that would assert that we are really, essentially, or metaphysically free. Lacan's theory cautions us against ever making such a proclamation. Yet despite the determinism implied by psychoanalytic theory, psychoanalytic practice is committed to the view that one can change the destiny a particular unconscious configuration (that Lacan calls the fundamental fantasy) creates for an individual. As Lacan put it in his second seminar—a seminar very keen on exploring the extent to which individuals are determined by unconscious structures—"the game is already played, the die already cast. It is already cast, with the following proviso, that we can pick it up again, and throw it anew" (II, 219). What Lacan was after with his theory of the act, which was one way in which he tried to describe what occurs during a psychoanalysis, was an account of the conditions under which such a rethrow emerges.

He conceived of the psychoanalytic act as a kind of signifying practice that would be "verbal to the second power" (XXIV, *Ornicar?*, 8: 12). I take this to refer to a signifying practice that goes beyond one of the characteristic features of speaking that he had always emphasized. According to Lacan, every act of speaking implies not only a speaker and an addressee but a third place, the Other, posited as a "site" that guarantees the truth and meaning of what is being said. Thus it is from within a fantasmatic framework that we communicate; always implicitly seeking, by communicating, some kind of recognition from this third-party Other, above and beyond whatever message we wish to convey to the concrete others to whom we speak. For a long time, Lacan considered this a structurally necessary state of affairs, so much so that many were and still are led to believe that his theory of the subject is strictly linguisticist and deterministic. This Other implied by the fact of speaking does always remain a structural necessity—that is, it is always a factor, something co-posited, in any signifying practice, but with the idea of the psychoanalytic act, Lacan was exploring signifying practices that exceeded this structure. There is, as we will see, still a relation to a type of Other in these acts, only it is a different relation to a different kind of Other. The subject of an act is a subject who does not receive recognition of its being, or identity, from the Other. I will argue, then, that an act represents a rupture with identity, and the term *subject* in this context does not designate the one who acts. Instead, it designates what an act does. An act "subjects" in a new way.

CHAPTER OUTLINE

This work aims to show in detail how the Lacanian subject is neither a constitutive transcendental subject nor a subject immanent in, or reducible to, the structures that constitute it: the Lacanian subject is an effect or a function of certain types of signifying practices. So this theory relies on an account of the structures wrapped up in these signifying practices. The first chapters of this book will be concerned with unpacking the most important features of these structures, with exploring how some signifying practices involve not only the structures that can be found in language itself (chapter 2), but also how they involve relations to others (chapter 3), and a relation to what I will call for now a "traumatic sexuality" (chapter 4). Since there are different ways in which these relations are configured, there are also different ways in which a subject comes about, as well as different kinds of subjects. I will then focus on two major ways in which the subject comes about: in what Lacan calls the "fundamental fantasy" (chapter 5) and in the act (chapter 6). The former gives us a portrait of a subject with an identity, pursuing recognition, while the latter is where Lacan's understanding of freedom can be found. A change in the way language is structured, a change in one's relation to the Other, and a change in one's relation to foundational traumatic experiences—these are the areas in which the emergence of the Lacanian act is to be located.

Lacan makes few pronouncements about the terms in which acts should happen, and thus again his theory seems to be antihumanist and apparently has no ability to make a meaningful intervention in contemporary practice. In other words, it is worth wondering, despite an increasing amount of studies on this topic, whether a Lacanian ethics is even possible. I want to suggest that this may actually be an advantage of Lacan's theory. In this sense Lacan is right to say, in that passage from 1960, given earlier, that "Freud's thinking" (and he certainly has his own thinking in mind too) protests against ethics. Lacan claimed that ethics can never succeed in doing more than furthering the interests of a moral order or "the State." This is because ethics puts an emphasis on recognition (of others, and of one's own goodness in recognizing others), and therefore relies upon and reinforces a relation to an Other who is, as Lacan described it, a subject-supposed-to-know.

Renata Salecl suggests that our historical moment is characterized both by the collapse of such an Other (which is already a basic feature of what is called "modernity," or the Nietzschean death of God) and by a variety of attempts to reestablish some kind of full, "premodern" Other (2000, 141–168). She wonders whether it would be possible to accept somehow that the Other does not know, while avoiding the temptation to "save" the Other from this fate. Is it at all possible for us to act socially and individually in such a way that we do not either implicitly rely on a notion of an Other who knows, or implicitly expect the reestablishment of such an Other? My discussions of the Lacanian act in chapters 7 and 8 try to outline in more detail what such acts might look like.

But these chapters also get into more detail about the nature of the subject. In chapter 7 I raise some objections to Slavoj Žižek's theorization of the subject in *The Ticklish Subject*. Žižek claims that the subject is negativity (1999, 159–160). This can be understood in both Hegelian and Sartrean terms: The subject is the power of the negative, or the subject is something like a negating power. I argue that such a portrayal of the subject is misleading, since the Lacanian subject should not be thought of as something that negates, which would place it too close to the transcendental, phenomenological subject. In this chapter, I argue that the subject is a consistency of some kind, and I present a theory of the subject worked out by Alain Badiou in his 1982 *Théorie du sujet* to follow through with this idea. Badiou theorizes the subject as a "destructive consistency," and I think this is a more accurate way of thinking about the Lacanian subject too.

If Žižek's portrayal of the Lacanian subject tends to make it too transcendental, constitutive, and phenomenological then the work of another prominent theorist of subjectivity, Judith Butler, tends to go in the other direction. In chapter 8, I argue that Butler theorizes a subject that is immanent in the discourses that constitute it. Furthermore, on Butler's terms, it is difficult to imagine a subject who ever does anything other than perform an identity. The Lacanian act shows us a subject involved in a practice beyond identity and the pursuit of recognition. In this discussion, I use an example from Alain Badiou's work to show how such an understanding of the act can be applied to the social and political questions that are often at issue in Butler's theory.

Since this theory of the subject is a bit counterintuitive, and since the whole project of subject theory itself may raise plenty of questions and suspicions for some readers, in my first chapter I will consider two influential criticisms of Lacan's work, which will present a common misunderstanding of Lacan's subject. These criticisms claim that Lacan's subject is equivalent to language, and that Lacan grants to language all the powers of the classical subject. I will begin making my case in the first chapter that this overlooks an entire tendency in Lacan's work that considers the subject not only as an effect of language but as an effect of language plus the real, which I will be thinking of primarily in terms of sexuality.

CHAPTER 1

Lacan's Subversion of the Subject

Lacan often insists that his use of the term *subject* goes against the traditional understanding of the subject: he is rather well known, in fact, for proclaiming a "subversion of the subject" (Lacan 1966, 793–827/Lacan 2002, 281–312). But Lacan does not only subvert the subject. As Alain Badiou has pointed out, Lacan was one of the few in his time to have gone beyond calling for a subversion of the (classical) subject: Lacan also rethought the subject (Badian 1989, 24–25). Two influential works on Lacan—Borch-Jacobsen's (1991) *Lacan: The Absolute Master* and Lacoue-Labarthe's and Nancy's (1992) *The Title of the Letter*—argue that Lacan's rethinking of the subject corrupted his subversion, such that the Lacanian subject is a traditional subject in a thin disguise. In particular, they claim that Lacan's subject, despite its new disguise, is still a subject who represents, who creates meanings, and seeks above all to represent itself. In order to introduce the issues and concepts involved in Lacan's theory of the subject, I will focus on a claim shared by Borch-Jacobsen and Lacoue-Labarthe and Nancy: that Lacan's subject is language *at work*. The subject, according to this erroneous reading, is identical to language understood as the process of creating meanings and representations.

In his description of Lacan's project, Borch-Jacobsen highlights an oddity intrinsic to it: Lacan tried to introduce the subject into a structuralist theory of language. Structuralist approaches to anything generally set the issue of subjectivity aside. Borch-Jacobsen argues that the major problem with Lacan's supposed subversion of the subject results from this forced inclusion or reintroduction of the subject into a structuralist understanding of language:

> The hypothesis here [...] is that the subject's reintroduction corresponds to the linguistic model's massive overdetermination by the philosophical problematic of the subject of representation, a problematic Cartesian in origin, of which Lacan provides an ultramodern version inspired by Kojève's commentary on Hegel. (1991, 187)

According to Borch-Jacobsen, by introducing the subject into a structuralist theory of language Lacan situates both the subject and language within the problematic of representation. Borch-Jacobsen explains what he means by "the subject of representation" as follows: it involves "a subject's intentionally *ex*-pressing himself within 'language,' manifesting himself in exteriority by passing through the medium of the other—in short [...] performing an autorepresentation" (1991, 188). Borch-Jacobsen does say that Lacan provides us with an "ultramodern" version of this subject of representation. That is, Lacan's subject is not a simple repetition of the Cartesian subject. But Lacan's subject is still "Cartesian in origin," and this mitigates its claim to subversion (1991, 187).

By calling Lacan's subject an "ultramodern" version of the Cartesian cogito, Borch-Jacobsen acknowledges that Lacan alters the subject as it had traditionally been understood. To its credit, Borch-Jacobsen finds that "the Lacanian cogito is from the very start a linguistic, social, and intersubjective cogito, a cogito in the first person plural" (1991, 189). Language, sociality, and intersubjectivity are attributes that are indeed difficult to attach to the Cartesian cogito. By making these attributes essential to the cogito, Borch-Jacobsen wants to say that Lacan upgraded the cogito, bringing it in line with contemporary concerns, while leaving the basic "problematic" of the cogito intact. Lacan's modernizations change nothing, then, about the subject's "structure as cogito, understood as the structure of the subject of representation. The subject of speech, for the Hegelian who was the young Lacan, continues to speak *himself* in the other to whom he speaks" (1991, 189). So, this Lacanian subject who speaks itself and represents itself in language is

> precisely what makes the otherwise sense-less machine of the signifier run, what makes the *langue* of the linguists speak—or, if you will, it is that "prodigious energy"—the negative—

> which makes langue signify, makes it "produce" meaning. And this meaning is once again, now and forever, the "subject = 0" who speaks himself in everything. (1991, 195)

According to Borch-Jacobsen, Lacan's view is that a meaningless system of signifiers is only able to produce meanings because of the work of a subject. Lacan may have modified and upgraded the Cartesian cogito by making it more "social, linguistic, and intersubjective," but since the subject is still seen as some kind of power that creates meanings in language, a power that fills empty signifiers with content, the representational model of subjectivity is still operative in Lacan's theory.

This does not jibe with what Lacan thought his theory of the subject was doing, and strictly speaking, signifiers, not subjects, are what produce meanings. A subject who produces meanings would usually be thought of as a subject who is somehow external to language: a subject with intentions, desires, and meanings who must use signifiers to express them. But by claiming that Lacan's subject remains classical, Borch-Jacobsen does not mean that the subject is external to language in this way. The Lacanian subject, according to Borch-Jacobsen, is engulfed in language. So how is one to think of a subject of representation who is not external to the medium in which it is represented? Borch-Jacobsen's solution is to claim that for Lacan, subject and language are actually the same thing. Lacan's introduction of the subject into a structuralist theory of language, according to Borch-Jacobsen, bestows upon language all the powers of the subject:

> This complete reabsorption of the subject into the "discourse of the Other" that represents him is what has made inattentive readers think that Lacan had finished once and for all with the subject of the cogito. But that simply is not true, as Lacan himself very well knew. To say that the subject *is* language is also to say that language *is* the subject "himself"—or, if you will, that the two are the *same*. (1991, 195, emphasis in original)

The claim that for Lacan "the subject *is* language" is erroneous, yet I would like to point out why this reading is an elegant solution to a genuine theoretical problem. If "the subject *is* language," if the two are the same, then one does not have to say that the subject is external to language (thus the subject remains profoundly linguistic). Yet the subject may still be something that expresses and represents itself; it can still be seen as the agent behind the significations produced by language, only it would be something like an unconscious agent.

In fact, if language and the subject are identical, then any use of language may be seen as a self-expression and self-representation, as Borch-Jacobsen goes on to argue: "In reality, language in Lacan speaks only of the subject. [. . .] Thus this language remains autoenunciative through and through" (1991, 195). However, Borch-Jacobsen's contention is erroneous. He gives no passage in support of his claim that the subject is the same as language, and I have not found one in Lacan's work either—quite the opposite, as we shall see. I believe Borch-Jacobsen is led to make this assertion because he wishes to do justice to the idea that the subject is not external to language in Lacanian theory. A persistent theme in Lacan's discussions of the subject is the view that the subject is an effect of signifiers, and so Borch-Jacobsen is right to wonder whether the subject is anything other than language. Borch-Jacobsen does not consider, however, that thinking of the subject as an effect does not have to mean that the subject is somehow immanent in, rather than external to, language. I will be arguing that Lacan's subject is an effect of language, but an effect that remains external to, and not reducible to, language. This is because the subject is not simply an effect of signifiers but an effect of signifiers themselves interacting with something nonlinguistic: sexuality.

In their widely read and influential work *The Title of the Letter*, Lacoue-Labarthe and Nancy arrive at roughly the same interpretation of the Lacanian subject as Borch-Jacobsen. They acknowledge that the Lacanian subject is not a "master of meaning," but they still claim that "the locus of the Lacanian signifier is nevertheless the subject" (1992, 65). If signifiers are located in a subject, then signifiers still somehow depend upon a subject for their meaning. As is the case with Borch-Jacobsen's critique of Lacan, it is the relation of the subject to language that maintains what Lacoue-Labarthe and Nancy call the "classical" notion of the subject in Lacan's work, and the classical subject was a subject who produced meaning (1992, 63).

Where Lacoue-Labarthe and Nancy say "classical," Borch-Jacobsen says "subject of representation," but the point is the same. Lacoue-Labarthe and Nancy argue that if signifiers are located "in" a subject, then the subject is something that creates meanings. Borch-Jacobsen argues that if the subject is identical to language, then the subject not only creates meanings but also represents itself whenever it speaks. In both cases, language is portrayed as a medium that represents and expresses (more or less) what a subject wants to represent and express. Also, both interpretations understand the subject to be something that makes language work. Lacan's subject is indeed deeply entangled with language, but according to these readings the subject is still the master of language, even if it is not the "master of meaning": it still makes language work, even if it does not have full control over what language produces. Here is how Lacoue-Labarthe and Nancy present their conclusion about Lacan's subject:

> The subject is defined as "what the signifier represents," which should be understood the following way: if the subject is the possibility of speech, and if this speech is actualized as a signifying chain, then the relation of a signifier to another signifier, or that which a signifier "represents," as Lacan says, for another signifier—namely, *the very structure of the chain—is what must be named "subject."* (1992, 69, emphasis added)

The subject is identified with the structure of the signifying chain. Roughly put, with language.

CRITIQUE OF THE CRITIQUES

What Borch-Jacobsen and Lacoue-Labarthe and Nancy all seem to agree on is that it is the particular way in which Lacan construes the relationship between the subject and language that makes his theory of the subject traditional, despite its innovation in introducing "social, linguistic, and intersubjective" aspects into the cogito. A point that seems to work in their favor is the definition Lacan often gave of "the signifier," a definition that puts the subject and language in a manifestly representational relationship to each other. What is a signifier? According to Lacan, in a definition repeated often in his work, "a signifier is what represents the subject to another signifier" (Lacan 1966, 819/Lacan 2002, 304). In this definition, the relation of the subject to language is put in terms of representation, and Lacan is saying explicitly that signifiers represent a subject. This definition understandably plays an important role in Borch-Jacobsen's interpretation of Lacan's theory of the subject, where it is used to show that Lacan, despite holding that "the subject is subjected to the signifier," also holds that "the signifier represents nothing but the subject, by means of which it [the signifier] is reinvested with that function of *representation* that Lacan so stringently denies elsewhere" (1991, 186, emphasis in original). Lacoue-Labarthe and Nancy also use this definition in their critique of Lacan: in fact, in the passage I cited earlier, they refer to it when making their point that the subject is equivalent to language (1992, 69).

I will respond in two ways to the claim that Lacan's subject is a subject of representation and self-expression: first, by taking a closer look at Lacan's definition of the signifier, and second, by looking at some passages in which Lacan expands upon the relation of the subject to language.

While the definition of the signifier expresses the relation between the subject and the signifier in terms of representation, it is not clear that the definition is making the subject into a subject of representation, since it does not at all imply that the subject is something that uses signifiers to represent or express itself. It merely says that a subject is something that gets represented by a signifier. In this respect, a subject might be no different from anything else that gets represented or said in language. True, the definition is privileging the subject in relation to signifiers. By definition, it is a *subject* that one signifier represents to another signifier, and one is not dealing with a signifier if it does not represent a subject. But still, the definition is not saying that there is a subject who aims to represent itself, or that it is a subject who accomplishes a self-representation through signifiers. The definition supports the view that the subject is a product of the interaction of signifiers just as much as it supports the view that the subject is engaged in auto-representation.

Further justification for this take on the matter can be found on the basis of what else Lacan says about the subject. Several passages make it quite clear that Lacan does not wish to equate the subject with language. At one point, Lacan characterizes the subject as something that has a "one foot in, one foot out articulation in the field of the Other" (XVI, 5/7/69). If "the Other" is, more or less, the field of language, then it is difficult to see how the subject could be identical to language if the subject has one foot in and one foot out of it.[1] The subject is in part "in" the Other but is also not in the Other: in other words, the subject has an important relation to language, but it is also external to language in some way.

In another passage, Lacan writes that "the subject that it [the signifier] represents is not univocal. It is represented, undoubtedly, but it is also not represented. [. . .] Something remains hidden in relation to this very signifier" (XVII, 101). Lacan is elaborating on the definition of the signifier here, indicating that the definition itself (which was, after all, supposed to be only a definition of "the signifier") does not give an adequate picture of the subject. The subject is not only represented by a signifier: a part of it is also not represented. Again, the suggestion is that the subject is not identical to language.

The final passage I will consider here is one of the clearest I have found concerning the relation of the subject to language in Lacan's work. In it, Lacan explicitly rejects the view that the subject is equivalent to language, while also bringing into his theory of the subject an element whose importance for Lacanian theory still needs to be weighed. In a moment of candor, Lacan asks:

> Where is the subject [. . .]? In radical, real individuality? [. . .]. In the organism [. . .] drawn in by the effects of the *ça parle*, by the fact that one living being among others has been called upon to become what Mr. Heidegger calls the "shepherd of being," having been taken up into the mechanisms of the signifier? Is it, at the other extreme, identifiable with the very play of the signifier? Is the subject only the subject of discourse, in some way torn out of its vital immanence, condemned to soar over it, to live in this sort of mirage [. . .] making it the case that everything s/he lives is not only spoken, but, in living it, s/he lives it by speaking it, and that already what s/he lives is inscribed in an *epos*, a saga woven throughout the length of his or her very act? Our effort this year, if it has a meaning, is to show, precisely, how the function of the subject, playing between the two, is articulated elsewhere than in one or the other of these poles. [. . .]. Does it suffice to know that the function of the subject is in the between-the-two, between the idealizing effects of the signifying function and this vital immanence which you will readily confuse again, I think, despite my warnings, with the function of the drive? What we are engaged in, precisely, and what we are trying to push further, is precisely this. (IX, 12/20/61)

The idea that the subject is identical to the play of signifiers, or to language, is flatly rejected here. Instead, the subject is portrayed as something articulated between two poles. One of the poles is language, while the other pole remains a bit vague. Lacan tells us not to confuse this second pole with the drive. But what is it? Is it the organism? Vital immanence (whatever that is)? Radical, real individuality?

THE SUBJECT BETWEEN LANGUAGE AND THE REAL

I would like to discuss briefly what Lacan had in mind with this second pole, since it plays an important part in my argument that Lacan's theory of the subject is not reducible to language and is even in some sense external to language. It will turn out that the subject is produced not only by an interaction of signifiers but by an interaction of signifiers with something nonlinguistic. Although the subject is not identical to either of the poles Lacan considers here, each pole designates something that is involved in the production of a subject—and language alone does not suffice.

Lacan's theory of the subject, then, can be presented in terms of two theses modeled on what is at stake in these two poles. One thesis is found relatively early in Lacan's work: the subject is a product or an effect of signifiers. This is what could be called the "linguistic" or "structuralist" thesis, and it is most clearly stated by the time of Lacan's ninth seminar: "The subject is the consequence of the fact that there is a signifier" (IX, 5/2/62). According to the second thesis on the subject, however, the production of the subject by signifiers needs to be complemented with an appreciation of a particular type of obstacle to signification. While Lacan in his ninth seminar used the terms *vital immanence*, *radical, real individuality*, and *the organism* to characterize this other, apparently nonlinguistic, pole of the subject, it would not be erroneous to understand this second pole in terms of sexuality, although I will not make this case until chapter 4. Let me point out that this does not violate Lacan's warning not to confuse the second pole with the drive, since the drives and the kind of sexuality I will describe are not the same thing.

Let us consider again what Lacan was up to in that passage. In a rare moment, he was trying to give a clear picture of his theory of the subject. The subject is not language, he says. It is not identical to the "play of signifiers." Then he considers whether the subject is biological. The answer, again, is no: the subject is not the organism, the real individual, or vital immanence. Is Lacan saying that a subject is between language and the body? The problem with this way of putting things is that it becomes clear later on in Lacan's work that the body is not really a suitable candidate for what he was trying to get at with this other pole either. In his fourteenth seminar, Lacan argues that the Other is the body: "The body itself is originally this site of the Other, insofar as it is there that the mark, as a signifier, is originally inscribed" (XIV, 5/30/67). As Bruce Fink puts it, the body, according to Lacan's conception of it, is always "overwritten" and "overridden" by language (1995a, 12). So "body" for Lacan is always a body that has already gone through language. One way to get at this second pole, nevertheless, is to consider the idea that there is something of the body that does not fit with the "socialized" body, the body that is overwritten with signifiers. Saying that a body is overwritten with signifiers suggests that there is something prior to signifiers on which the writing occurs, something that gets besieged by signifiers at some moment of its existence. This could be thought of as a body prior to the body that is linguistically and socially carved up, thus a body that is presymbolic and perhaps to be thought of in terms of what Lacan called the real. In *Beyond Gender*, Paul Verhaeghe considers the body in Lacan's work from this point of view, arguing that

> as long as Lacan was emphasizing the determining influence of the symbolic order, the body was thought of as a mere effect, that is, as a signified body, an imaginarised body. Indeed, we have a body as an effect of language and the distance created by this language. Once Lacan takes the Real seriously, another body enters into play, one for which the signifier "body" isn't even really appropriate. If the Real is our starting-point, it is not the body that is operative, but the organism, or organs. (2001, 79, emphasis in original)

Verhaeghe suggests speaking of the organism instead of the body when thinking about what I want to say is at stake in that second pole Lacan mentioned. But whatever term is settled upon, the category under which this organism or body is to be thought is the real, and not the symbolic.

But does the real always mean the presymbolic? The real is a much-contested term, and I would point out, with Fink and others, that there are two versions of the real in Lacan's work. There is a first real ($real_1$), prior to the acquisition of language, which is "*progressively symbolized* in the course of a child's life," and there is another "second-order" real ($real_2$), which is an effect of the symbolic order itself (Fink 1995a, 26–27, emphasis in original). $Real_1$ sounds like a typically "realist" notion: the real consists of stuff "out there" that language tries to symbolize. $Real_2$, however, is not outside the symbolic, as $real_1$ seems to be. This second-order real "is characterized by impasses and impossibilities" that occur in the symbolic order itself (1995a, 27). In what I think is his best definition of this understanding of the real, Lacan said that "the real can only be inscribed on the basis of an impasse of formalization" (XX, 93). Instead of being a field of referents that language aims at, this version of the real is a stumbling block in the field of signification itself.

Which notion of the real applies to the second pole of the subject as Lacan considered it in his ninth seminar? It is not clear. If the second pole is meant to be nonlinguistic and prior to symbolization, then would it have to be thought of in terms of the presymbolic $real_1$? Lacan gave no indication that the subject's second pole entails a resistance to signification (except, perhaps, by the fact that he himself had a hard time settling on a good name for it!), and he did consider the possibility that the subject is something "condemned to soar over" its own vital immanence—its ineffable, presumably prelinguistic body. This would suggest that this second pole is prior to signification, thus making it into something that would fit under the category of $real_1$. But it should be recalled that Lacan only entertained this possibility when he was considering the subject to be identifiable with language. If the subject were identical to language, then Lacan's view was that it would indeed be condemned to soar over its vital immanence. This vital immanence would be radically excluded from the order of language, and thus from the subject, making it into something like a $real_1$. But Lacan rejects this idea, and so there is an entirely different implication.

If the subject is not to be identified with language, then the subject can also not be seen as something that simply "soars over" some ineffable vital immanence. In other words, if the subject is not identical to language, then this second pole also cannot be seen as something totally excluded from both the order of signification and the subject's structure itself. On the contrary, a subject who is not identical to language would dwell in a domain constituted by remnants of this real pole, which is present in language without fully fitting into it. This pole—whether it is thought of as the body, the real, the organism, or vital immanence—is a factor for a subject then, insofar as it has effects upon and within language, so we can already see that "subject" in Lacan's theory names neither what is going on in language itself nor what is going on in the biological individual but the effects of the latter on the former and the former on the latter. All of this is very well summarized by saying that the subject is between the two poles.

But why should this strange effect between two poles still be given the name "subject"? There has been a consensus for some time now that the classical theory of the subject—which Borch-Jacobsen characterized as "representationalist"—is inadequate. Such a view of the subject grants too much power to it and fails to take into account the subject's own constitution by and subjection to its world, language, and culture. Methodologically, what Lacan does with the term *subject* in his work is not unlike what Derrida calls a "paleonymy"—the preservation (for strategic purposes) of an old, metaphysical name. But can a deconstructive paleonymy be done with a term such as subject? Derrida's answer is ambiguous, while Lacan's is not.

DERRIDA ON THE SUBJECT

In his discussion of paleonymy from the collection of interviews published in *Positions*, Derrida speaks of it as a "strategic necessity that requires the occasional maintenance of an old name in order to launch a new concept" (1981, 71). He explains further:

> Taking into account the fact that a name does not name the punctual simplicity of a concept, but rather a system of predicates defining a concept, a conceptual structure *centered* on a given predicate, we proceed: (1) to the extraction of a reduced predicative trait that is held in reserve, limited in a given conceptual structure (limited for motivations and relations of force to be analyzed), *named X*; (2) to the delimitation, the grafting and regulated extension of the extracted predicate, the name *being maintained as a kind of lever of intervention* in order to maintain a grasp on the previous organization, which is to be effectively transformed. (1981, 71, emphasis in original)

A paleonymy proceeds by continuing to use an old, traditional name while making the name different from what it always was, because one or more of the predicates associated with that name is being rethought and reworked. The technique of paleonymy should not be confused with another operation of deconstructive strategy, which consists of showing how a term that was thought to be inessential or only supplementary is actually central for the functioning of a system and at the same time disrupts the closure of the system in question. Deconstructive strategy is usually thought to consist of taking a weak, dispensable, or regrettable term in a metaphysical system—writing over voice, difference over identity, and so on—and demonstrating this term's secret necessity for the system, in order to bring about disruptions and to highlight the chronic instability of the system. What makes paleonymy a slightly different operation, even though from the earlier passage it is clear that it contains this aspect of deconstruction within it, is the fact that it can, in principle, involve using a strong or dominant concept from the philosophical, metaphysical tradition, changing its attributes with an eye to abandoning the concept altogether someday. The concept in question would always be in scare quotes.

Lacan's theory of the subject is taking a central philosophical and metaphysical concept and trying to understand it differently, without hoping for a better, more appropriate name for it. As a result, from Derrida's perspective, Lacan runs the risk of simply repeating what was metaphysical about the subject. This is precisely the point of the critiques of Lacan's theory that I have been considering in this chapter, according to which Lacan's subversion of the subject was also too much of a preservation of the (classical, representationalist) subject. A deconstructive paleonymy does not set out to preserve an old name: it uses the name out of grim necessity and acts as if there is something about the name itself that will always be suspect. This is what I think can be called into question: Is it really necessary to await or invent a new name?

Derrida doubts the feasibility and desirability of reworking the concept of the subject at all. Consider the following passage, in which Derrida is discussing his concept of writing:

> Constituting and dislocating it at the same time, writing is other than the subject, in whatever sense the latter is understood. Writing can never be thought under the category of the subject: however it [the subject] is modified, however it is endowed with consciousness or unconsciousness, it will refer, by the entire thread of its history, to the substantiality of a presence unperturbed by accidents, or to the identity of the self-same in the presence of self-relationship. (1976, 68–69)

The history of the subject poisons it. No matter how one modifies the subject, it will persist in being what it has always been: "by the entire thread of its history." This suggests that as far as Derrida is concerned, a reworking of the concept of the subject would be if not impossible, at least foolhardy and useless. The subject cannot be reworked, it cannot be opened up and extended outside of the metaphysical system it is part of, because the subject is always understood as substance, self-presence, and so on. The history of the concept saturates it. This suggests, oddly, that the meaning of the subject is once and for all fixed, that there is a meaning for it that persists, no matter how much the concept of the subject is reworked. Is there a peculiar Derridean essentialism when it comes to the question of the subject?

Derrida seems to be deciding *a priori* that a future extension or transformation of the concept is doomed to failure because the history of the concept is so corrupting. If Derrida is excluding the possibility of any fruitful extension of the concept "subject," then this can only be read as a foreclosing of a possible opening of the concept. It is striking that someone who has taught all of us about the essential dissemination of meaning at the same time speaks of the subject always meaning x, y, and z. Whatever meanings attach to the concept of the subject are maintained only by means of signifying practices which, as Derrida himself should argue, I believe, are always open to interruption and can always be altered.

In an interview with Jean-Luc Nancy in *Who Comes After the Subject?*, Derrida ultimately grants that it may be possible to rework the concept of the subject in a useful way, but he continues to be suspicious of the desire to keep the name "subject." The following is a fairly representative quote for his position in this interview: "I would keep the name [subject] provisionally as an index for the discussion, but I don't see the necessity of keeping the word 'subject' at any price, especially if the context and conventions of discourse risk re-introducing precisely what is in question" (1991, 99). The provisional preservation of the name "subject" indicates that such a use might qualify as paleonymic, but once again it is the term itself that seems to threaten a return to what was metaphysical about the subject.

Furthermore, we see in this passage that Derrida finds an insistence on keeping the name "subject" strange. Indeed, why would one insist on keeping an old, suspicious name when something better might come along? Derrida is right, I believe, to question such an insistence. If Derrida is saying this out of disagreement with philosophers who would say that abandoning the concept of the subject is tantamount to some kind of nihilism or antihumanism, then I follow him. But is the only alternative to be eternally suspicious about the name? By continuing to think about the subject, and by continuing to use the name, Lacan adopted a different strategy, at the same time suggesting that the hope for a more innocent name may be just as strange as an insistence on keeping an old name.

Lacan's method supposes that it is not impossible to make something else be understood by an old name. In a certain sense, this results in making a new name of the old name anyway. So instead of a bizarre insistence on keeping the name "subject" at any cost, and also instead of an equally bizarre insistence that the name "subject" will always be dirty, and that we should therefore keep our eyes open for a better, more innocent name, there is the more optimistic and perhaps more cavalier Lacanian path. Lacan once said that he could make any word mean anything he wanted, as long as he kept talking about it long enough. On a more general level, though, this is precisely how the meanings of words actually change: by means of ongoing signifying practices. This also demonstrates something about the theory of freedom that can be found hidden in Lacan's theory. Freedom, from this perspective, is intimately bound up with something like the invention and repetition of new signifiers. In chapter 6 and the later chapters, the effects of such an invention will be studied in detail.

CHAPTER 2

The First Thesis

> The subject is the consequence of the fact that there is a signifier. (IX, 5/2/62)

In the last chapter, I claimed that Lacan's theory of the subject could be presented in terms of two theses. What I call Lacan's first thesis is the idea that a subject is an effect or a product of signifiers. To understand this thesis it is a good idea to discuss what signifiers are. Lacan has a unique conception of signifiers, and they play a role in his work that they do not play in most theories of language. I will begin with an analysis of his conception of signifiers and move on to discuss the ways in which signifiers are productive of meanings in two kinds of figures of speech—metaphor and metonymy. Once it is established that such figures of speech are capable of producing meanings, I think the counterintuitive claim that an interaction of signifiers can produce something like a subject will be more compelling. In one respect, signifiers produce a subject in the same way that signifiers produce a meaning. Does this mean that the subject is just a meaning? In part, yes, but this does not give us a full picture of Lacan's theory of the subject, as I will go on to show in chapters 3 and 4.

THE TRACE AND THE SIGN

I will begin with a look at what Lacan calls the "trace," a concept that in a certain sense is the starting point for his notions of the sign and the signifier. All sorts of things in the natural world leave traces: a pebble rolling down a sand dune leaves a trace, for example. For Lacan's purposes, the important property of a trace is that it is self-sufficient (XVI, 5/14/69). A rolling pebble may have caused a trace, but *as* a trace the trace is self-sufficient: what we observe is simply a mark left in the sand. In this respect, a trace differs from a sign and a signifier. While a sign and a signifier may originally be traces and may always possess some self-sufficiency, some tracelike aspect, they are what they are because they are not wholly self-sufficient. Both refer to something other than themselves, and in this respect they depart from their origin in traces.[1]

First let us look at how this reference to something else occurs in the case of signs. *Sign* is the term Lacan uses to describe the most familiar and obvious aspect of communication. "A sign," Lacan tells us in an oft-repeated definition, "represents something to someone" (Lacan 1966, 840/Lacan 1996, 268).[2] This is a simple, commonsense view of the sign and its role in communication. In any communication there is a sender, a message, and a receiver. A sign represents something (a message from the sender) to someone (the receiver). Such a description of the sign actually covers a wide variety of communications. Not only would words qualify as signs according to this view, but gestures, pictures, and even a dog's bark could also function as signs insofar as all are bearers of a message, however obscure it may be to us.

Lacan refers to a scene from Defoe's *Robinson Crusoe* quite often when discussing the sign in relation to the trace. Robinson Crusoe, believing that he is on an uninhabited island, one day comes across a footprint in the sand that he knows cannot be his own. Crusoe could have seen this footprint as a brute trace: that is, he could have seen it as a peculiar shape that the sand just happened to take on, and it could have been taken as a self-sufficient, nonreferential form. Yet the footprint could also have been taken as a sign of someone else's passage: indeed, this is how Crusoe ultimately, and rightly, took it. We can see the difference between a sign and a trace on this basis. To borrow a term from phenomenology, a trace can be called a "reduced" sign: a trace is a sign reduced to a pure materiality without signification. If Crusoe had not taken the footstep to be the sign of someone's passage, then it would have qualified as a mere trace. Such a material trace becomes a sign—a unit of communication and no longer a mere natural phenomenon—when it is seen as a mark that an absent object has created. A trace can always be subordinated to its cause, so to speak, and it is always possible to take a trace to be "pointing at" its cause or "referring to" it. When this occurs, however, one is no longer dealing with a mere trace but a sign. Lacan describes a sign, then, as a trace that an "object, gone elsewhere, has left behind" (III, 188/167, translation modified). What makes a sign differ from a pure trace is this reference to and dependence upon an object, which makes it the case that a trace is now something that refers to something else and is no longer a self-sufficient entity. To paraphrase Lacan's definition, a sign refers to something for someone, unlike a trace, which does not refer to anything. It should be noted that any trace can in fact be taken as a sign, and that any sign can have its meaning or referential context bracketed and be reduced to a mere trace. A sign is reduced to being a mere trace if it is taken as it is in its pure positivity. When abstracted from its referential structure, a sign is just a trace.

SIGNIFIERS

How do signifiers differ from both traces and signs? Lacan gave his first account of how signifiers differ from signs and traces in his third seminar. Later in Lacan's work, this difference was accounted for in another way, and I will consider this change in what follows. Like the sign, in his third seminar Lacan also called the signifier "the sign of an absence. But insofar as it forms part of language, the signifier is a sign which refers to another sign, which is as such structured to signify the absence of another sign" (III, 188/167). The signifier is here called the "sign of an absence," and it is said to refer to another *sign*, and not to any other sort of object. The footstep on the beach qualified as a sign because it recorded a foot's passage, indicating that a sign could be nonlinguistic and still communicative. A signifier, in contrast, refers to other *signs*, and this makes it more specifically linguistic. So at this point in Lacan's theory, there is a difference between signifiers and signs, but it is not a strong difference.

Lacan calls attention to a stronger difference between signifiers and signs a few years later. He had previously called the signifier "a sign that refers to another sign" (III, 188/167). He says later in his career that what is characteristic of a signifier is that we find in it *the annulment of the sign's function altogether*. In seminar nine, Lacan says explicitly: "The signifier is not at all a sign" (IX, 12/6/61). What he is calling attention to here is the idea that a signifier does not possess the central feature of a sign, which is to refer to a *specific* thing. A signifier is at this point of Lacan's work defined as that which shows "the presence of difference as such and nothing else. The first thing that it implies is that the relation of the sign to the thing is effaced" (IX, 12/6/61). Traces are self-sufficient, but signifiers are radically dependent (on other signifiers, as we shall see, although they are independent of any particular signified or referent): and, unlike signs, signifiers do not relate, point to, or refer to specific things (objects, meanings, or referents). This lack of a specific reference is the major difference between signifiers and signs.

What motivated this change in Lacan's view of signifiers? Whereas a sign is dependent upon what it refers to and can be said to subordinate what would otherwise be a trace to its object or referent, a signifier effaces both the trace as a pure positivity and the sign as a reference to a particular object or meaning. What a signifier gives us is neither a full presence (like the trace) nor a reference to a "full" absence—a specific object that caused the trace, as the sign does. Rather, it presents us with what Lacan calls an "absolute difference:" "Nothing else founds the function of the signifier except being an absolute difference. It is only by the way in which the others differ from it that the signifier is sustained" (XVI, 2/26/69).[3] In his third seminar, when Lacan saw signifiers as members of the class of signs, they still referred to something—to other signs. But including the signifier within a system of difference like this actually downplays the importance of reference for signifiers. Traces, according to Lacan, were self-sufficient. Signs implied the ruin of this self-sufficiency by subordinating traces to objects. Signifiers go even farther: signifiers are not dependent upon merely one object but upon *every other signifier*. For this reason, it is not entirely appropriate to speak of a signifier "referring" to other signifiers: it does not refer to them as a sign refers to an object. Rather, all the other signifiers absorb it, and its particularity is always vanishing because of this absorption. What is being described in this movement from traces to signs to signifiers is a movement from the self-sufficiency of the trace to the referential structure of the sign to the radical difference constitutive of the signifier. Of course, this radical difference could just as well be called a "hyper-referentiality." Certainly, unlike a sign, a signifier is not fixed to a *particular* object, but in its inclusion within a system of other signifiers there is still an extreme form of reference at work. A signifier's reference is not to a specific object or to a specific sign but to all other signifiers, or to the mere fact that signifiers exist.

Once this point about signifiers is understood, the heuristic aims of the other two ideas—trace and sign—have served their purpose and can no longer be maintained as rigorous concepts. When the signifier is conceived of in terms of radical difference the signifier becomes primary, and the structure of a sign can be said to presuppose this differential system of signifiers. Similarly, the self-sufficiency of a trace can only be found by abstracting from a primary field of difference. Here we see a typically Lacanian idea: once in language, there is no way out.

Although the story began with traces, signifiers are actually there all along, and they are not there in isolation but there "with" an entire differential system of signifiers.[4]

LACAN VERSUS SAUSSURE ON THE MEANINGLESSNESS OF SIGNIFIERS

With what we have seen so far of signifiers—they are not signs, and they are what they are in a field of difference—we are left wondering whether signifiers really have anything to do with meaning at all, as one would expect them to in most theories involving language. Do they ever refer to meanings? If they do, how do they acquire meanings according to Lacan's theory? Is a signifier's meaning the other signifiers to which a signifier "hyper-refers"? Before giving Lacan's position on these questions, a review of Saussure's account of meaning may be helpful. Let me note before going on that Lacan does have a theory of meaning, and it is in some way indebted to Saussurean linguistics, but not in a straightforward way.

According to Saussurean linguistics, a signifier is always attached to a signified. Of course, it is not primarily signifiers that are important in Saussure's work but signs, which are conceived of as unions of signifiers (sound patterns) and signifieds (concepts or thoughts). This latter notion—the signified—is where Saussure locates meaning. So the fact that one sign differs from other signs in a linguistic system does not lead one to an apprehension of a sign's *meaning* (as is the case for Lacan's understanding of signifiers). Rather it leads one to an apprehension of a sign's value. This value is distinct from a sign's meaning and is not immediately bound by the internal link between the signifier and signified but by "what exists outside" this link, namely, all the other signs (Saussure 1986, 114). The function of meaning in Saussure's theory, in contrast, can be described in terms of a closed relation between a sound pattern (signifier) and an idea or a concept (signified). The function of value, however, is more "sociable" and brings us outside of the sign's solipsistic meaning.

The value of a sign is determined by the sign's place in the linguistic system, which is in turn determined by the position of all the other signs in the system. For example, "*mouton*" in French and "sheep" in English are words that have the same meaning but not the same value. This is because the French word is also the word for the meat that comes from sheep, whereas the English word only names the animal and not the meat that comes from it ("mutton") (1986, 114). Thus the meatiness or edibility of sheep is not directly evoked in English, while it is in French.

This example, which is straight from Saussure, indicates that meaning in Saussure's theory has something to do with the object to which a word refers. Otherwise, what sense would there be in saying that "mouton" and "sheep" have the same meaning? What makes them have the same meaning is the fact that they both refer to the same animals. But it must be the case that what Saussure calls "value" is more than just a part of meaning—that is, it is not just any part, a part that a sign could do without. Saussure himself claims that "language itself can be nothing other than a system of pure values" (1986, 110). In fact, we are not able to discern the meaning of a sign in abstraction from its relation to other signs, in abstraction from its value. Thus value is more than just a disposable part of meaning. It serves to color the meaning of a sign. Just as there is no form without color, there would be no meaning without a value coloring it. So Saussure claims that although meaning is to be found in the direct link between signifier and signified, "the content of a word is determined in the final analysis, not by what it contains [i.e., meaning, or the signified] but by what exists outside it. As an element in a system, the word has not only a meaning but also—above all—a value. And that is something quite different" (1986, 114).

Despite this view of the importance of value, Saussure still adheres to a conception of meaning that involves a one-to-one link between signifier and signified. This is something Lacan rejects. In fact, Lacan collapses the distinction between value and meaning in Saussure's work and chooses instead to speak of what Saussure called value as *meaning*. In other words, "value" in Saussure's theory—arguably his most important contribution to linguistics—becomes "meaning" in Lacan's theory, and Saussurean meaning, as a unity of signifier and signified, has no real place in Lacan's theory. In fact, in Lacan's opinion, it is mythical. According to Lacan's view, the signifier alone, as a meaningless unit, is a constituent in a process of meaning production, or what I will also be calling a signified effect.[5]

In Lacan's theory, a signifier's difference from other signifiers is considered to be prior to any possible link between a signifier and whatever meaning or signified might end up being associated with it. Saussure says of language that in it "there are only differences [. . .] *and no positive terms*" (1986, 118 emphasis in original). This is Lacan's position too, only Saussure then goes on to say that this is true only of the signifier and signified "considered separately" (ibid.). That is, signifiers on their own are not "positive" terms but terms steeped in difference: they exist in what I called earlier a "hyper-referential" structure.

But the sign, the unity of these two "negative terms" (signifier and signified), is indeed a positive unit in Saussure's theory. It is able to be isolated, and it forms the basic unit of linguistics. Perhaps Lacan can be characterized as a radical Saussurean: According to Lacan's view, there are nothing but signifiers and signified effects in language. This follows, of course, from his rejection of the distinction made in Saussure's work between value and meaning. There is really nothing but value.

So the concept of the signifier as such does not play as important a role in Saussure's work as it does in Lacan's. It is most often reduced in Saussure's work to being a sound pattern that conveys a meaning. The sign, a union of signifier and signified, is the central concept for Saussure. By emphasizing the distinction between a sign and a signifier, Lacan departs from Saussure, since it is not clear that for Saussure a signifier could be treated independently of its position in the linguistic sign: after all, a signifier is not a "positive term."[6] So the Lacanian signifier is not just another name for the Saussurean sign, because the Lacanian signifier is essentially meaningless. Saussure's sign is not meaningless—it is the primary unit of meaning.

The fate of meaning in Lacan's view of the signifier should now be clear. Lacan's signifier cannot be understood to possess what Saussure meant by either meaning or value. In his third seminar, Lacan put his cards on the table: "Every real signifier is, as such, a signifier that signifies nothing" (III, 210/185). The difference between signs and signifiers can then be described in another way: "It isn't as all or nothing that something is a signifier, it's to the extent that something constituting a whole, the sign, exists and signifies precisely nothing. This is where the order of the signifier, insofar as it differs from the order of meaning, begins" (III, 213/189). The signifier "begins" when the sign is taken out of the referential structure in which it is situated, when the meaning of the sign is "reduced." The signifier then is a purely meaningless and purely differential unit, and unlike the trace, it is not self-sufficient but hyper-referential. As such, it is also distinguished from the sign, whose reference is more or less fixed.

THE PRODUCTIVITY OF SIGNIFIERS

With such a view of the signifier, Lacan is still compelled to give an account of how meaning (Saussurean "value") occurs, since it is not simply given with a signifier. Although Lacan rejects the Saussurean notion of the sign—a union of signifier and signified—this does not prevent him from granting that some sort of signified effect is an important aspect of language. Although there may never be a strict union of signifier and signified, signifiers, according to Lacan, give the *impression* that there is meaning somewhere, however elusive it may be. In fact, this is precisely what signifiers do: they give an *impression* of meaning. As Lacan said in "Function and Field of Speech and Language," "the function of language in speech is not to inform but to evoke" (Lacan 1966, 299/Lacan 2002, 84).

The essential features of signifiers have now been introduced. First, signifiers are not signs. They originate in a destruction of the one-to-one reference that is constitutive of signs. Also, signifiers are constituted by difference, and their uniqueness consists of their difference from other signifiers: this makes them unlike traces. A signifier is, moreover, meaningless. Since Lacan rejects the notion that a signifier and signified (meaning) are united in a single unit, meaning is never ultimately pinned to a signifier. So whatever meaning is, it is not reducible to or identifiable with a particular signifier. According to Lacan, signifiers generate a signified effect or meaning effect that cannot itself be situated within the order of signifiers.

This unfixed meaning effect or signified effect is produced by an interaction of signifiers with each other in what Lacan calls, following Saussure, a signifying chain (Saussure 1986, 70). A signifying chain is nothing other than a succession of signifiers, but as we will see chain is perhaps an inaccurate term. A chain suggests a horizontal series of interlocking parts, but the signifying chain would also have an elaborate vertical dimension. Lacan says as much in "L'instance de la lettre" when he suggests that it would be better to think of a signifying chain in terms of a musical staff (Lacan 1966, 503/Lacan 2002, 146). The two main procedures by which meaning is created, which I will study in the next section (metaphor and metonymy), involve what could be called a latent dimension of signifiers in a spoken or written signifying chain and show us that it is not the case that "signifying chain" simply means "the signifiers that appear in a discursive utterance." For example, there are more signifiers at work in a phrase such as "Pick up some fries for me" than appear manifestly in the phrase. Even according to Saussure, the value of the signifiers in this phrase depends upon other signifiers not included in the phrase itself. In the operations of metaphor and metonymy, as we shall see, use is made of both manifest signifiers and implied or latent signifiers. *Neither of the two is to be conflated with the signified effect or meaning effect produced by the operation.*

Saussure uses a piece of paper as a model for explaining the relation between the signifier and the signified: "Thought is one side of the sheet and sound the reverse side. Just as it is impossible to take a pair of scissors and cut one side of paper without at the same time cutting the other, so it is impossible in a language to isolate sound from thought, or thought from sound" (1986, 111). In this model, the signifier, as "sound," cannot be said to produce the signified. It is bound to the signified, the signified is its flip side, and there is a natural connection between the two. Thus the signifier does not *produce* meaning, because for Saussure meaning "is simply the counterpart of a sound-pattern"—that which is called thought in the example of the piece of paper (ibid.). We can understand Lacan's theory here by saying that Lacan does with the signifier what Saussure thought it was impossible to do. Whereas for Saussure signifier and signified are as closely bound to each other as two sides of a sheet of paper, for Lacan one side of the Saussurean piece of paper is effectively cut away from the other. A signifier is not only something radically independent of any signified—no attachment to any particular signified at all is necessary for it. A signifier can always signify something else, and for this reason on its own it, strictly speaking, signifies nothing.[7]

So if Lacan cuts the sheet of paper in half the "impossible" way, the production of meaning cannot be said to occur by means of a signifier simply being united to a signified. Consider also the image from Saussure's *Course in General Linguistics* in which the sign is presented as that which introduces order into the two otherwise indeterminate fields of thought and sound (1986, 111). On Lacan's view, according to which signifiers are productive, signifiers cannot be understood in similar terms. His "impossible" cutting of one side of the paper from the other means that the production of meaning occurs within and among the network of signifiers. Saussure's diagram gives the impression that sound patterns and meanings preexist the sign in some way, and that signs function to make thoughts and sounds more determinate and distinct. According to Lacan's theory, there is no need to conceive of the sign as something that unites and gives determination to two radically distinct dimensions such as sound and meaning, or signifier and signified. One dimension (sound/signifier) creates the other (thought/signified). A signified is consequently seen as a product or an effect of a signifying chain. As I mentioned earlier, this is ultimately something with which Saussure would not agree. This leads me to suggest, following Marc Darmon, that a suitable image for Lacan's view of the functioning of signifiers is not the Saussurean piece of paper but a Möbius strip, a one-sided surface (1990, 41–43). I will first take a closer look at the functions of metaphor and metonymy as Lacan presents them before going further with this one-sided image of the signifying chain.

These topics will then lead me to a preliminary discussion of the subject in Lacan's work.

But before I do this, it might be important to discuss a bit further just what a signified is in Lacan's theory. Lacan often uses this concept in his work, and I believe that when it is used, it is usually used in the sense of the "signified effect" of which I am speaking here. That is, when Lacan does use the concept "signified," when he is not criticizing it as something that does not exist (there are only ever signifiers), he is using it in the sense of a "signified effect" generated by signifiers. This cannot exactly be characterized, as it was for Saussure, as a "concept" or a "thought." And it is not simply what we would normally call a word's meaning. Certainly, meanings can be quite clear at times. By saying "pass me the salt," my intention is probably clear, and we might want to say that the meaning of the phrase is unambiguous. But the idea of a meaning or signified effect recalls to us that there is always more evoked by words than what one wants them to mean, and it is not always possible to reduce evocation down to the kind of fixed meaning possessed by signs. The point here is that even when I say "pass me the salt," there is still more said than what we might normally take the phrase to mean. For example, the phrase may evoke certain signifiers on the part of various listeners, it may get them to wonder about my intentions. Perhaps the meaning of the phrase is after all fundamentally ambiguous, in that it cannot be asserted with absolute certainty that I actually *mean* "pass me the salt" when I say "pass me the salt." Maybe I am quoting someone, or maybe "pass me the salt" is an idiomatic expression from my part of the country meaning "how great!" or something entirely different. Granted, this is rather silly. But I am simply trying to illustrate that what is being spoken of here as the signified—always really just a signified effect—is something other than what we might take the more or less easily determinable meaning of a signifier or phrase to be. This "easily determinable meaning" never completely does away with the aura of ambiguity surrounding every signifier and every signifying chain. This aura of ambiguity is just what Lacan's idea of a signified effect is trying to account for. In his later works, Lacan expressed this in a phrase: "qu'on dise reste oublié derrière ce qui se dit dans ce qui s'entend" (Lacan 2001, 449). Very roughly translated, Lacan is saying here that there is (or should be?) always something that remains forgotten behind what is said in what we hear or understand.

In what follows, I will try to be rigorous in my use of the terms *signified effect* and *signified*. I will use the former to speak of the evocativeness produced by an interaction of signifiers, and I will use the latter to speak of what one ends up with when one attempts to reduce this evocativeness. In this case, we have an apparently stable meaning and the appearance of a one-to-one correspondence of a signifier and a meaning. Of course, such an idea is mythical, but it does nevertheless play an important role in our lived experience of language. But this fixed meaning is in fact always just another signifier, evoking others, generating yet another signified effect.

METAPHOR AND METONYMY

What I wish to do now is show how signifiers are able to produce signified effects and how these have a strange status with respect to the signifying chain itself: they are not quite within it but not simply beyond it either. Metaphor and metonymy are two figures of speech that produce signified effects that resonate "beyond" the signifying chain itself, effects that are created in the signifying chain but that are also in excess of it.

Lacan defines metaphor as the substitution of one signifier for another in a signifying chain: a substitution that, he says, is productive of a signified effect. Metaphor does not work by juxtaposing two different images, or two signifiers (Lacan 1966, 507/Lacan 2002, 148). Lacan wishes to say that *substitution* of one signifier for another is essential to metaphor: a substitution that leads to one signifier being effectively covered up by another in a signifying chain. Here the image of a signifying chain as a musical staff must be used, since it allows us to imagine how two signifiers—one manifest and one suggested—can coexist. Metonymy will also reinforce the necessity for such an image of the signifying chain, as we shall soon see.

Consider an example: Upon their arrival to America, Freud allegedly said to Jung, "They don't know that we're bringing them the plague" (Lacan 1966, 403/Lacan 2002, 109). What is the metaphor here? The plague, of course, is psychoanalysis. The signifier "psychoanalysis," however, is not present in what Freud said. The signifier "plague" covers it up. This example can be used to illustrate the distinction between the signified and the signified effect. The "signified" that is produced by this metaphor is simply another signifier. In other words, Freud was talking about psychoanalysis without using the word explicitly. However there is a signified effect, a resonance, created by this substitution that is not reducible to the signifier acting as a signified ("psychoanalysis") but is instead something that neither the signifier "psychoanalysis" or the signifier "plague" is able to convey on its own: the idea that psychoanalysis is a devastating and highly contagious disease, as well as what Freud's own opinions about psychoanalysis were (did he believe it was justifiably seen as a plague, or was he just anticipating America's response to his work?). To put it in terms of that passage from "Function and Field of Speech and Language," cited earlier, if this metaphor manages to inform us about psychoanalysis, telling us that it is a plague, then it does not inform us enough. It evokes more than it informs, or what it evokes is not reducible to the information we glean from it.

Metonymy also produces a signified effect. Whereas metaphor can be characterized as a process in which a signified effect is created by putting one signifier in place of another, metonymy differs, according to Lacan, by being a "word to word" process (Lacan 1966, 506/Lacan 2002, 148). However, Lacan gives a definition of metonymy in his third seminar that only seems to confuse it with metaphor by using the term *substitution*: "The rhetorical form that is the opposite of metaphor has a name—it's called metonymy. It involves substitution for something that has to be named [...]. One thing is named by another that is its container, or its part, or that is connected to it" (III, 250/220-221). This is a typical understanding of metonymy, and Lacan's view changes a few years later.[8] Lacan gives more specificity to his concept of metonymy in his fifth seminar, where we find out that what is important in metonymy is contiguity in the signifying chain itself and not necessarily any "conceptual" or real contiguity. According to most understandings of metonymy, metonymy exploits some kind of conceptual or real relation between part and whole. This way, for example, "sail," a part of a ship, is used to name the whole ship in a phrase from *El Cid*: "thirty sails in the harbor" (V, 73). Lacan diverges from the normal view of metonymy by situating the contiguity at stake in the signifying chain itself and not in a conceptual or real relation. He points out that ships often have more than one sail, so the phrase in question could be referring to one ship. And if there are in fact thirty ships in the harbor, then there are probably more than thirty sails in the harbor (V, 73). For these reasons, Lacan claims that "the function given to the sail in relation to the ship is in a signifying chain, and not in the reference to the real; in the continuity of this chain and not in a substitution. It's a matter, then [...] of a transfer of signification along this chain" (V, 74). Curiously, however, "ship" does not occur manifestly in the signifying chain being considered in this example of metonymy, and this could lead one to think that "sails" is indeed being substituted for it in some way. Lacan conceded in his third seminar, as we have seen, that there is something like a substitution going on in metonymy. Why does Lacan want to deny that substitution occurs in metonymy?

Substitution is a very bad way to account for the difference between metaphor and metonymy. If we think of a metaphor as a comparison, it is easier to keep metaphor and metonymy distinct from each other. "Thirty sails in the harbor" does not involve a comparison of ships with sails but uses "sail" as a name for a ship. When Lacan refers to "the function given to the sail in relation to the ship" it is this nominating function he has in mind. "Sail" functions as a new way of naming "ship," and the signifying chain itself makes this signifier function as a name, by simply using it as such. Metonymy, then, operates by using a new name without relying on a substitution. It just gives "ships" another name and is not comparing ships to sails. In a metaphor, in contrast, there is always a comparison going on, and a comparison is a metaphor when it substitutes one signifier for another.

The important point to bear in mind is that metaphor and metonymy both occur in a signifying chain, and it is not any reference to reality, to anything "outside" the chain, that makes these figures of speech do what they do. But it is difficult to see how this is the case, since both metaphor and metonymy rely upon signifiers that are not part of what can be called the manifest signifying chain. In what way, then, do they occur "in" a signifying chain? This difficulty can be resolved, I think, if we recall that a signifying chain is a "multidimensional" structure involving both manifest and latent dimensions.

But even such a structure does not give us a representation of the space of the signified effect. It simply describes the interaction of signifiers among themselves in vertical and horizontal dimensions, both being temporal dimensions representing synchrony and diachrony, respectively. Really, this is all there is for Lacan. But the whole machine, when set to working, produces a little ghost. This is what I am calling the signified effect. What place can we give to the signified effect in metaphor and metonymy?

THE FORMULAS FOR METONYMY AND METAPHOR AND THE PLACE OF THE SIGNIFIED EFFECT

The formulas that Lacan developed during his fifth seminar and published in "L'instance de la lettre" try to describe how metaphor and metonymy bring about their signified effects differently. What I will try to explain here is how metonymy creates an absent or a withdrawn signified effect, while metaphor creates a verbal incarnation of a signified effect in a signifier by conflating a signifier with this effect, making that signifier act as a signified.

Lacan gives the following formula for metonymy:

$$f(S\ldots S')S \cong S\,(-)\,s$$

The Ss stand for signifiers, and the *s* for a signified effect. This formula expresses much that we already know about metonymy: the movement from one signifier to another in the signifying chain (S . . . S') is congruent to or tantamount to (S≅) one signifier giving the effect of there being a signified somewhere, an effect that is not placed in the signifying chain but that "resonates" beyond the signifying chain, indeed, beyond the signifier itself (S−*s*) (V, 145). The bar between S and *s* can then be taken to represent a gap between signifiers and the signified effect but also as a minus sign, such that metonymy gives us signifiers with an absent signified effect. "Resonance" is perhaps the ideal term for expressing what it is that metonymy achieves.

The formula for metaphor is given as follows:

$$f(S'/S)S \cong S\,(+)\,s$$

This formula indicates that a signified effect is produced by a substitution of one signifier for another signifier, and that one of the signifiers in the operation becomes the stand-in for this effect itself, as indicated by the fragment of the formula: S ≅ S (+) *s*: here S is a signifier charged with a signified (Lacan 1966, 515/Lacan 2002, 155–156). Metaphor does not only create a signified effect that exceeds any particular signifier, it also achieves an incarnation of this effect in a particular signifier, which then acts as the "signified" of the metaphor. This is evoked by the plus sign in the formula which, Lacan explains, manifests "the crossing of the bar" between the signifier and the signified (515/156). The elusiveness that characterizes the kind of signified effect produced by metonymy is, in metaphor, incarnated in one signifier.

On this basis, we can see why the difference between metonymy and metaphor was so important for Lacan. For one thing, Lacan sees metonymy as the framework "within which something new and creative can be produced, which is metaphor. Even if something originally metonymic is put in a position of substitution, as is the case with thirty sails, it is something other than a metaphor. In other words, there would not be metaphor if it weren't for metonymy" (V, 75). In metonymy, the illusion is created that a signified is there just beyond the next signifier, so to speak, only no signifier manages to incarnate it. By making a signified effect "resonate" throughout the signifying chain, the arrival of a full signified is put off into the future. The realization that "thirty sails" means "thirty ships" does not exhaust the signified effect that this figure of speech brings about. The signifying resonance that metonymy produces suffuses the entire chain with the absence of a signified. So whereas from a normal point of view the metonymy would amount to saying "ships" without actually saying it, making ships into the signified of the metonymy in question, on Lacan's view a signified effect is produced that is different from either "ships" or "sails." Even when we know that "ships" is meant by "sails," Lacan argues that we are still clueless about why the ships are there, and exactly how many ships there are in the first place (V, 75). What Lacan emphasizes in metonymy is a "glissement de sens"—the signified flees from us, leaving something enigmatic about the metonymy as a whole.

With this understanding of metonymy, Lacan is able to claim that metonymy affects the structure of any signifying chain. Insofar as it takes time for a signifying chain to unfold, there is always something like a metonymic relation established among all the signifiers of a signifying chain. For this reason, metaphor must be said to presuppose metonymy. And here we see one reason for Lacan's insistence on the difference between metonymy and metaphor. Metonymy is a primary structure for any signifying chain, and metaphor presupposes this structure. Every metaphor occurs within a signifying chain that already presumes a metonymic context. This also means that without first establishing a lack of a signified there would be no possibility for metaphor's verbal incarnation of a signified. In a metaphor, what we have is a signifier that stands in for the ambiguity of the signified. Thus a metaphor is a kind of hieroglyph, an enigma, presented in a signifier. Another way to put this is to say that for interpreting a metaphor we have nothing else to go on but the metaphor itself. In metonymy, the context is always there to help us, and we can always expect more signifiers to come that might offer clarification. Consider the signifying fragments reported in Freud's case study of Schreber. Lacan describes such fragments (incomplete phrases such as "Factum est...," which would insistently pop into Schreber's head) in terms of contiguity, a central concept for his understanding of metonymy (III, 249/220). Schreber was at a loss as to the meaning of these fragments, but we can say that they definitely created a signified effect, that is, he felt that they meant something, only he did not know what.

To put all this another way, if metonymy may be characterized as messianic, promising a full meaning that never really comes but is just around the corner, metaphor could be characterized as Pauline. St. Paul's works, of course, cannot be characterized as messianic insofar as they announce the arrival, *which has already happened*, of the kingdom of God. As Paul said, "the kingdom of heaven comes like a thief in the night." In a metaphor, the "kingdom" of the signified is suddenly there in a signifier that incarnates a meaning whose effects you are now living in—only this all happened while you were sleeping, as it were, and once again you missed its full presence! Instead, you simply live in its effects. Metonymy also creates an enigma, but this is more an enigma in the form of a "glissement de sens" that does not manage to incarnate a signified effect in a signifier. In his third seminar, Lacan discusses a particular type of aphasia that helps illustrate my point here:

> You are all familiar with Wernicke's aphasia. The aphasic links together a sequence of sentences of an extraordinarily developed grammatical nature. He will say—*Yes, I understand. Yesterday, when I was up there, already he said, and I wanted, I said to him, that's not it, the date, not exactly, not that one. . . .*
>
> The subject thereby demonstrates complete mastery of everything articulated, organized, subordinated, and structured in the sentence, but what he says is always wide of what he wants to say. Not for an instant can you be in any doubt that what he wants to say is present, but he never manages to give verbal incarnation to what he is aiming at in the sentence. (III, 249/219, emphasis in original)

Just as is the case with metonymy, a full meaning is promised in this case of Wernicke's aphasia, but it remains entirely evasive. The distinction Lacan makes here between what is present in the utterance (a promise of meaning) and a "verbal incarnation" is interesting. Despite the fact that we do not know exactly what the aphasic wanted to say, we do not doubt that he wanted to say something, and this "wanting" is itself evident in the clumsiness of the utterance. The aphasic's statements create a signified effect that is not incarnated anywhere. Metaphor, in contrast, would achieve a "verbal incarnation" (this formulation should strike the reader—an incarnation of what is promised in the Word) for the signified effect Lacan speaks of here, although even in the case of metaphors the full signified remains something that one does not simply "have."

Have we learned anything about the nature of a signified effect from this? Even though metaphor, in contrast to metonymy, achieves a "verbal incarnation" of meaning, a signified is still not fully, or simply, present in it. In Saussure's work, the signifier and signified were as impossible to separate from each other as the two sides of a piece of paper. The edge of the paper can be used to represent the bar between the signifier and signified. In Saussure's work, this bar is always in some sense crossed: there is no signifier without a signified, just as there are no one-sided pieces of paper. Given that Lacan promotes the independence of the signifier from the signified, the bar cannot have exactly the same function for him as it does for Saussure. For Saussure, the bar couples and does not separate. Even though Lacan does speak of a "crossing of the bar" in metaphor, the bar is for him something that maintains a distance, something that functions to separate signifiers from the signified. This is implied by his claim that metonymy is a structure on which metaphor depends: in other words, metaphor requires a signifying chain (something in which a bar between signifier and signified is established and maintained) in order to create the effect of a crossing of the bar. In metonymy, the signified slides away from signifiers and is always absent from signifiers, even though it is always suggested by them. Metaphor presupposes this arrangement but produces a "verbal incarnation" of the signified effect by making one signifier pose as the signified: the "plague" *is* "psychoanalysis."

What I wish to avoid with this reading is the idea that a signified effect can actually be reduced to a signifier, which Lacan's formulas (particularly the one for metaphor) may lead one to believe. Samuel Weber, in his *Return to Freud*, makes it sound as if this were the case: "As a result of substitution, the repressed signifier is banned to the realm of the signified, or more precisely, to a 'place' where it functions as a signified, while, however, remaining as a signifier" (1991, 68). This is true, insofar as metaphor makes one signifier act as a stand-in for the signified effect. As I have been saying, the term *signified* is appropriate for what happens here, even though what we have with this "signified" is simply another signifier. But what Weber is saying may be misleading in that it does not discuss what I am calling here the "signified effect," the lower-case, italicized "s" in Lacan's formulas, for the signified effect of a metaphor is not one of the signifiers involved in its production, be it "plague" or the "repressed" signifier "psychoanalysis." So the repressed signifier is not equivalent to the signified-effect, and what functions as a signified effect does not remain in the signifying chain as a signifier. "Psychoanalysis" is not the signified effect of the metaphor we considered earlier. The signified effect can perhaps be characterized as a new resonance that gets incarnated by the "signified" "psychoanalysis."

So Weber has a point if we want to talk not about the signified effect but the determination or fixing of this effect—then, indeed, we have a signifier acting as a signified. And Weber is certainly right to speak of a "place" for the signified. Lacan thinks of this place as something in excess of any signifier. To return to the image of the Möbius strip, the strip could be taken as the signifying chain, and the void that the strip surrounds would be where the signified effect should be placed. This also helps explain why Lacan, in his explanation of the formula for metonymy, speaks of it as introducing a "lack of being" with respect to an object. The maintenance of a bar between signifier and signified amounts to the creation of something beyond the signifying chain, which can be said to lack therein despite attempts to incarnate it (in metaphor). Thus unlike in the Saussurean model, where the signified is available on the other side of the sheet of paper, in Lacan's theory what is on the other side is always another signifier just posing as the meaning or signified (a Möbius strip is, after all, a one-sided surface), and one keeps going around the signified effect without actually getting to it. As Marc Darmon puts it, "The signified of saying, for its part, ex-sists in relation to the said, that is, it is to be situated elsewhere, beyond the edge of the strip" (1990, 43). According to Lacan, the "other side" of signifiers is in fact produced by the order of signifiers. The main point is that the order of signifiers produces the effect that there is an order of final signifieds beyond signifiers. In imagining the space of this signified effect, we must not be misled into thinking the "beyond" of the Möbius strip of signifiers as something that exists prior to signifiers, or as something that the chain of signifiers is attached to as a sign is supposed to be attached to its referent. In fact, the signifying chain itself forges the signified effect's space.

THE FALSE FALSE

I would like, in conclusion, to give a hint as to how signifiers produce a subject effect and not just a signified effect, which will be the topic of chapter 3. Lacan's definition of the signifier is bound up with a conception of the subject. In the previous chapter, I introduced Lacan's claim that a signifier represents a subject, but I argued that this is not because signifiers represent that subject's intentions. Signifiers are not a medium that a subject uses to communicate. Rather, just as meaning, rigorously speaking, never occurs as a hard and fast relation between a signifier and signified, although there is a meaning effect or signified effect, there is also a subject effect that occurs due to the interaction of signifiers.

Lacan uses an example at different moments in his work that is meant to explain the sense in which signifiers produce a subject. But at first sight, the example only presents problems. It is known that certain animals are capable of hiding their tracks. Now, Lacan once described the creation of a signifier in terms of a crossing out of a trace. Why? Because crossing out a trace gives us a difference between two traces—the trace that crosses out, and the trace that is crossed out. This crossing out makes one trace refer to another trace, and so there is a resemblance to a signifier here. Recall that Lacan at one time defined a signifier as a sign that refers to another sign.

The example of an animal that crosses out its tracks raises the following question: By virtue of covering up its tracks, does this animal create signifiers? Lacan says no, but the justification for this answer is not immediately obvious. If these covered-up tracks do not qualify as signifiers, then it must be because they still primarily function as marks of an absent presence and thus must still be signs. When the animal covers up its tracks, it does not efface the potential signlike nature of the tracks. In order to justify this claim, Lacan is forced to introduce another understanding of what signifiers do, and this links signifiers directly to subjects.

This idea is the following: An animal can certainly cover up its tracks, but it does not make false false tracks. If we discover the covered-up tracks of an animal we may be certain that the animal went the way the (previously hidden) tracks indicate. What an animal cannot do is leave tracks that lead us to think it went a certain way, but since the tracks look false, we believe that the animal must have gone another way, when in fact it did go the first way after all.[9] In other words, "Traces made so that they are believed to be false but are nevertheless the traces of my true passage [. . .] this is what I mean by saying that in them a subject is made present, when a trace has been made so that it is taken for a false trace," but is in fact the true one (IX, 12/12/62). A sign simply refers to an absent presence. A signifier does something different, because signifiers are differential by nature. A signifier gives and hides at the same time. Such giving and hiding, such presence and absence, is also a key property of the subject effect.[10]

This adds something to our understanding of what a signifier is. A signifier is not only characterized by its radical difference and its participation in a hyper-referential structure. What makes a signifier a signifier, according to Lacan, is its "presentation" or creation of a subject effect. This is not a subject whose intentions are represented by the signifier, but a subject that is itself nothing but something represented by the signifier, a subject as an indeterminate product, something supposed behind the signifier.

This is perhaps an overcomplicated way of making a very simple point about how the unconscious functions. Freud's article "Negation" gives us another way of seeing the close relation between the signifier and a subject effect, as well as a way of seeing how a subject effect is presented in signifiers (which is the point Lacan was trying to make with his example). Freud argues that when someone in an analysis says something like "You ask me who this person in the dream can be. It's *not* my mother," the smart money is on that person in the dream being the patient's mother after all (1961b [1925h], 235, emphasis in original). Negation, according to Freud, is a mechanism by means of which unconscious thoughts and desires enter consciousness, and the truth of the unconscious shows through despite the attempt on the part of the conscious ego to negate it. Although the signifier in question enters consciousness in negative terms, what is important is the entrance of that particular signifier at that particular moment, regardless of whether the signifier is affirmed or negated by consciousness. The "not" is an attempt to efface the signifier "mother" and to lead the analyst to believe that the analysand's true thoughts are elsewhere, that the dream had nothing to do with his or her mother. This battle against a signifier in signifiers allows us to see how the conscious subject, the ego, is at odds with another tendency, a tendency that the signifier "mother" manages to represent. Signifiers, despite our conscious use of them, despite our illusory control over their emergence and our illusory belief in our control over how they are to be taken and read, reveal that there is a subject in a place other than the conscious speaking subject's place. This is the kind of subject Lacan theorizes.

Signifiers, then, are indifferent to the conscious subject's (the ego's) intentions. Where the analysand wishes to deceive the analyst is where there is truth: this is the very structure of the "false false" and is in fact the structure of the basic functions of the unconscious—puns, parapraxes, dreams, and slips of the tongue. The unconscious produces signifiers that can be embellished by negations, but which are in fact true. The truth appears despite our attempts to falsify it, or rather, the truth appears *because* of our attempts to falsify it. One always says more than one intends. So the signifier is in excess of the intention of the conscious subject. It is in this signifying excess, in saying more than we meant to, that the subject effect is to be situated, and not in consciousness, where we struggle to use signifiers to get a meaning across.

CONCLUSION

Something must be added here, however, because it is still possible to think that even this kind of subject exists prior to the signifiers that reveal it. Is it not simply another *intention* that is shown when the signifier "mother" is blurted out, especially in an analysis? This might suggest that the only real difference between the conscious subject and the Lacanian subject is one of position. According to this reading, it could be granted that the ego is conscious and the subject is unconscious, but both would still appear to have intentions that are expressed in signifiers. This is Borch-Jacobsen's and Lacoue-Labarthe and Nancy's point, in fact. If this were the case, there would be no essential difference between the Lacanian subject and the classical subject regarding the relation of the subject to signifiers: both would be using signifiers to represent their intentions. And so both subjects are subjects who have a certain mastery over signifiers. Lacan wants to claim that signifiers produce a subject effect that does not preexist its presentation by signifiers but is produced and sustained by a signifying consistency. In other words, signifiers are the mode of the subject's being. Insofar as the subject has some sort of being or consistency, this being or consistency is "of signifiers," but again, this is not a complete picture of the subject in Lacan's work.

According to Borch-Jacobsen, signifiers in Lacan's theory are purified of any *specific* communication or message. This means that signifiers are independent of any specific signified. But what we do have with Lacan's understanding of the signifier, according to him, is something boiled down to a pure intention to communicate—which is why, Borch-Jacobsen explains, a signifier represents the subject and nothing else. According to Borch-Jacobsen, "The subject is now the *elusive* signified of all signifiers, what they all represent in his absence; but he is none the less their signified, to which their references refer" (1991, 187, emphasis in original). The subject is a signified in the sense of being a fundamental referent, a fundamental ground for all utterances. The subject is, then, something to which all signifiers refer. If the subject is the fundamental referent of signifiers, then this is because the subject uses signifiers in order to express itself—to announce if not any specific communication or message at least its very existence as a subject. The subject, then, is something that wants to express itself.

What Borch-Jacobsen's reading fails to consider is why Lacan finishes his definition of the signifier ("the signifier represents a subject . . . ") with the phrase "to another signifier." The point is not that the subject has left a trace that must then be deciphered (by other subjects, presumably) as being the trace of a subject, a trace of a hidden intention running counter to what the conscious individual wanted to say—in this case, all the subject could ever leave behind it are signs, and we would be forgetting the distinction between signifiers and signs. If we take seriously the idea that signifiers produce a subject effect (instead of saying the reverse—that a subject leaves signifiers of its "passage," its true intentions, behind it), then we must call into question the idea, implied by Borch-Jacobsen's reading, that there is a subject that exists prior to its expression, a subject who leaves traces of its hidden intentions in conscious discourse. What is at stake here, in fact, is a good understanding of the nature and status of the unconscious.[11] Is the unconscious an eternally existing, deep nether-region that contains the true intentions and meanings of the subject? Lacan is vehemently opposed to such an interpretation of the unconscious, such that, according to his view, the unconscious cannot even be said to express itself.[12] It does not consist of a region of intentions that can only achieve expression between the lines, as it were, of a conscious, spoken discourse. The unconscious "consists" of nothing but interruptions, bursts, and gaps in signifying practices: "Discontinuity, then, is the essential form in which the unconscious first appears to us as a phenomenon—discontinuity, in which something is manifested as a vacillation" (XI, 34/25). If this is the case for the unconscious, then what must we think about the subject of the unconscious?

I have been saying that the subject is a product of signifiers. This still needs to be explained. For now it should be noted that if it is a product of signifiers, then we have no reason to suppose that this subject has any intentions whatsoever, or that it is a subject that uses signifiers in an attempt to communicate something.

CHAPTER 3

Identity, or the Subject-as-Meaning

The subject is the consequence of the fact that there is a signifier. And [. . .] the birth of the subject holds good [*se tient*] only insofar as it can be thought of as excluded from the signifier that determines it. (IX, 2/5/62)

In this chapter I will discuss in more detail what is bound up with the idea of a subject being represented by a signifier. Despite what Lacan's definition of the signifier implies, he also insists that a subject is never identical to any signifier: "The subject that [the signifier] represents is not univocal; [the subject] is represented, undoubtedly, but it is also not represented" (XVII, 101). Represented but also not represented: my claim that the subject is like a signified effect is able to account for both of these ideas and will be able to show how a subject has both metonymic and metaphoric characteristics. In the last chapter, we saw how metonymy and metaphor produce signified effects that are both present and absent from a signifying chain. In metaphor, a particular signifier stands in for the more diffuse signified effect, marking the presence of that effect in the signifying chain. Metonymy marks rather the perpetual absence of the signified while at the same time succeeding in creating a signified *effect*.

At the end of chapter 2, I said a little about the subject not being represented by signifiers. If a subject is something like a signified effect, then this means that it never has a hard and fast place in a signifying chain and is not reducible to any point, any signifier, of a signifying chain. But a subject is also represented nonetheless, and there are certain signifiers to which a subject gets fixated. Certain signifiers then are more important for the subject than others, and these are the signifiers involved in the identity of a subject.

A central tenet of this theory of the subject can be put as follows: a subject has an identity, but it is not identical to its identity. In this respect, Lacan's theory of the subject is not unlike a traditional theory of the subject. Even the Cartesian cogito was distinct from at least some of its attributes. But the subject theorized by Lacan is not a conscious, reflecting subject. Such a point is often made about the subject in Lacan's theory, but it is easily forgotten or set aside, and we can easily continue to think that this subject is still something like a conscious subject—a subject who wishes to express itself, who represents the world to itself, a subject who interprets, and so on, albeit on another level. I am studying the subject as a product of signifiers here partly in order to avoid this mistaken impression about Lacan's conception of the subject. The subject in Lacan's theory is a function of signifiers. In order to gain clarity on what this means, the structures involved in using signifiers have to be studied. What structures are involved in using signifiers? In the previous chapter, I explained the different ways in which signifiers produce a signified effect. In this chapter, we will see how a relation to others in general is also implied by any use of signifiers. In the next chapter, a relation to the body, affects, trauma, and the real will be studied.

This relation to others in general is central for understanding what is at stake in the subject's representation by a signifier. As the critics I discussed in chapter 1 argue, representation is an important topic in Lacan's theory, and the subject is indeed represented by a signifier. But it is not its intentions that are represented. Rather, its mere existence as a *desired* subject is what gets represented. So representation and identification are closely related. Identity, according to Lacan, always involves being desired by others: more specifically, our identities are what enable us to think we are desirable.

According to Lacan, "The subject is born insofar as the signifier emerges in the field of the Other" (XI, 223/198). Taking this idea strictly, a subject is born when there is a name for a child—or a mere expectation, wish, or regret on the part of its parents. When a signifier emerges for a child to be, that child is fixed to that signifier at birth. Gradually, the child-subject "se fige en signifiant"; he or she gets congealed into this signifier (XI, 223/199). In his 1959 article "Jeunesse de Gide," Lacan in fact referred to the Other as a place "where the subject is constituted as signified" (Lacan 1966, 751). Fixing the subject to a signifier is a step toward making a subject who is a signified in the Other.

INTRODUCTION TO THE SUBJECT-AS-MEANING

What does it mean to say that subjects are produced by signifiers? Are subjects not produced by sex acts, pregnancies, and birthing? According to Lacan's theory, a flesh-and-blood individual is not the same as a subject. Certainly a subject is not possible without flesh and blood. But, curiously, there can be an individual without this individual being a subject. This at least is one consequence of Lacan's theory of the subject. The subject is a particular kind of effect of signifiers on a real individual.[1]

One way to approach the idea that a subject is produced by an interaction of signifiers is to consider the signifying context that precedes the birth of an individual. There is usually already a chain of signifiers ("a sea of language," as Lacan says) existing for a child before he or she is born. While the social, economic, and material conditions of a child's environment are important factors in his or her life, as well as his or her genetic makeup, Lacan holds that it is what is said that is important for determining what conditions the *subject* will exist under. Odile Bernard-DeSoria has a provocative way of illustrating what I am getting at here. "A child is not born of a sexual act between two beings, male and female, but of the signifying encounter between two subjects" (1992, 23). What is being called a subject here is "born" from what is said between two subjects, that is, in the parental discourse preceding the child's birth. This is the signifying chain from which the subject is produced:

> "If it's a boy, I'll name him after my brother who died in the war," one mother says.
>
> "I've always dreamt of a girl who would ride horses well," expresses another mother.
>
> Predictions, admissions of attachment, narcissistic wishes, these words show what anticipates the coming into the world of every human subject.
>
> Most often not expressed, sometimes mortifying—"I don't want a girl, I hate girls," was said during one young woman's analysis—the child to come is preceded by the effects of unconscious words, which are themselves the remainders, the scoria of an entire history, belonging to previous generations. A child's umbilical cord is made up of nothing but these signifiers produced by his or her ancestors and transmitted at the same time as the color of his or her eyes or the shape of his or her cranium. (1992, 23–24)

Catherine Mathelin puts things even more dramatically. Describing the changes that psychoanalysis with children underwent in the 1960s in France, largely due to Lacan's work, she claims, "for the very first time, it was recognized that the child could be its parents' symptom" (1999, 4). Mathelin's work makes it clear that the symptoms children bring into the clinic are often determined by what is repressed on the part of their parents. So in analyses of children we find cases where the unconscious of one (or both?) of the parents exists "on" the child, so to speak.

Consider the case of "Xénophon," a boy Mathelin had in analysis for more than six years, beginning at age four. When Mathelin first met him, Xénophon did not speak at all. His parents brought him to Mathelin when doctors and psychiatrists suggested having him put into an institution, after having diagnosed him with autism.[2] How do you analyze someone who does not speak? As is usually the case in the analysis of a child, the analysis began with drawing. In particular, for Xénophon, the analysis began when he would mark with a cross (X) the notes Mathelin would read out to him, notes she made while Xénophon's mother was speaking. (Mathelin would begin the session with both Xénophon and his mother: his mother would do the talking. Then Mathelin would do what she could with the child alone. She began by simply reading out loud to Xénophon the notes she had made when his mother was talking.) Xénophon seemed very interested in what Mathelin was saying and ended each session by putting a cross at the bottom of her page of notes. He would not make any other communications, nor any other drawings. For a long time, this was his only act in the analysis. It was as if he were signing her observations, agreeing to them, and entering into a contractual relationship with her.

The importance of the signifier "cross" became increasingly clear in the course of the analysis. As a grave marker, it was bound up with the death of the younger sister of Xénophon's mother, which his mother never got over. Mathelin's interpretation is that Xénophon had become this dead child for his mother. In fact, he always already was this dead child, and Xénophon had simply assumed a position that was made for him. As Mathelin puts it, "a child always identifies with what concerns the mother most. Xénophon had identified with the object in the tomb. Thus there was no need for him to talk" (1999, 100). Certainly Xénophon would not have been able to have the position he had if it were not for his mother's acute feelings of guilt at the death of her sister. It may seem like Xénophon did not actually have to do anything to assume this role at all. It was put onto him, it was already there for him, in many different ways: in his mother's constant fear that her child would die, in the fact that his mother never left him alone, in the many visits both made to her sister's grave, and in who knows what else was said, implied, and hinted at. Yet his "signing" of Mathelin's notes with an "X" also indicates an assumption of this role of the dead child on his part.

The analytic cure generally proceeds by shifting the value of such "mortifying," deterministic signifiers. They become relativized: no longer the oppressive force they once were, in the course of analysis they are able to take on different meanings. As we shall see, something like this is also at work in the notion of the psychoanalytic act that I will be discussing in chapter 6. In the case of Xénophon, this shift in meaning was clear in how the "cross" changed its role in his drawings. As the analysis progressed, the crosses became, as he put it (once he was finally speaking), "star crosses, and you need them to live. It's not like crosses for dead people" (1999, 99). One sees such a result often in Mathelin's fascinating case studies: analysis manages to relativize the signifiers that were once oppressive for the child. Through the analysis, these signifiers wind up generating different meanings, beyond the meaning that had been determined for them by the Other.

What this case shows us is that an interaction among signifiers is of capital importance for the subject. True, a real child is not produced by signifiers, but no child exists, lives, or suffers without their interaction. If human beings did not speak, then children would still come into being. But the fact that something comes into being in language and through language first (for example, by saying, thinking, or dreaming "I want a child . . . "; or, with the signifying configuration "dead child," into which the flesh-and-blood Xénophon "fell into") makes for all the difference between individuals and what are being called here "subjects."

Such signifying chains are the stuff of the unconscious. According to Lacan, the unconscious is, famously, "the Other's discourse." This should be taken literally, and my brief discussion of the case of Xénophon hopefully makes it clear how. "Dead child" is an example of a meaning for the Other, a signifying chain making up part of the Other's discourse. This signifying chain was an important aspect of Xénophon's unconscious: an Other discourse that was determining his existence, yet one that he also in some way agreed to.

THE SUBJECT-AS-MEANING

This case study gives us a clearer picture of how a subject is produced by signifiers. In part, and first of all, a subject is a meaning for the

Other. But Lacan's theory of the subject is in fact much more complicated, as we might guess from the fact that this meaning, in this case, was transformed by manipulating signifiers in a psychoanalytic cure. Through a talking cure, Xénophon went from being a dead child to being a living, speaking child.

To begin complicating the picture, consider the following passage from Lacan's fourteenth seminar. Lacan says that "the barred subject as such is what represents a meaning to a signifier, this signifier from which it has emerged" (XIV, 11/16/66).[3] We can take a guess at what Lacan means here based on the case of Xénophon. Xénophon represents the meaning "dead child" to his mother. But this passage from the fourteenth seminar raises some questions about the relation between a subject and signifiers. The passage states that a subject represents a meaning to another signifier. But how can a subject represent a meaning? After all, *signifiers* represent. If a subject represents, is the subject acting like a signifier? And does this not go against the idea that a subject is not reducible or identical to a signifier?

If we recall Lacan's definition of the signifier—according to which it is *the signifier* that "represents the subject to another signifier"—then there is something peculiar about this passage from the fourteenth seminar. According to this passage, a subject is playing the role of a signifier: it represents a meaning to another signifier. Yet this is indeed one way in which the subject appears in Lacan's work: it describes a subject involved in identification. Identification, in turn, is wrapped up with gaining recognition from the Other; it confirms or affirms the meaning that is already carved out for me in the Other. In the next chapter, I will study the motivations behind making such an identification in the first place.

ON IDENTIFICATION

So the subject-as-meaning, or the subject as a signifier representing a meaning to another signifier, is the identity of a subject. Early in his career, Lacan described identification in terms of the mirror stage. This stage concerns a time in the child's development (between six and eighteen months of age) during which the child is fascinated by its image in mirrors (Lacan 1966, 93–100/Lacan 2002, 3–9). Lacan took note of the fact that this interest is unique to human beings—our closest relatives in the animal kingdom may be able to recognize their own images, but they take only a passing interest in their reflections in mirrors. Infants of a certain age are captivated by them. Why is this? Lacan claims that this interest arises from the child's *de facto* underdevelopment. Humans are born prematurely in comparison to other animals: we cannot yet walk, and our nervous systems have not yet developed to a point where other movements can be well coordinated and controlled. The mirror image allows the child to anticipate a coordination, gracefulness, and control that it does not yet have over itself. Not only does it see itself as a unified form in the mirror (already at odds with how the child actually must be experiencing itself), the image also responds directly to the child's movements and intentions.

Ethologists have discovered that images are often crucial in the development of organisms. Female pigeons in captivity, for example, will not ovulate unless they are presented with an image of another pigeon, and this may be a real pigeon, a reflection in a mirror, or even a cardboard cutout. Lacan argues that images also have a developmental importance for humans—and these do not always need to be mirror images. The adults in the child's environment, or the sight of other children, suffice to offer the child the experience of unified forms. To stick to the specific case of the mirror image for the moment, Lacan argues that the child assumes or introjects the mirror image, and this becomes the foundation of the child's ego, the basis for his or her own image of himself or herself (Lacan 1966, 94–5/Lacan 2002, 4). One must in fact maintain a distinction between the child's ego and the images upon which it is founded. The images become what Lacan calls the "ideal ego," where "ideal" is used here in the same sense as in the phrase "ideal car." "This is not an ideal of the car," Lacan explains, "nor the dream of the car when it is all alone in the garage. It is really a good, solid, car" (VIII, 389). The ideal ego, then, is a set of images to which the ego is always trying to correspond—it is what the ego should be. Hence Lacan speaks of alienation, rivalry, aggression, and jealousy in the child's relation to the others it comes across. These others (not to be confused with the symbolic, linguistic Other) are what we are not but are trying to be. These others have already "got it," so to speak, and this supposed possession of a perfection we lack may arouse the affects I just mentioned. In connection with this Lacan spoke in his seventh seminar of the fundamentally ridiculous way in which we tend to consider others: "the reference the subject makes to any other, whomever it may be, is always a bit ridiculous [. . .]. [W]e see him or her continually compare him- or herself to the other as to someone who lives in equilibrium, is in any case happier than him- or herself, does not ask any questions, and rests easy" (VII, 278/237, translation modified).

But the ego and the ideal ego are not the only factors involved in the child's identifications. The ideal ego concerns what can be called the "imaginary register" of identification, but the ego of the child is not only structured in imaginary terms, but in symbolic terms. That is, signifiers are also important factors in identification. To explain the symbolic dimension of the development of the ego, Lacan uses Freud's term *ego ideal* (in French, *idéal du moi*, in German, *Ichideal*). As we shall see, Lacan later calls this the "unary trait," a signifier that marks the child and holds a place or a meaning in the Other for him or her. The ego ideal is the symbolic or linguistic foundation of identification. It plays, in the symbolic order, roughly the same role that the mirror image plays in the imaginary order—it is something that the ego strives to be but is not. Lacan provides an illustrative and a humorous way of understanding the difference between the ego ideal and the ideal ego in his eighth seminar. "The ideal ego," he explains,

> is the son of the family out driving around in his little sports car. He's going to show you the country with it. He's going to show off [*faire le malin*]. He's going to exercise his sense of risk [. . .] his taste for sport, as one says [. . .].
>
> Whatever the case may be, this is the register where he will have to show himself [. . .] stronger than the others [. . .]. This is the ideal ego. (VIII, 397)

Several factors here are evocative of the imaginary register—being stronger, faster, more daring, proving oneself. Such is the stuff of the ideal ego, the image upon which our egos are founded and the model to which they aspire. Notice that the terms used here are highly imagistic: speed, strength, beauty, defiance, pride. The ego ideal, in contrast, takes into account the function of signifiers in identification. Lacan continues with his example:

> The ego ideal is constituted by the fact that to begin with, if he has his little sports car, it is because he is the son of the family, because he is daddy's boy [fils à papa]; that, to change the example, if Marie-Chantal, as you know [Marie-Chantal was a popular young singer in France at the time], joins the Communist Party, it's to piss her father off [. . .].
>
> The one and the other, Marie-Chantal and the daddy's boy cruising around in his little car, would be simply engulfed in the world organized by the father, if there were not precisely the signifier "father," which permits them, if I may say, to extract themselves from it in order to imagine themselves pissing him off, and to even succeed in doing so. This is what

> is expressed by saying that he or she introjects the paternal image here.
>
> Isn't this also to say that it is the instrument thanks to which the two characters, masculine and feminine, can "extroject" themselves from the objective situation? Introjection is just that, in short—organizing themselves subjectively in such a way that the father [...] in the form of the ego ideal, not so wicked as all that, is a signifier in which the little person, male or female, comes to contemplate him or herself without too much disadvantage when cruising around in his little car or brandishing her Communist Party card." (VIII, 398)

Lacan here speaks of the *image* of the father being introjected, but it is also clearly stated that what is at stake here is the signifier "father." As he says, it is because "father" is a signifier that the daddy's boy and Marie-Chantal can extract themselves from it and establish a position for themselves that is more complex and nuanced than what is possible with respect to the ideal ego. Because the ego ideal is a signifier, the daddy's boy and Marie-Chantal can extract themselves from it, so to speak, and believe they are defying it—pissing the poor old man off or satisfying him—without any of this at all entailing anything "narcissistically disadvantageous" (VII, 398). That is, even though they set themselves up in a defiant relation to the ego ideal, the ego ideal is still for them the point of view from which they have a place and are "seen" by the Other, and this is still, whether they are seen by the Other as good or bad, narcissistically satisfying. Defiant or not, the common factor here is that in these examples they remain seen by the Other, and their actions occur entirely within the Other's scope. Indeed, their actions are for the Other, even when they appear to be against the Other.

What is important here is the notion that the ego ideal is a signifier in the Other from whose "point of view" the individual is given a meaning and a place. In his eighth seminar, Lacan even revises his theory of the mirror stage to include this notion. In Lacan's revision of the mirror stage, the child is compelled or encouraged to identify its mirror image (ideal ego) as itself by a parent (or someone else) saying something like "That's you Jimmy! Yes it is!" In the two kinds of identification I just looked at, it seemed as if there was only one thing at work: a mirror image, or a signifier ("father"). With this revision of the mirror stage, it is clear that there is also something else at work in identification. Not only is there something offered to the child—the name, or, in the imaginary register, the mirror image itself, there is also what

Lacan calls "*l'assentiment de l'Autre*," the Other's assent to this, in the form of: "Yes, that's you . . . " (VIII, 414).

It can be supposed that before this primary identification a child is already making demands and articulating its needs in the Other's language, the child's mother tongue: all of this will be studied in the next chapter. But the child finds that it has a place in this symbolic Other by means of the Other's affirmation of a place for the child. The child is told by the Other what he or she is.

THE UNARY TRAIT AND THE PROPER NAME

In light of what has been said about Lacan's revision of the mirror stage, I would like to consider in more detail how an interaction of signifiers produces a subject. The idea of a signifier that represents the subject in the Other is discussed by Lacan at the end of his eighth seminar and afterward in terms of the "*trait unaire*," which is how he translated a phrase that occurred in Freud's work: "*einziger Zug*." In English, Lacan's phrase is usually translated as the "unary trait." The unary trait is another name for a signifier that represents a subject to another signifier.

How does Freud use this term? In chapter 7 of *Group Psychology and the Analysis of the Ego*, Freud wrote of a "partial and extremely limited" form of identification, which "only borrows a *single trait* from the person who is its object" (1955 [1921c], 107, emphasis added). Freud found this kind of identification to be present in certain types of symptoms, where, say, a child adopts its mother's cough. Such a symptom, Freud wrote, "brings about a realization of her [the child's] desire to take her mother's place: 'You wanted to be your mother, and now you *are*—anyhow so far as your sufferings are concerned'" (106). What I would like to emphasize here is the "single trait"—the cough—that is central in such an identification. In Lacanian terms, this "single trait," the unary trait, is taken to be a signifier that manages to represent a subject to another signifier—in this case, perhaps, the other signifier is "father." A subject-as-meaning is produced by means of this interplay between two signifiers.

Another way in which Lacan approaches identity is by studying the proper name. Erik Porge sketches Lacan's theory as follows:

> When the subject wants to grasp her identity by means of her proper name, she encounters this name as an exterior determination that surpasses her and forms an obstacle to the self-

> apprehension of her identity. The first and last name that identify her come to her from her parents, and the apprehension of her identity by this means confronts her with the Other's desire. [...] One's name fixes one's destiny. This is why the first name is generally chosen with great care, even if this great care is not without ambiguities. (1997, 16)

In fact, the proper name has already been seen in action in my discussion of Lacan's modification of the mirror stage. The child's identification with the mirror image is motivated by "l'assentiment de l'Autre." In this "assentiment," we can imagine that the child's name is used: "That's you, Jimmy!" Put this way, we can see how there are actually two signifiers at work in this example. There is both the name (a "unary trait") and the Other's assent, which should be taken to be a signifier to which the subject who falls under the unary trait is represented. Lacan often uses the proper name as a model for the unary trait: "If something is a proper name, it is inasmuch as it is not the meaning of the subject that it brings with it, but something that is of the order of the mark applied in some way to the object, superimposed on it" (IX, 12/20/61). As a simple mark, as a unary trait, a proper name is meaningless, just as any signifier on its own is meaningless. A name is nothing but a meaningless "trait."

According to Lacan "the subject is constituted, or not, as a bearer of this unary trait" (IX, 2/28/62). When there is a subject that is constituted as the bearer of this trait, there is a subject-as-meaning, despite the fact that the name itself is meaningless. My name precedes me, and to this extent my place in the linguistic and social Other is given before my birth. This is all my name does—it gives me a place. This meaningless signifier, however, is also the bearer of a string of meanings provided that other signifiers enter into the picture, bringing about an operation similar to what happens in metaphor. Here again, the other signifier at work would be the place in the Other from which I am looked at and possibly desired, for example, the Other's affirmation of the signifier that gives me a place. So to the extent that I am talked about and desired (or not) by means of this meaningless "trait" existing in most cases before I am born, a discursive place is already carved out for me in the Other. My name functions as the representative point of this "talk," this knot of signifiers whose consistency makes up the stuff of the subject-as-meaning. Once again, we see that the construction of the subject-as-meaning may thus precede the actual birth of the individual.

CHAPTER 4

The Second Thesis

> Sexuality is always traumatic as such. (Lacan, 1976, 22)

While explaining the first thesis on the subject in Lacan's work, it was necessary to consider a few key concepts, among them the signifier, metaphor, metonymy, the signified, and the signified effect. The second thesis on the subject, which I have described as a thesis that involves a reference to sexuality, requires an exploration of more of Lacan's concepts. Furthermore, the second thesis requires a bit of construction or invention: it is not as easy to find in Lacan's work as the idea that the subject is an effect of signifiers is. Readings such as Borch-Jacobsen's and Lacoue-Labarthe's and Nancy's, which take Lacan's subject to be language, are no surprise then.

The gist of what I am calling the second thesis is that the subject is not only produced by an interaction of signifiers but by an interaction of signifiers with another "pole," as Lacan referred to it in his ninth seminar, that can go by a variety of names. In chapter 1 I discussed some of the issues surrounding the naming of this pole and settled on the idea that it should be thought of as the real, understood as a resistance to signification.

The resistance to signification offered by the real differs from the way the signified effect studied earlier might be said to resist signification. A signified effect can always get "signified" by having signifiers put in its place, without any of these signifiers being able to exhaust the signified effect. A signified effect can, therefore, be characterized as a surplus of meaning. A signified effect has many possible meanings that can be nailed down or specified with various signifiers, even though there is always still a surplus of meaning that is not exhausted by this action. What is being explored by this "second pole" of the subject involves a more radical resistance to signification. The difference could be put this way: Where a signified effect gives the impression of a surplus of meaning, and the signifiers that take its place are so many attempts to pin down that surplus of meaning, the resistance to signification involved here entails a radical absence of meaning, or an impasse in meaning, such that any attempt to put a signifier in its place bears the mark of a failure, and not a (partial) success. Not a surplus of meaning, then, but a radical failure of meaning, hence, something for which signifiers cannot be given. In order for this to be able to take on signification, in order for it to be "integrated" into a signifying chain, some sort of signifying invention must occur. But in itself, this resistance offered by the real is something other than a signified effect, and the distinction between the two ought to be kept in mind.

THE OTHER AND THE BODY

My presentation so far has been emphasizing language, signifiers, and meanings. This could lead one to believe that Lacan's theory of the subject is indeed "intellectualist" and "linguisticist." Certainly, the objection would go, there is more to people than language. What about affects? Drives? And what about bodies, without which people are unthinkable?

Although it is certainly the case that signifiers are important elements in Lacan's theory of the subject, they do not operate in a vacuum. One way to begin correcting the "intellectualist" or "linguisticist" slant of my account thus far is to reconsider a passage I gave in chapter 1, concerning the relation of the Other and the body.

> What is this Other? What is its substance? [. . .]. For a long time, I've been told that I camouflaged the mind [*l'ésprit*] in this site of the Other. [*Je me suis laissé dire . . . pendant un temps, que je camouflais dans ce lieu de l'Autre l'esprit.*] The annoying thing is that this is false. The Other, in the final analysis—you haven't guessed it yet—is the body. (XIV, 5/10/67)

Is it admitted here that Lacan's conception of the Other, prior to this point, had been slanted toward the "mental"? Had the Other been intellectualized? The charge may seem appropriate—the symbolic Other is assuredly not a real other. Lacan also claims that it is not a subject, although we like to think that it is (IX, 1/15/61). Usually the

Other is simply described as the site or "treasure trove" of signifiers. All of this seems to give weight to the charge Lacan is considering here—that the Other is the mind, or perhaps even something like Hegelian Spirit, thinly disguised. But here he says that the Other is the body.

My aim for the moment is to show that such an idea of the Other is compatible with Lacan's discussions of the Other as a treasure trove of signifiers. Although it may be the case that the connection between the Other and the body in Lacan's work was never explicit before the fourteenth seminar, I hope to show that the assertion of their identity does not come from out of the blue either and is not part of a desperate attempt on Lacan's part to save his theory from an unattractive position. This is important for my discussion of the second thesis. Explaining this thesis will require a discussion of Lacan's account of the dynamic relation between a child and its others, and the body, of course, plays a crucial role in this relation. It is the site of the first irruptions of what he calls "jouissance," which is the primary mode in which the kind of impasse in signification involved in the production of the subject appears.

Some hints that the body is the Other are to be found in the way that Lacan had always portrayed the order of signifiers. In chapter 2 I spoke of signifiers in relation to traces, and in chapter 3 we saw that one of the key signifiers in identification—the unary trait—could be characterized as a simple mark, like a name, that gives a "place" to the child in the Other as a set of signifiers. If the unary trait is a mark, then do we have to imagine that such a mark must actually be made on something? Or is this just a figurative way of speaking? In fact, Lacan had often spoken of the body as the site where such a marking takes place. This is one reason Lacan was led to say that the Other is actually the body and not some transcendent Mind or Spirit. The body, in fact, is to be seen as the surface where such a marking signifier is first "inscribed": "The body itself is originally this site of the Other insofar as it is there that the mark as signifier is originally inscribed" (XIV, 5/30/67). Lacan was fond of such images of signifiers being literally inscribed on bodies. At one point, he spoke of the unary trait as a tattoo (XI, 230/205–206). He also spoke of the subject's destiny (the unconscious, and what I was calling the subject-as-meaning in the last chapter) as a codicil imprinted on someone's head, to illustrate the point that one is the bearer of a message from and for others that only others can read—like a "Kick Me" sign on your back, perhaps, explaining why you are always receiving kicks from everyone (II, 323/280). Such ideas emphasize the signifier's materiality, as well as the necessity for a signifier to be a mark somewhere, on something. Here, this something is the body.

This still seems obscure and figurative, and one has to wonder whether one can really speak of the body as the "treasure trove" signifiers. Certainly, the body could be thought of without too much difficulty as a site where signifiers are inscribed or placed. Classical psychoanalytic symptoms illustrate what this would look like. One of Freud's fundamental premises was that such symptoms, like hysterical pregnancies, or false paralyses, are messages and have meanings. Lacan simply takes this farther and sees these symptoms as knots of signifiers on the body (Lacan 1975b, 22). This does not mean that the body itself is the treasure trove of signifiers. This is a body, however, that suffers from signifiers, and in doing so this body seems to belong, in part, to the Other.

I have already introduced the notion that there is another idea of the body in Lacan's work, one that would be something other than this body that suffers from signifiers. In Lacan's discussion of the classic psychoanalytic developmental stages—oral, anal, and genital—we can see how both notions of the body play important roles in Lacan's attempt to theorize the subject. In what follows I will consider how signifiers always produce a subject-effect in a particular context: originally, this is a context of demands exchanged between a child and its caregivers. Within this context, something emerges that gives the final kick necessary for the production of the subject.

NEED, DEMAND, AND DESIRE

Lacan's discussion of the oral, anal, and genital stages is impossible to follow without a preliminary discussion of the key terms he uses to describe those stages: need, demand, and desire. A child has biological needs, and since the child cannot yet help himself or herself and cannot yet speak, these needs are communicated to others through cries. Need motivates a child's first communications. If need is about a simple biological requirement—a need to be fed, for example—then an essential modification of this kind of need occurs with what Lacan calls demand. As soon as a need is put into signifiers, we are dealing with what Lacan calls a demand. A demand, then, is a spoken, articulated need and is no longer merely a cry that communicates some kind of biological requirement. In articulating a demand, a child puts its need into the language of the others around it. Because of this articulation a split occurs in the child, a split that places the child into a "beyond" and an "on this side" (*en deçà*) with respect to the demand (VIII, 235). The beyond of demand concerns the fact that a "demand in itself bears on something other than the satisfactions it calls for" (Lacan 1966, 690–691/Lacan 2002, 276). Demand does preserve one of the basic features of need: a demand may still be about a need to be fed. But, by virtue of the fact that it uses signifiers, there is also something else at stake in a demand. What is this something else? A need can be communicated to someone through cries. A need becomes a demand when it is put into the Other's terms, when it is put into language. A demand, therefore, involves an address to someone, an other, in that other's terms. So articulating a demand implies that a child has "entered" the Other. The beyond that demand introduces concerns this entrance into the Other, a realm that is "beyond the child.

To whom is a demand addressed? According to Lacan, to the Other itself, specifically, an Other who is taken to be omnipotent, one who is thought to be able to respond to our demand. This notion of an Other capable of responding to demand will be very important for what follows. Demand "institutes the other to whom it is addressed as one who may be present or absent" (VI, 5/27/59). By virtue of making demands, I institute an Other who is possibly present or possibly absent, one who may or may not be there to respond to my demands. Because of this, if a particular other satisfies my need to be fed, for example, then that other is also satisfying something else that is latent in my demand: a demand to be simply present and attentive to me. Lacan calls this demand latent within every demand a demand for love. By giving me what I demand, the Other instituted by my demand not only satisfies my needs but also indicates to me that I am loved. Thus beyond the satisfaction of my needs, demand brings about a kind of signifying satisfaction, an assurance that I have some position for the Other, that my speech—indeed, my very being—is recognized by the Other. In other words, my use of the Other's terms in the articulation of my demand is legitimized by the Other's answer. The Other responds to my attempts to articulate my needs into demands, indicating that I have a place in this Other.[1]

What we are getting here is an account of how a subject is not only produced by signifiers, or how a representation is made for the subject by the Other's discourse, but also how representations may be sought after on the part of an individual. Thus we are finding out something about the motivations for identification. There may be a difference between the representation and meaning I am given by the Other and the representation I seek, or no difference at all. At any rate, recognition is sought after as a kind of legitimation of my entry into the Other as a speaking being.

So demands bring about a sort of satisfaction that does not directly arise from the satisfaction of need. They bring a signifying satisfaction, which involves the affirmation of a place for the child within the Other (as the "treasure trove" of signifiers and a site of possible recognition). Lacan said at one point that "what is demanded is never anything but a place" (XVI, 5/14/69). When the Other responds to my demands, I have a place in the Other, and I can see myself as loved by the Other. In this respect, demand is a demand for love, and within every demand lies not only a demand to satisfy some biological need but also a demand to be shown that I have a place in the Other, to be shown that I have some status for the Other. This gives us a further idea of what is at stake in the beyond opened up by demand. Beyond the satisfaction of a need, demand seeks a representation in the Other, acceptance by the Other, and a recognition of my speech, my use of the Other's signifiers.

According to Lacan there is also something "on this side" of demand, and this is where he situates what he calls desire. The "on this side" refers to something on the part of the individual, as opposed to the beyond of demand, which concerned the Other. However, the famous Lacanian concept of desire, although something different from demand, is never independent of this beyond of demand: "It is not that demand separates us from desire [...] its signifying articulation determines me, conditions me as desire" (IX, 5/9/62). In fact, my own desire is articulated only after an exposure to the Other's desire occurs within the exchange of demands between the Other and me. It is impossible, in Lacanian terms, to conceive of a desire that is not indebted to the structure of demand. Desire should not be taken to precede demand. Yet desire does open up something beyond the conditions of demand.

So what is desire in Lacanian theory? It remains a tricky concept. Is it something biological, or something linguistic, or both? What role does it play in the interaction between child and Other? Of course, Lacan's position can be characterized as one according to which there is nothing of desire without signifiers. This means that signifiers produce desire, but what they produce in desire is different from what is produced in demand. Demand involves getting recognition from the Other. Desire involves something else. While a demand is also always a demand to be given a place in the Other, to have my use of signifiers recognized and legitimized, desire is partly about not having a place in the Other, and, early in Lacan's career at least, it is thought of as something that sustains the possibility of a detachment from any place or recognition in the Other. Desire entails the possible suspension of the significations and representations forged by a signifying chain, for example, a suspension of the kind of signifying destiny discussed in the case of Xénophon. When "cross" was given a new signification in the course of his analysis, the early Lacan would have been inclined to speak of this as an emergence of a desire on the part of Xénophon. But desire, because of its origins in the structure of demand, ends up playing a more ambiguous role as Lacan's theory progresses. At some points, desire is understood to be something that can free one from determination by and subjection to the Other. Desire, then, would be another word for freedom. At other moments of his work, however, Lacan thinks of desire as something that only manages to strengthen one's subjection to the Other.

If I were to give a history of the concept of desire in Lacan's work, I would say that it enjoyed a steady increase in importance from seminars one to six and reached its apotheosis in the seventh seminar, only to be humbled considerably in the very next seminar. What we see over the course of the 1960s is a continuation of this humbling, and, in the late 1960s and 1970s a near absence of the concept altogether. Accounting for this would require a study of its own. In short, I think the concept arrived at something like the deadlock with demand that I have just pointed out. Moreover, as we will see in chapter 6, Lacan develops a theory of the act in the 1960s that is largely able to replace desire when he wants to think about what happens during a psychoanalysis. In the 1950s, Lacan spoke about the end of analysis as a realization of one's desire. In the 1960s, he speaks about analysis ending in an act.

To understand something about desire in Lacan's work, we have to see how desire comes about from the experience of not having a place in the Other after one already experiences having a place. According to Lacan, such an experience is in fact contingent upon experiencing the Other's desire. So the Other's desire is always first with respect to the emergence of my desire. Apart from its close relations to demand, it may also be because of this priority of the Other's desire that desire stops being the term Lacan uses for what happens at the end of analysis.

Desire ultimately ends up being ambiguous: it always remains in part a desire to be recognized by the Other after an encounter with the Other's desire, but at the same time it is interested in canceling out any placing and recognition in the Other. In the chapters that follow, I will be making use of the conceptual distinction Lacan used in the 1960s to express the difference between determination and freedom. Instead of using the distinction between demand and desire to think about this difference, Lacan made a distinction between fantasy and act. We will see that what Lacan calls an act is something that cannot be reduced to a demand structure: in fact, the difference between fantasy and act is defined, I will argue, by the presence or absence of demand. An act, unlike the fantasy, does not make a demand on the Other and is not aimed at acquiring recognition by the Other.

Yet desire is a crucially important concept, since Lacan finds in his studies of the emergence of desire something that provides him with the stuff for his second thesis on the subject: a resistance to signification. This resistance is found twice: once in the concept of the Other's desire, and again in the concept of jouissance.

ORAL

In his eighth seminar, Lacan begins his explanation of oral demand by considering a child's demand to be fed. I explained earlier how a demand addresses the Other, but in Lacan's explanation of oral demand, we see that there is also something else at work. A demand is an address to an Other who is supposed to be able to respond to our demand. In his eighth seminar, Lacan puts this idea in the following way: a demand implies a counter-demand on the part of the Other. When making a demand, we presuppose or construct some possible response on the part of the Other, and this amounts to imagining some demand coming from the Other itself. To my demand for food might correspond a demand from the Other to let myself be fed (VIII, 238). For example, I want food: the counter-demand is found when I imagine an Other who will give it to me, or an Other who wants me to be fed.

It is not entirely accurate to say that such a counter-demand always "corresponds" to my demand, for it is not the case that every demand to be fed meets with a positive response, a positive counter-demand on the part of the Other to let oneself be fed. The Other may refuse to feed me when I want to be fed, and when I do not want to be fed, the Other may want me to eat. So there is always a possible dissonance between the two demands. In fact, Lacan thinks that there is an essential lack of correspondence between the two demands: "What is there that responds better, apparently, to the demand to be fed than that of letting oneself be fed? We know, however, that it is in the very mode of confrontation of the two demands that this tiny gap, this abyss, this tearing, lies, where discordance is introduced" (VIII, 238). According to Lacan, even when the two demands complement one another—I demand to be fed and the Other actually demands that I let myself be fed—there is still a discordance between the two demands. What accounts for this discord? The "tiny gap" between the two demands that Lacan just mentioned is a desire that overruns the explicit and implicit content of the child's demand to be fed: explicitly, there is a simple demand for food, but implicitly there is also a demand to be recognized. Desire creates a condition in which a child might not let himself or herself be fed, a condition in which a child may refuse to let his or her demand to be fed be satisfied.

Why would a child do this? In order to sustain his or her desire. According to Lacan the desire lying within demand would be extinguished if the demand were also extinguished—that is, if the demand were satisfied, there would be no more desire. As Lacan puts it, the child "refuses in a certain way to disappear as desire by the fact of being satisfied as demand" (VIII, 238). So the child may refuse the Other's demand.

But what is the desire at stake here? Why would this desire be extinguished with the satisfaction of the demand? Why would the child be so interested in maintaining such a desire in the first place? And does it not seem as if this desire precedes any manifestation of the Other's desire, going against what I argued earlier, and will continue to argue? Here we have to look more closely into the structure of oral demand. The counter-demand raises another question: What is the child for the Other? This counter-demand is not only a demand to let oneself be fed at certain times. Lacan argues that in this counter-demand the "Other is constituted as the reflection of the subject's hunger" (VIII, 255). The child demanding to be fed sees in the Other a reflection of her own hunger, and thus sees the Other itself as hungry, as a hunger that demands something of the child. Furthermore, the child sees herself as the object of the Other's hunger: the child can be said to situate herself on a "cannibalistic menu" (VIII, 256). Since the child's own demands are wrapped up in demands coming from the Other, when she makes her own demand to be fed she posits herself as an object that satisfies the Other's hunger. We can see now what Lacan might mean when he talks about disappearing with the satisfaction of demand. If, in her own oral demand, a child takes herself to be the object that satisfies the Other's demand, then when the child's own oral demand is satisfied the child herself can be said to vanish into the Other. There is no "room" for her to desire, since she is annihilated, reduced to being an object for the Other.

It may still be difficult to understand the justification for this point of view. Let us begin by positing the child's demand as a starting point. To this demand corresponds a (posited or actual, it does not matter) demand on the part of the Other for the child to let herself be fed. In other words, when I demand to be fed, I also always suppose that there is some Other there (or not) to feed me. My demand is always related then to what the Other will demand of me: perhaps I will not get fed, in which case the Other is demanding that I eat at another time. Moreover, Lacan argues that a child experiences the Other's demand that he or she be fed at certain times as an encounter with the Other's own hunger. In other words, my hunger is not sufficient to make the Other satisfy my demand. Something we can call "the Other's hunger" determines when my hunger will be satisfied and when it will not be. This is why any satisfaction of my own demand to be fed implies at the same time the satisfaction of the Other's demand, or the Other's hunger. And here we can see more clearly why, even when the two demands complement one another, there is still a discord. When the Other's demand matches my demand, not only is my hunger satisfied, but the Other's is as well. I myself become a satisfying object for the Other, an object that satisfies the Other's hunger. Notice that I become this satisfying object when I am satisfying my own demand to be fed! Because of the involvement of a demand on the part of the Other within every oral demand that I make, when my own demand is satisfied I disappear, in that I also become an object of the Other's satisfaction, and my satisfaction is also the Other's satisfaction. For this reason, Lacan portrays the relation between these two demands in terms of discord, not harmony. (Lacan does not see this as a shared satisfaction but as an appropriation of my satisfaction by the Other.)

We still do not know why the child would be interested in sustaining her desire, and why the preservation of the "tiny gap" between the two demands would be of such importance to her. The way Lacan puts it, it seems simply to be a matter of life and death. Perhaps the Spinozistic roots of this concept of desire are visible here. Spinoza claimed that desire is the essence of man. In *The Ethics*, desire (*conatus*) is concerned with staying in being, with maintaining one's existence (III, Proposition 6). Something like this is present in Lacan's conception of desire too. Although he claimed that "what is demanded is never anything but a place," Lacan also held that being "placed" is unbearable. Desire is in many respects about a suspension of any place for me in the Other and is about maintaining some kind of existence outside of the Other, as much as this is possible. True, this is, strictly speaking, impossible unless some kind of distinction is introduced into Lacan's concept of the Other—a distinction I will discuss in chapter 6, when I introduce Lacan's concept of the act. This much is clear: Desire involves a questioning of any position in the Other. Demand requests such a position. For a child to maintain herself independently of the Other, a refusal of demand's satisfaction is required. In this respect, desire seems to have something to do with freedom. The child disappears into the Other when an oral demand is satisfied. Thus in order to preserve herself, the child may try to preserve a gap between the two demands, for example, by refusing to be fed. Anorexia is a good illustration of what Lacan means by desire.

Yet once again I seem to be speaking here of a desire that precedes any appearance of the Other's desire. It should be noted that what I have spoken of as the Other's demand and the Other's hunger cannot in any way be considered exemplars of the Other's desire. We will see that the Other's desire is fundamentally different from any demand that might come from the Other. According to Lacan, what is going on in the oral and anal stages is retroactively constructed after an encounter with the Other's desire during or before the genital stage. It is with this encounter that desire proper is actually constituted (VIII, 243). So the desire Lacan speaks of in the oral stage is actually based on a reconstruction of an oral situation after an encounter with the Other's desire at the genital stage. At the time of the oral stage, let us say, there is nothing but a possible "gap" that can be maintained between the two demands. Its nature and its importance are not yet clear. The importance of this gap gets "rewritten" after the genital stage and an encounter with the Other's desire, and it is in this rewrite that the "gap" gets rewritten in terms of desire, becoming a gap necessary for the subject's existence in distinction to the Other.

The oral situation does not succeed in maintaining such a space. Even if my oral demand is satisfied, it becomes the Other's satisfaction: I ate at the right time, the Other's time, thereby satisfying the Other's hunger. And, by satisfying the Other, I become an object for the Other. I get annihilated and eaten up by the Other. Refusing to be fed is a perfectly logical response to this frustrating situation, but it has rather drastic consequences. In the next stage a mediation is possible, but it also has frustrating results.

ANAL AND GENITAL

In the anal stage, the Other's demand comes before the child's. We began our look at oral demand with the child's own demand to be fed, which then got wrapped up in a demand from the Other. In the anal stage, the Other's demand is already there, first, in the Other's demand to the child to relieve himself at certain times and certain places. Here too the child effectively satisfies the Other's demand when his own need is satisfied. But this time it is not the child himself who is the object of satisfaction, who is an object on a "cannibalistic menu."

Instead, what satisfies the Other is the object produced. The child's need to relieve himself gets routed through the Other, and leads again, as in the oral situation, to the Other's satisfaction: here, "the subject only satisfies a need for the satisfaction of an Other" (VIII, 241). Also, "the satisfaction of caring for the infant [la satisfaction du pouponnage], of which wiping is a part, is first that of the other" (ibid.). In the oral stage, the (potential) desire "on this side" of the demand was extinguished when the demand was satisfied, since the child himself was "eaten up" by the Other in the satisfaction of the oral demand. Here, in the anal stage, desire "goes away in little turds" (VIII, 242). And it is the child himself who is symbolized in the little turds.

How so? At this stage, the child is able to satisfy the Other's demand by producing little objects. In the oral stage, it was the child himself who was the object satisfying the Other's demand. So in the anal stage there is a mediation: what the child makes is what satisfies the Other. The anal stage is a moment at which the child can satisfy the Other by his activity. This makes it easier to maintain a gap between the two demands, for it is not the child himself who is directly annihilated in the satisfaction of its demand. In the anal stage, satisfaction comes about by means of an identification: the child satisfies the Other not with his very being, but with something he produces. And yet, this identification is also destined to frustrate. These little objects in which the child sees himself as pleasing to the Other, on the basis of which he is given a place within the symbolic universe, and for which he may sometimes even be praised, are also objects that the child is not allowed to enjoy too much, and cannot identify with too closely. The child goes away in the little turds. If the child is not directly annihilated by the satisfaction of his demand in this case, he is annihilated vicariously, through the fate of the anal object with which he identifies. So if the child identifies with the anal object, he still gets annihilated when the Other's demand is satisfied. Just as in the oral stage, it is as if there is no space for the child to be here.

The genital stage allows for the creation of a space between the nascent subject and the Other, although again it does not at all resolve the fundamental discord between the two. What is different about this stage is that in it instead of being confronted with the Other's demand the child is confronted with the Other's desire—an enigma that appears between the lines of the Other's demands. Once the Other's desire is introduced we can speak about the production of a subject. The earlier stages fail to bring about this production. It is only with the radical lack of a place for the child, a lack that the Other's desire implies, that a subject can get produced. The oral and anal stages offer a place for the child in the Other, but the production of a subject occurs only when the Other offers no place at all. Without this trigger, there would only be a strictly determined subject-as-meaning, a fate determined by a signifying chain. Without this interruption, the subject would be nothing but a series of signifiers working like sheet music in a player piano, and attempts to separate from those signifiers would always be frustrated.

CHÈ VUOI? AND THE OTHER'S DESIRE

In the oral stage, the Other's demand was a response to the child's demand, and the child could see himself as the object of this demand, satisfying the Other to his own chagrin. In the anal stage, the Other's demand to the child, which was first, was also readily answered, again to the child's chagrin. The genital stage involves a demand from the Other that the child simply cannot answer. This "absolute" demand is in fact what Lacan calls the Other's desire. This is not a desire for anything specific, and it is not necessarily a desire directed toward the child (although it may well be concerned with a part of the child, as we will see). It presents the child with an enigma, and as a result it puts the child's relation to the Other, and the child's very being, into question. Without this, there would be no possible space apart from the Other.

Lacan characterizes this episode in the following way. Prior to this episode,

> the Other is already installed [. . .] as the one where the sign reposes. And the sign suffices to instate the question *Chè Vuoi?* [What do you want?] [. . .] to which the subject at first has no answer.
>
> A sign represents something to someone, and for want of knowing what the sign represents, the subject, faced with this question, when sexual desire appears, loses the someone to whom the desire is addressed: namely, himself. (VIII, 257–258)

It seems that it is when sexual desire appears that the child is faced with the question of what the Other wants. But whose sexual desire, the child's or the Other's?

First, the question of what the Other wants—the question *Chè Vuoi?*—should be explored on its own. Different manifestations of this question appear throughout Lacan's work. The first appearance of the phrase *Chè Vuoi?* in Lacan's work is in his fourth seminar, but I think we do not see its full significance emerge until seminar six (IV, 169). The phrase actually comes from the eighteenth-century novel *Le diable amoureux*. The story concerns a man named Alvaro who one day conjures up the devil. The devil grants him three wishes. After the first two wishes are used up, Alvaro does not know what to wish for next. The devil takes a guess and assumes the form of a beautiful woman, named Biondetta, who will not stop following the poor man around. Alvaro is annoyed by this, and so is the wealthy courtesan Olympia, who had taken an interest in Alvaro. Olympia gets jealous of the devil-Biondetta and kills her. In her dying moments, Alvaro, who had always been indifferent to Biondetta's charms, is finally struck by her beauty, and, as if forgetting for a moment who she really is, utters her name in a moment of tenderness, when he realizes he is going to lose her. He had never said her name before. At that instant, the devil vanishes.

The *Chè Vuoi?* episode occurs in the scene when the devil is first conjured up. The devil appears to Alvaro in the form of a camel's head with huge ears and asks in a booming voice "*Chè Vuoi?*," "What do you want?" Alvaro stumbles and is not sure what to say. He comes up with a few wishes (a nice dinner for his friends, a harp player to entertain them) but does not wish for anything else. It is then that the devil decides to incarnate himself in the form of Biondetta. This point is important: The devil, by incarnating himself as Biondetta, gives Alvaro a desire he did not know he had, or did not want to admit. In this sense, desire is the Other's desire—it comes from the Other.[2]

Some important modifications in Lacan's use of the phrase "*Chè Vuoi?*" occur between the fourth and sixth seminars. In Cazotte's story, *Chè Vuoi?* was a question that the devil asked to his conjurer. In seminar four, Lacan treated the question *Chè Vuoi?* in terms of how it occurred in Cazotte's work—*Chè Vuoi?* as a question the Other asks of me. For this reason Lacan associated it then with the superego; the nagging, insatiable voice of conscience. In seminar six, after referring to the context in which it appears in *Le diable amoureux*, Lacan describes *Chè Vuoi?* in distinctly opposite terms as "the question posed to the Other of what he or she wants" (VI, 11/12/58). Here the direction of the question is reversed—it is as if Alvaro were asking the devil what the devil wanted.

In fact, this reversal is already prepared for in seminar five. There Lacan explained the relation of demand between mother and child in the following way:

> The mother comes and goes. It is because I am a little being already taken up into the symbolic, and because I have learned how to symbolize, that one can say that she comes and goes. In other words, I sense her or do not sense her, the world varies with her arrival, and can go away. (V, 175)

The mother comes and goes for the child and does or does not answer the child's demands. She incarnates an Other who has the power to answer the child's demands. At this same point in his fifth seminar, Lacan is trying to account for the function of the father in psychic life and is trying to do so solely in terms of the mother's discourse. In other words, according to Lacan, the paternal function comes into being by virtue of what the mother says of the father: real fathers, apparently, have little to do with it.[3]

Upon encountering this signifier of the father in the mother's speech, the child is led to ask a question. Speaking in the child's voice, Lacan says:

> The question is—what is the signified [of this signifier]? What does she want, that one? I would certainly like it to be me that she wants, but it is quite clear that it is not only me that she wants. There is something else bothering her [*Il y a autre chose qui la travaille*]. What bothers her is the x, the signified. And the signified of the comings and goings of the mother is the phallus. (V, 175)

Let us imagine that the child is going along quite fine in the oral and anal stages: it knows how to resist the Other's demand, how to be happy submitting to it, what chances its own demands have of being answered. In all of this, the child can imagine that it is a satisfying object for the Other. Let us continue speaking in the child's voice, as Lacan did: Maybe I am satisfying for her, but what exactly am I for her? She wants other things, has interests that have nothing at all to do with me, and seems particularly interested in this "father" character. So what is my position for her exactly? I understand everything in terms of demands. I can refuse them or submit to them, I can make them and refuse to have them satisfied. But what is this peculiar feature of the Other that apparently has nothing to do with me? If this is a demand, then it is one that I cannot satisfy, one to which I cannot relate.

Such is the Other's desire, and when the phrase "the Other's desire" is used, one should think not only of the Other desiring but also of the whole line of questioning that this desiring elicits in the child. This line of questioning, the panic-stricken signifying production that it may bring about, as well as the suspension of a place for me in the Other implied by it—all of this is what Lacan means by the Other's desire.

We can imagine how such an episode might be precipitated by coming across the signifier of the father in the mother's discourse. It is quite well known that children are often puzzled about what exactly their fathers are for their mothers and what role the father has for her generally. This puzzlement is precisely about the significance, or the signified, of the father for the mother. What is he for her? What does she want in him? Such a signifier, of at least some importance to the mother in many (most? all?) cases, forces me to question my own position for the mother. The father as a signifier encountered in the mother's discourse is associated with the reason for the mother's comings and goings. In this way, "father" becomes a metaphor for the Other's desire. It is an answer to that desire, as well as the incarnation in a signifier of the enigma of that desire. Is this a construction on the part of the child? Is it something the child observes? This much is clear: being compelled to search for a reason for her "comings and goings," for the fact that she responds and sometimes does not respond to my demand, is what the encounter with the Other's desire is all about. We could call this whole signifying proliferation, this whole incitement to discourse, a quest for the signified of the mother's behavior. Note that even though the phrase *Chè Vuoi?* is not given explicitly in this account from the fifth seminar, it can easily be put to work there and could easily have been used in Lacan's description of the child's wonderings about his mother. So Lacan adapts the phrase *Chè Vuoi?* to his theoretical needs, even though its literary origin does not justify his use of the phrase.

THE PRODUCTION OF THE SUBJECT

Before moving on to study some further issues, I would like to make a point about how the Other's desire fits into Lacan's theoretical edifice. As we have seen, Lacan develops this concept in the late 1950s. He already had a theory of imaginary and symbolic identification at the time, both of which were explained in terms of the mirror stage. Yet this stage only accounts for the production of the ego. In the mirror stage, I am presented with an image (or a signifier, a unary trait, in Lacan's later revision of the mirror stage), and I get identified with it.

Lacan's article on the mirror stage does not offer a very satisfactory account of how this identification happens. It just seems to happen. In Lacan's later discussions of the mirror stage, we do get an account of why mirror-stage identification occurs. It occurs because the Other identifies me with the image. This is my motivation to identify with the image. It is as if my identity is already "out there," affirmed by the Other as "me" before I have anything to do with it.

We might imagine that despite this identification the lived experience of the child is not taken up into the identification and does not quite jibe with it. And we might imagine that this forms the basis for what Lacan calls the subject. But this raw "lived experience" is not what is behind Lacan's theory of the subject either. A subject is not consciousness, nor is it some kind of "vital immanence." We have already seen that Lacan rejects these ideas.

When the idea of the Other's desire is added to this account of identity, the subject can finally be conceived as something that is neither consciousness nor an ineffable lived experience. In other words, the Other's desire makes it possible to account for how a subject is something other than its identity or its ego. In the encounter with the Other's desire I am given neither an image nor a signifier for what I am, and I am not encouraged by the Other to identify with anything. The Other's desire is in this way different from the Other's affirmation of a place for me in identification. With respect to the Other's desire, I am without a place. I am not even really addressed by the Other. The Other's desire "does not recognize me, as Hegel believed [. . .] it does not recognize me, nor does it misrecognize me [. . .]. It calls me into question" (X, 179–180). Even though, as Lacan often claimed early in his career, desire is always a desire for recognition, the initial encounter with the Other's desire is something in which recognition is not an issue. The Other's desire is not at all directed toward me. Here we can point out an important difference between Lacan and Lévinas. Many commentators on Lévinas, as well as Lévinas himself, have tried to ground the subject in an address from the Other. This makes the subject fundamentally ethical, fundamentally indebted to the Other and compelled to recognize or respect the Other. To make the difference between Lacan and Lévinas clear, what is called the subject in Lacan's theory begins when the Other no longer addresses you. According to Lévinas, what is traumatic is the encroachment of the Other on my own psychic space. According to Lacan, what is traumatic is finding out that the Other's desire concerns something that leaves you out of the picture. Being "touched" by the Other is traumatic too, but not being touched at all is at least as bad, and in this absence of a touch can be found the core of Lacan's theory of the subject.

This encounter with the Other's desire motivates a quest for a signified and an eventual identification with that signified. The Other's desire plays a role different from that played by the image in the mirror stage. In imaginary and symbolic identifications, a meaning or an identity is produced, and an individual is presented with a place that is already his or hers. In the encounter with the Other's desire, I am not given any place at all, and my very being is put into question. The Other's desire is a mirror that does not return my reflection. Because of this, the subject in Lacan's work is not just something determined. It is also a position with respect to a determination, an affirmation or a rejection of it. The subject is some kind of negation of determination. But this negation actually originates from the resistance to signification that is found in the Other's desire. The Other's desire is opaque and abyssal. For this reason, it makes any determination appealing, because it is something I can always fall back on. In the next chapter, we will see how Lacan's theory of fantasy is largely an account of how the place offered by the Other's discourse gets reaffirmed after an encounter with the Other's desire. However, the Other's desire also makes any determination and any recognition, strictly speaking, impossible. Lacan's theory of the act gives an account of how this aspect of the Other's desire can be preserved in a signifying practice, as we will see.

THE LINK BETWEEN THE OTHER'S DESIRE AND JOUISSANCE

In a passage I gave earlier from the eighth seminar, Lacan hinted at a connection between the appearance of the question "What do you want?"—a question I have used to introduce the concept of the Other's desire—and the appearance of sexual desire (VIII, 257–258). What was called "sexual desire" in that passage is, I believe, a reference to what Lacan elsewhere calls "jouissance." This concept also helps shed some light on the theoretical impasse of desire. In the 1960s, Lacan sides desire with fantasy, and thus with determination and the achievement of recognition. This means that desire cannot serve as a model for freedom, if the end of analysis is more or less concerned with the emergence of a practice of freedom. Desire becomes just another way of getting recognized. When Lacan focuses on jouissance, he is able to give his view of the end of analysis another basis and another slant. This leads him to develop his notion of the act.

What is jouissance exactly? In Jacques-Alain Miller's seminar *Extimité*, Diana Rabinovich pointed out that around the time of his seventh seminar Lacan ceases speaking about the satisfaction of need and instead talks about jouissance (1986–1987, 2/26/86). This does not mean that the two are identical, that jouissance is a replacement for what was earlier called the satisfaction of a need. Jouissance is not simply the satisfaction of a need but the satisfaction of a drive. Lacan explains that it is

> presented as hidden in a central field, with characteristics of inaccessibility, obscurity, and opacity, in a field encompassed by a barrier that makes access to it the most difficult for the subject, inaccessible perhaps inasmuch as jouissance is presented not purely and simply as the satisfaction of a need, but as the satisfaction of a drive. (VII, 247–248/209, translation modified)

The idea that jouissance is the satisfaction of a drive leads me to my next point, which is that jouissance is antagonistic to desire. Lacan associates the drive with a transgression of the pleasure principle. The drive is in fact described as "the only form of transgression permitted to the subject in relation to the pleasure principle" (XI, 205/183). To the extent that the pleasure principle is the domain of desire, desire and jouissance must then be at odds.[4] Desire is in fact an attempt to avoid jouissance.[5]

Jouissance could just as well be seen as displeasure, since it is a radical disruption of the pleasure principle, but Lacan also described it as an extreme pleasure:

> The dialectic of pleasure itself, namely what it possesses of a level of stimulation simultaneously looked for and avoided [...] implies the centrality of a prohibited zone [...] because the pleasure there would be too intense. (XVI, 3/12/69)

Since jouissance is beyond the pleasure principle, it is appropriate that there should be some uncertainty as to whether this zone beyond the pleasure principle should be called pleasurable or unpleasant: it is the pleasure principle that determines what qualifies as pleasure or pain. Lacan also calls jouissance flat out an *Unlust* (X, 148). The best way to see it is probably as an excessive, unbearable "tension" for which the language of pleasure and displeasure is not adequate. This would also help explain the way in which jouissance is beyond the pleasure principle. It is a "tension" that does not go away, a "tension" that cannot be "relieved" by means of signifiers, because there is no signifier for it.[6] There is thus a radical tension between this jouissance beyond the pleasure principle and the order of signifiers.

Yet there is at least a theoretical resemblance between jouissance and the Other's desire. While the two concepts are quite different—one accounts for something affective and drivelike, the other involves a lack of a symbolic place—both entail a signifying suspension, or an impasse in signification. The point of the second thesis on the subject is that the subject is only produced by signifiers being confronted with a resistance to signification. Concerning jouissance, Lacan in fact says that "in the subject's system, it is not symbolized anywhere, nor is it able to be symbolized either" (XVI, 5/14/69). Much the same could be said for the Other's desire.

In a passage from seminar eight, cited earlier, Lacan seems to suggest that there is in fact more than just a resemblance between jouissance and the Other's desire, but some kind of connection. That is, there seems to be some causal link between the encounter with the Other's desire and the first appearance of "sexual desire," or what we could just as well call jouissance. Elsewhere in his work he makes similar claims: "It is at this precise point [...] where this positivization of erotic jouissance is produced, that the positivization of the subject is also correlatively produced, as dependent [...] [on] the Other's desire" (XVI, 5/14/69). Here it sounds as if jouissance emerges as an answer to the Other's desire and affords an individual the opportunity to reestablish a position with respect to the Other's desire.

Lacan often refers to the case of Little Hans in this context. When Hans discovered the pleasurable sensations arising from the stimulation of his genitals, he also found that that pleasure was not to be shared. There was a demand expressed by the Other in relation to this: "That's disgusting." Quantitative factors aside, Hans would have realized that this pleasure was unlike others because of how the Other responded to it. Such pleasures or enjoyments remained without a place in the Other, and insofar as Hans was interested in pursuing them, he was pursuing something that led to being without a place in the Other, thus something that led to his own disappearance.

The important point is that Hans's experience of his mother's desire was not provoked by an encounter with the signifier of the father in his mother's discourse but by this prohibited, placeless jouissance itself. In other words, here an experience of jouissance led to a question of what the child is for the Other. Inversely, the Other's desire may also lead the child to wonder not only about his or her symbolic place with respect to the Other but also about the place of these particular satisfactions. "I satisfy her in many ways, but not with that." The child finds there is a limit to what can be shared with others: that is not what they want. So what is the place of *that*? What is its function? What is to be done with it? And what am I for the Other if *that* has no place?

What, then, is the connection between the Other's desire and jouissance? Is jouissance itself traumatic, or is it a confrontation with the question of the Other's desire that makes jouissance traumatic? Sometimes Lacan's answer to this question is unambiguous. In response to a question forwarded by Ed Casey on Lacan's visit to Yale in 1975, Lacan said the following about sexuality:

> Sexuality is always traumatic as such. The first kind of trauma is obviously the one Freud tells us about [. . .]. Of what does Little Hans's phobia consist? He suddenly notices that he has a little organ that moves. It's perfectly clear. And he wants to give it a meaning. But, whatever this meaning might be, no little boy ever experiences this penis as something that is attached to him naturally. He always considers the penis as traumatic. I mean, he thinks it is external to the body. (Lacan 1976, 22–23)

Lacan argues that when Hans experiences an autoerotic jouissance, his penis is not experienced as his—it becomes his only later, through a symbolic identification with the father. For this reason Lacan argues elsewhere that the jouissance at stake here cannot even be called autoerotic: "This [. . .] does not deserve to be labeled 'autoerotism' under the sole pretext that after all this *Wiwimacher* [Hans's word for his penis] is somewhere stuck onto him, below his belly. The enjoyment that has resulted from this *Wiwimacher* is alien to him" (Lacan 1988, 13). It sounds as if this jouissance is essentially alien, and is thus traumatic in itself. But what accounts for its "alienness"? It is always from the perspective of given symbolic configurations that jouissance is alien and unable to be named, which is also to say that it always appears with, or against, signifiers. For this reason, jouissance should be thought of in terms of $real_2$—something that is not prior to and outside of signifiers but that appears within signifiers as an impasse in signification.

Again, which comes first, jouissance or the Other's desire? It looks like jouissance is first, because of Lacan's claim that sexuality as such is traumatic. The first manifestations of sexuality force one to reconsider one's position for the Other—they occur before one can do anything with them symbolically. It seems to make sense to say, then, that it is in the wake of these manifestations that one encounters the question of what it is that the Other wants with respect to them. However, it should also be noted that unless there is already some encounter with a lack in the signifying chain, unless there is already some encounter with the question of what the Other desires, sexuality might not be traumatic at all. Worse, it would be the stuff of psychotic ruptures. Jouissance is an impasse in the fabric of meaning, but in neurosis it is at least put into a relation with that fabric. In psychosis, this relation is missing, and there is a radical gulf between the symbolic and the real. In neurosis, there is also a gulf, but there is also a project to build a bridge across the gulf, an attempt to elaborate on a relation between the two.

This study has at least given an indication now of how the body plays a role in Lacan's theory of the subject. The body is the site and origin of a signifying impasse. Now this is not what Lacan usually calls the body in his theory. As we have seen, the body is usually for Lacan something "overwritten" with signifiers. For this reason, Lacan was not inclined to say that the "stirring" in Little Hans's genitals was something that involved his body. Little Hans already had a body image prior to this stirring. The emergence of genital sexuality introduced something that did not fit into this image—and so, Hans's penis, when it started acting up, was not something he experienced as "his." Nevertheless, from another point of view, this jouissance was indeed coming from Hans's body. What needs to be explained now is how this impasse originating in the body—an impasse that can be abbreviated under the heading of sexuality—plays a role in the production of the subject.

A DEFINITION OF THE SUBJECT

In chapter 3, I described the subject as a meaning. What I am saying here adds an important supplement to this notion of a subject represented in and for the Other. First, there is a meaning: I am something for the Other, an object that satisfies the Other's demands, or a significant, desirable object for the Other (like Xénophon). Then, either because of bodily experiences that cannot be signified or an encounter with the Other's desire, or both, this position as a meaning is called into question. In the wake of these encounters, there are two major possibilities. My position as a satisfying object or meaning for the Other can be reaffirmed. Fantasy is Lacan's account of how this happens. In fantasy I try to reassert my position as the object of the Other's desire, and my own desire is to remain such an object. Another way is possible, and Lacan's theory of the act discusses this. An act involves a different reaction to both the Other's desire and the meaning constructed for us in the Other.

For now I will introduce a general definition of the subject that occurs in Lacan's work from the mid-1960s, when he was developing his notions of fantasy and act. Of course, this is not the only theory of the subject going in Lacan's work. "Subject" is used in many different ways by Lacan. It sometimes means something as simple as "child" or "individual," and it often just means "patient" or "analysand." When used in all of these senses, "subject" seems to mean nothing more than "that which undergoes an experience." In other words, it is not used in a precise theoretical manner. On my reading, Lacan does not come up with a unique and rigorous theory of the subject until his fourteenth and fifteenth seminars.

In his early seminars, Lacan was always a bit sketchy about the subject. Consider a typical example from his second seminar: "I am giving you a possible definition of subjectivity, by formulating it as an organized system of symbols, aiming to cover the whole of an experience, to animate it, to give it its meaning. And what are we trying to realize here, if not a subjectivity?" (II, 56/40–41). "Subject," according to this, would simply mean "system." A subject is identified here with the working of a signifying chain, and analysis is about unearthing this chain. Indeed, here Lacan does seem to be equating the subject with language. But the subject here is also, even more strikingly, associated with what gives meaning to experience, and not with something that itself has meaning or is a meaning. It is safe to say that this is nothing but a phenomenological view of the subject, one that is far removed from thinking of the subject as something produced by signifiers. This is just one aspect of this definition, though, and it is an aspect that is abandoned by Lacan later on. Another aspect of this definition from seminar two will remain active throughout Lacan's discussions of the subject. A subject will always have something to do with a consistency of signifiers, with an "organized system of symbols." What will disappear from Lacan's work is the notion that a subject is something that gives meaning.

The idea that the subject is a product of signifiers can be found unambiguously in seminar nine: "Nothing else supports the traditional philosophical idea of the subject except the existence of the signifier and its effects" (IX, 11/15/61). This subject can still be thought of as an "organized system of symbols," but it is not something that gives this order meaning. Rather, the subject is identified with a meaning. This corresponds to what I spoke of in chapter 3 as the "subject-as-meaning," a subject represented in the Other, and part of the Other's discourse.

But I have been claiming that Lacan was not satisfied with this version of the subject either. Again, the subject is always something like a consistency of signifiers in Lacan's opinion, but this is actually only one aspect of the subject. Lacan's ultimate vision of the subject is achieved when the subject is portrayed as something between an organized system of symbols and what motivates that organization in the first place—events such as sexuality, jouissance, and the Other's desire, all of which can be correlated with the real. In fact, in a passage I discussed in chapter 1, in the ninth seminar itself Lacan very clearly expresses his dissatisfaction with the idea that a subject is reducible to language.

The definition of the subject that I want to focus on now comes from Lacan's fourteenth seminar. There he says that a subject "is situated at the junction—or, in better terms, the disjunction—of the body and jouissance" (XIV, 6/7/67). We have seen in this chapter that in seminar fourteen the Other is the body. I would suggest that "body" in this definition is the body overwritten with signifiers, in contrast to the jouissance that pervades it. It is not so much of a stretch, then, to suggest that when Lacan says "body" here, we could also just as well say language. So not only does this definition reaffirm that a subject is neither language nor jouissance, it also tells us more about the structure of the subject. As I argued in chapter 1, in his ninth seminar Lacan was content with saying that the subject is between the two poles of language and the real. In this definition, the subject's position is given more elaboration. The subject is situated at a junction and disjunction of the two with each other. The next two chapters will study two major elaborations of this junction-disjunction structure.

CHAPTER 5

The Fundamental Fantasy

There is no subject of desire. There is a subject of fantasy. (Résponses, 9)

The definition of the subject Lacan gives in his fourteenth seminar takes into account both the fact that a subject is produced by an interaction of signifiers, and the fact that it is contingent upon a particular kind of event within a signifying chain. In the next two chapters, I will consider how Lacan's conceptions of fantasy and the act represent different ways in which this definition takes shape, and how they allow us to flesh out the subject's structure.

The term *fantasy* can be a bit misleading. It tends to connote some kind of active imagining on the part of an individual, usually opposed to reality. Lacan's notion of fantasy, however, involves something different. In "La diréction de la cure," he writes, "Any temptation to reduce fantasy to imagination [...] is a permanent misconception. [...] However, the notion of the unconscious fantasy no longer presents any difficulty once it is defined as an image set to work in the signifying structure" (Lacan 1966, 637/Lacan 2002, 260). Saying that this understanding of fantasy no longer presents us with any difficulties is an exaggeration, certainly, but we see that although Lacan does not consider fantasy to be something consciously imagined, it remains an image—albeit an image that has been filtered through what Lacan calls a "signifying structure." I will be arguing that fantasy—or the configuration that often goes by the name "fundamental fantasy"—is actually a particular way in which language and resistances to signification get mixed together, creating a junctive and disjunctive situation for a subject.

RECENT DISCUSSIONS OF FANTASY: BAAS, BERNET, AND ŽIŽEK

Freud describes fantasy as an "imaginary situation" (1961a [1919e], 179). This gives us the idea that fantasy is something like a satisfaction aid actively imagined by an individual. Daydreams would provide good examples of this. While daydreams would certainly fit under the heading "imaginings" and are commonly called "fantasies," what Lacan calls fantasy, and sometimes the "fundamental fantasy," is something quite different and has a much more restricted meaning—one that is nevertheless based on Freud's theory of fantasy. Rudolf Bernet points out that in Freud's work there is a

> progressive differentiation between imagination understood as "imaginativeness" [*fantaisie*] and imagination understood as "fantasy" [*fantasme*]. "Imaginativeness" [*fantaisie*] refers to an autonomous psychic activity, characterized by the fact that its intentional objects do not "really" exist. [. . .] With the progressive exploration by Freud of what must really be called the "psychic reality" of the unconscious, however, this opposition between the subjective imaginary and an objective reality loses much of its importance. Far from being a flight from reality, imaginary activity is associated more and more with a necessary work of psychic representation [. . .]. It is no longer a matter here, then, of free imaginativeness, but of *fantasy*. (Bernet 1993, 193)

In Lacan's work, I suggest that what goes by the name of fantasy is also an example of an imaginary activity that is part of a "necessary work of psychic representation." Fantasy in its everyday sense would be more akin to what Bernet refers to as a free imaginativeness. In what follows, I will only be using the term *fantasy* in the former sense.

Bernet's account has the virtue of emphasizing that fantasy in Freud's work is not a distortion of a real relation or a wished-for relation to others and the world. It is, rather, an active invention of such relations. Bernet later argues that fantasy is "a sort of schema—in the Kantian sense of the word—of a possible object of desire" (1993, 196). Certainly fantasy does seem close to a Kantian schema, whose arts are "concealed in the depths of the human soul" and cannot be viewed as a simple conscious, reflective activity (Kant 1965 [1787], B180). Other commentators have made a similar point. Žižek also claims that "the role of fantasy in the economy of desire is homologous to that of transcendental schematism in the process of knowledge" (1989, 119). Žižek too describes the function of fantasy in terms of how it prepares an object for desire: Fantasy makes an empirical object—in itself perhaps of little interest—into an object of desire, as if a kind of screen is put over an otherwise neutral object, making it into something desirable. Bernard Baas has done the most work on the connection between fantasy and schematism, but he differs from Žižek and Bernet by situating the schema in a specific part of what can be called a fantasy structure and not in fantasy itself. "Fantasy makes the synthesis of the *a priori* faculty of desiring and the empirical object possible, a synthesis brought about by object *a* in its articulation with the barred subject of desire. This is exactly the same mechanism [*dispositif*] as the one from which the transcendental synthesis in the Kantian theory of knowledge proceeds" (Baas 1992, 71). "Object *a*" is Lacan's term for the object in a fantasy. Baas sees object *a* as a Kantian schema, because object *a* is what makes a transition to an empirical object of desire possible, which Baas calls an "epithemon" (his word for an object of desire, modeled on the Kantian terms "noumenon" and "phenomenon").

Note the distinction Baas makes between a *fantasy* that makes a synthesis possible and an object *a* that "brings about" the synthesis in question. Fantasy "makes possible" the synthesis of what Baas is calling the "a priori" faculty of desiring with the empirical object of desire, but the synthesis is *brought about* [*opérée*] by object *a*. There is, of course, a difference between "making possible" and "bringing about." Fantasy makes the synthesis Baas is talking about possible, but the synthesis is not brought about without object *a*. Object *a* is, according to Baas, the agent of the fantasy. For this reason, Baas is inclined to understand object *a*, and not fantasy itself, as a Kantian schema.

In contrast to Baas, I will argue that fantasy is an operation that actually produces object *a*, and we will soon see why this is important. My disagreement with Baas may be due to the fact that he is asking an essentially Kantian question such as "How is desire possible?," which leads him to posit an "a priori faculty of desiring" and requires him to give an account of how desire for mere *empirical* objects is possible. Baas knows that desire in Lacan's work is never really *for* an object. Instead, what he is asking is how it is possible for desire to see itself as desiring a particular object, even though, essentially, it does not. His answer is fantasy. So fantasy is portrayed by Baas as a corruption of what he calls "pure desire." Pure desire is a desire not lured by fantasy, it is a desire for what is "absolutely unpresentable, absolutely beyond figuration" (1992, 71). According to Baas, Lacan's ethic is about the cultivation of such a pure desire.

Whether this may be Lacan's ethic around the time of the seventh seminar and the article "Kant avec Sade" or not (and I have my doubts, although many take that to be Lacan's position), I believe that it is clear later on that such a pure desire is not anything Lacan is aiming at. So is it fair to say that fantasy corrupts a desire that would otherwise be pure? Lacan is usually insistent on the fact that fantasy structures and gives rise to desire: "Fantasy is the support of desire, it is not the object that is the support of desire" (XI, 207/185). This should be taken to mean that there is no desire before fantasy. The problem with Baas's presentation is with his presupposition of an "*a priori* faculty of desiring" preexisting the fantasy. On this basis, he understands fantasy to be something that introduces an impurity into an otherwise pure desire. If, however, fantasy is something that enables desire, then we can draw different consequences from fantasy. Fantasy will also form object *a* (understood later in Lacan's work not only as the object of fantasy but also as the cause of desire) and a certain type of consistency for a subject. I hope to show, then, that fantasy does much more than offer a schema for "a possible object of desire." If fantasy did this, then it would leave open the possibility that there is still a subject distinct from fantasy who would be possessing an "a priori faculty of desiring" that gets rendered empirical in fantasy. Instead, I wish to show that fantasy, far from presupposing either a desire or a subject capable of desiring, produces both desire and a particular kind of subject-effect.

So fantasy's scope is wider, and at the same time more limited, than Kant's schematism. The Kantian schema only provided a framework for possible objects of experience. Fantasy, according to Lacan, does not set up objects of experience—that is not what it is about. It sets up objects of desire, but it also "sets up" a position for jouissance in the Other (which is to say, in signifiers) and a representation or place for the subject itself in the Other. With this understanding of fantasy, the subject is certainly not an agent transcendent to fantasy, constituting the fantasy as a noematic object, but something found and achieved in the consistency of the fantasy itself.

Žižek describes fantasy as "the kernel of the subject's being [. . .] in an irreducible way decentered with regard to the symbolic texture which defines the subject's identity" (1992, 162). According to this view, I may consciously believe myself to be a certain type of individual with certain characteristics and desires, but my fundamental fantasy (in its Freudian-Lacanian sense) reveals what I really am: an already-dead child, someone who wants to be beaten, and so on. It is certainly the case that fantasy in this sense is different from the kinds of things we might consciously fantasize about. What is problematic with Žižek's account, however, is his description of the subject's encounter with its own fantasy. Žižek writes: "The subject can confront this extimate kernel [fantasy] only at the price of his temporary *aphanisis*" (ibid.). That is, when I encounter my fantasy my symbolic identifications and meanings are disrupted. Fantasy contests the way I (consciously and reflectively) understand myself. Thus an encounter with fantasy brings about a disappearance or fading (an *aphanisis*) of what I think I am, but also effects a fading of the (conscious) subject as such, who no longer knows what he or she is. It is as if fantasy itself has the same effects as the resistances to signification I discussed in the previous chapter. However, while it is certainly difficult to articulate the kind of fantasies Lacan is talking about—because they are embarrassing and unpleasant, not to mention unconscious—fantasy should not be seen as a resistance to signification in the way jouissance, the Other's desire, or the real in general is. I will be arguing here that fantasy has much more in common with a signified effect. It is an attempt to situate a meaning and value for both the subject and jouissance. If it is hard to articulate, this is because of the difference between the identity and image a conscious individual has of himself or herself and the unconscious foundation of these, found in fantasy.

The problem with Žižek's account of fantasy, then, stems from his double use of the term *subject*. On the one hand, Žižek calls fantasy a subject's "kernel of being." In a sense, this kernel is the subject itself, the subject as it really is. But fantasy is also something that Žižek portrays as "extimate" with respect to what the conscious, reflecting subject thinks of itself. Such a presentation can lead to confusion about the nature of the subject in Lacan's theory, and I will return to this topic in chapter 7. Žižek uses the term *subject* sometimes in the traditional sense, to refer to a conscious, reflecting individual, and he also uses the term *subject* to refer to the fantasy itself: the fantasy is the truth of the subject, it is what the subject really is. So the encounter about which Žižek is speaking is an encounter of the subject with itself, not fundamentally unlike any other reflective or conscious experience, although it is surely noteworthy for its disruptive nature.

I am trying here to avoid using the term *subject* to refer to the conscious, reflecting individual. A subject is not something situated on either side of a fantasy—it is not the object in the fantasy, nor is it the actor who plays a role in the fantasmatic scenario, nor is it the conscious individual (or ego) who encounters fantasy as a foreign entity. Where is the subject to be found in fantasy? I will be arguing here that it is to be found in the very consistency and structuring relation that the fantasy establishes for an individual—a junction and disjunction of language and jouissance. Does a subject encounter itself in fantasy? Only if one allows the term *subject* to name what should be seen as two different things: the reflecting individual and what a fantasy provides for that individual. If the term *subject* is restricted to the latter, then it is senseless to speak of a subject encountering itself in fantasy.

Žižek's account of fantasy does have the merit of showing us that the constitution of an object is not fantasy's most important function, as Baas and Bernet would have it. This is certainly one of its effects, but if attention is not paid to the way in which fantasy also constitutes the subject, then one could still believe that the subject is something that contemplates either the fantasy or the object in the fantasy. The difference between the Lacanian fantasy and Kantian schematism may be more important than their similarity. The fantasy is surely something like a "schema" that achieves a symbolic position for both the subject and jouissance. It provides the basis for the subject's identification, and it also provides a symbolic meaning for jouissance by associating jouissance with a particular object or signifier desired by the Other. But, as I said earlier, its scope is both wider and more limited than Kantian schemtaism.

"A CHILD IS BEING BEATEN"

Let us consider how this function of fantasy is illustrated in the paradigmatic example of fantasy for Lacan: Freud's study of the fantasy "a child is being beaten." Freud studied three fantasies that he claims to have come across frequently in his practice. In each case, "a child is being beaten" turns out to be a modification of earlier fantasies in his patients' development—first, "my father is beating the child *whom I hate*," and then "*I am being beaten by my father*" (1961a [1919e], 185). The latter fantasy is seen by Freud as "the most important and the most momentous of all" (ibid.). Freud repeatedly refers to it as an *unconscious* fantasy. This is not the case with the other two fantasies: The fantasy "a child is being beaten" is conscious and was used explicitly in the masturbatory practices of the patients Freud presented in his article. The fact that the fundamental fantasy "I am being beaten by my father" is unconscious means that it is the basis of a conscious fantasy like "a child is being beaten." Freud explains the transformations of the fantasy in terms of repression. The content of the fantasy "I am being beaten by my father" concerns a punishment for incestuous desires too difficult to admit to and is accordingly repressed. The more innocent and generic fantasy "a child is being beaten" is put in its place. Since it is more neutral, it is more amenable to consciousness, even more than "my father is beating the child whom I hate."

The true kernel of this fantasy remains, however, "I am being beaten by my father." According to Lacan, two important things are going on in this unconscious fantasy. One is that jouissance (which, again, should be thought of here also as a resistance to signification) is given a place in the Other and gets symbolized. In this particular fantasy, Lacan says that the child receives his or her message in an inverted form, from the Other (XVII, 73–74). The "message" in question is a response to a question about the status of jouissance itself. In the previous chapter, I discussed how jouissance is placeless and resistant to symbolization. Its first irruptions essentially put the child's position with respect to the Other into question. Inventing a place and function for jouissance in symbolic terms provides the "solution" to this. Fantasy does this by attributing jouissance to the Other. Lacan's point here is that in the fantasy "I am being beaten by my father," it is the father who is imagined to enjoy the act of beating. Thus in fantasy the child receives a message about jouissance. Fantasy makes jouissance into something the Other is after, and it makes me the object that provides the Other with jouissance. Here we find the second important achievement of this fantasy. In it, the child himself or herself also receives a place by being situated as the object that procures the Other's jouissance. In this fantasy, the father is "enjoying" the child, we could say. So this fantasy gives a double lesson—it tells us that jouissance is the Other's, and that we are the objects that make it possible for the Other to enjoy.

The place given to the child in fantasy is much like the subject-as-meaning discussed in chapter 3. The difference is that jouissance plays a role in this position now. Fantasy is developed in response to the signifying impasse of jouissance. For this reason, fantasy is something like a filter: Lacan calls it a "window on the real" (Lacan 2001, 254). If we expand on this a bit, we can see how fantasy illustrates the way in which a subject is situated at a junction and disjunction of language and jouissance. The fantasy's placing of jouissance in language also creates a subject of the fantasy—a subject situated in a particular relation to the Other and to jouissance. In this respect, the subject of fantasy is situated at the junction of language and jouissance, but also at their disjunction, since something of jouissance continues to escape the fantasmatic situation of jouissance. This part that escapes is where we can find the possibility for a different structuration of the subject, in an act. In fantasy, the subject is not put into a relation with this part of jouissance that does not get "written" in the fantasy. For this reason, the fantasy is indeed something like a window on the real. It permits access to the real under controlled conditions, conditions that effectively protect us from the real, while allowing access to a colonized, tamed real.

ALIENATION

In his eleventh seminar, Lacan develops a way of speaking about how the fantasy is constructed. He comes up with what he calls two "operations" of the subject that, together, result in a fantasy structure: alienation and separation. Before I discuss these two operations, I would first like to consider Lacan's formula for fantasy: $\$\Diamond a$. The two sides of this formula for fantasy can be taken to represent the child and the Other. The "lozenge" found in the formula—the diamond shape—reveals to us the situation or structure of the subject between the two.

Lacan explains this lozenge in various ways throughout his seminars and publications. In his eleventh seminar, he renders the bottom half of the diamond into an arrow going from barred-S to *a*, and the top half into an arrow going from *a* to the barred-S in order to describe how the operations of alienation and separation work (XI, 231/209). The bottom arrow describes the movement that constitutes alienation, and the top arrow separation.

Alienation is a rather familiar concept. According to Marx, alienation is the result of a particular social configuration. Specifically, it is due to the fact that in capitalist economies the product of a worker's labor is stolen from him or her. Self-consciousness requires an object in order to achieve itself and to be recognized as such, and in capitalism the object in which it would be recognized is turned into a commodity:

> The worker puts his life into the object: but now his life no longer belongs to him but to the object. Hence, the greater this activity, the greater is the worker's lack of objects. Whatever the product of his labor is, he is not. Therefore the greater this product, the less is he himself. The alienation of the worker in his product means not only that his labor becomes an object, an external existence, but that it exists "outside him," independently, as something alien to him, and that it becomes a power of its own confronting him; it means that the life which he has conferred on the object confronts him as something hostile and alien. (Marx 1978, 72)

Alienation, then, is essentially a self-alienation (Marx 1978, 133). Communism, the abolition of private property, would transform this condition, such that humanity would no longer be alienated from its essence—the product of labor would no longer be appropriated by the capitalist and would no longer have a power independent of its producers. The worker can achieve recognition through his or her labor in communism, then, not because the product is finally his or her property, but because it no longer takes on a power independent to the worker, dominating him or her.

Thus alienation is not a necessary condition, according to Marx. It is the result of a specific social and economic system. Is this also the case for Lacan's concept of alienation? Not at all. Lacan uses the term *alienation* to speak about a more fundamental human condition. Alienation is not what Marx understood it to be, nor is it, Lacan claims, an "existential" idea. That is, "alienation has a patent side, which is not that we are the Other, or that others [...] by capturing us [*en nous reprenant*] disfigure or deform us" (XIV, 1/11/67). Lacanian alienation is clearly an attempt to describe the child's "entry" into the Other, in the sense that a child becomes a speaking being, using the Other's signifiers. But alienation is not alienating because we are a meaning for others, even before we are born. Rather alienation is alienating because of what is given up upon such an entry into the Other.

What is given up in Lacanian alienation? Lacan imagines that at some point a child is confronted with an either/or choice. He or she can either choose to adopt language or to remain immersed in what Lacan calls "being." This opposition between language and being is, I believe, just another way of describing the opposition between language and jouissance. In seminar nine, Lacan situated the subject between language and the body. In seminar fourteen, he situates it at a junction and disjunction of the body (language) and jouissance. Alienation describes a transition from the body, jouissance, or the real, to language (the Other).

Alienation is not just about choosing language, then, but also about choosing what language implies: an acceptance of the Other's terms, an acceptance or assumption of the Other's determination of me as a subject-as-meaning. By speaking of alienation as a choice, Lacan can claim that a child either chooses this place already established for him or her in the Other's discourse or refuses it; only this is a forced choice. Lacan characterizes the result of refusing to choose language as a choice for being. We might put it this way: If a child refuses language, all he or she will have is a being with no symbolic place, no recognition by the Other. This is perhaps why Lacan speaks of the choice as a "forced" choice, because even if language is refused, there is still a symbolic position carved out for the child. For example, even if Xénophon had refused to be situated at the place of the "dead child," he still would have been in fact situated at that place for his mother. In this sense, perhaps, the choice between being and language is forced: No matter what you choose, there is some symbolic place carved out for you. What is lost in the operation of alienation, then, is any kind of "being" independent of the Other.

But there is not a total loss of this being either. Consider how things would sound if instead of using the term *being* Lacan had used the term *real.* A total loss of the real might only be conceivable if we think of the real as $real_1$, a kind of real prior to symbolization. But Lacan points out that the "lost" real or being leaves a mark on language. A child can choose to remain in being or to become a speaking being. In either case, some field is rejected, but not totally lost. This field that is rejected is not described by Lacan as "meaning-being" or some other term that would express the idea of a union of the two regions. Instead, the term *nonsense* or *non-meaning* is used to describe the consequences of the forced choice on either region (XI, 236/211). If a child chooses being, then the child is left with a being that has no symbolic place, a being with no meaning that is in fact haunted by the symbolic. If a child chooses meaning, then the child has a symbolic place, but this order of meaning will also always be haunted by a kind of non-meaning, Lacan's name for the effects of lost being on the symbolic. In this way, we see that "being" more closely resembles what was described earlier as $real_2$. This is a real that has effects on the symbolic and is not a real that is totally lost when language is assumed by a child.

So whatever is chosen—being or meaning—is also marked by what was not chosen. The field chosen is scarred by what is lost. This scar marks a place where something of being persists even after the forced choice of meaning, and similarly, for being, this scar marks a place where something of meaning is present in being. In either case, this way of thinking about the being and meaning shows that the real and the symbolic are not radically separable from each other in Lacanian theory. They are intertwined, such that one is always present in the other. The real has effects on the symbolic, and, conversely, the symbolic has effects on the real.

SEPARATION

Lacan claims that separation "achieves the circularity of the relation of the subject to the Other" (XI, 238/213, translation modified). If alienation is represented in the "lozenge" by an arrow going from the side of the child to the side of the Other, then separation tells us about the return trip. So whereas alienation tells us about what is given up upon entrance into the Other, separation tells us about how the child tries to regain this "lost being" after being alienated in the Other. Alienation implies a loss, and separation tries to redress this loss. Another way of putting it is to say that separation tells us about how the kind of traumatic "impasse in formalization" that is the real's presence in the symbolic achieves some kind of symbolization. Fantasy as a whole, produced by the operations of alienation and separation, is precisely the structure that constructs a real "regained" by the symbolic.

Of course, Lacan warns against taking the relation between alienation and separation to be complementary. It is not the case that separation gives back what was lost in alienation. He calls the relation between the operations one that is "circular, yet non-reciprocal" (Lacan 1966, 840/ Lacan 1996, 268). What separation manages to "regain" is some kind of symbolic status for the being lost in alienation, or for the real's essential resistance to symbolization.

In fact, Lacan describes separation as something that happens as a result of an encounter with the Other's desire, which is, I argued, a type of signifying impasse:

> Lack is encountered by the subject in the Other, in the very intimation that the Other makes to him or her by his or her discourse. In the intervals of the Other's discourse, the following arises in the experience of the child, which is radically able to be situated in that experience—"s/he tells me that, but what does s/he want?"
>
> In this interval cutting up the signifiers, which is part of the very structure of the signifier, is the heart of what, in other registers of my development, I called metonymy. It is there that what we call desire creeps, glides, and flees, like a ferret. The Other's desire is apprehended by the subject in what does not stick, in the gaps of the Other's discourse, and all the child's "whys" testify less to an avidity for the reason of things than they constitute a putting to the test of the adult, a "why are you telling me that?" always resuscitated in its foundation, which is the enigma of the adult's desire.
>
> Now, to respond to this capture [prise] the child, like Gribouille, answers with the anteceding lack, of his or her own disappearance, which s/he comes to situate at the point of the lack perceived in the Other. The first object that s/he proposes

> to this parental desire whose object is unknown is his or her own loss—"Does s/he want to lose me?" The fantasy of his or her death, of his or her disappearance, is the first object that the subject has which can be put into play in this dialectic, and s/he puts it into play in fact—we know it by a thousand facts, even if we only knew it from anorexia nervosa. We also know that the fantasy of his or her death is commonly aroused by the child in his or her love relations with his or her parents. (XI, 239–240/214–215, translation modified).[1]

This passage occurs in the context of Lacan's first discussion of separation in his eleventh seminar. Even though separation is not mentioned by name in this passage, the movement that is essential to separation is described. Separation describes what happens in a child's first attempt to come up with an answer to the Other's desire. So the operation of separation includes the Other's desire within it—it is motivated and spurred by this signifying impasse.

The general purpose of fantasy, I argued, is twofold. On the one hand, it is an attempt to stage oneself as the object of the Other's desire. In the passage just cited, the child's question about the Other's desire is answered by the fantasy of his or her own death, which turns the question "What does the Other want?" into "Does the Other want to lose me?" or "Can the Other afford to lose me?" My disappearance can be an object put into play in the encounter with the Other's desire, and it may succeed in situating me as something that the Other might desire: I suppose that my disappearance would cause the Other pain. On the other hand, fantasy also tries to give some symbolic place to jouissance. In Lacan's discussions of the case of Little Hans, jouissance is described as something that entailed Hans's disappearance—it put his status for the Other into question. Jouissance is at the root of the child's own perception of his or her possible disappearance. In other words, jouissance is something like an encounter with mortality, insofar as it entails a "fading" of the symbolically situated subject. The fantasy Lacan describes in the passage just quoted also manages to give this disappearance and mortality itself a symbolic status, making them into things that would have an effect on the Other.

But why exactly is the operation that results in the construction of a fantasy called separation? It seems to have more to do with putting oneself into a relation to the Other, to joining with the Other, than separating. In fact, Lacan claims that separation involves an "intersection" with the Other (Lacan 1966, 842/Lacan 1996, 271). In the diagrams used to illustrate alienation, we saw that something is lost, but that this lost thing also continues to have effects on what is chosen, thus the real persists within the symbolic, and the symbolic has effects on the real. Separation can be seen as an attempt to account for this persistence, and thus can be said to come up with an "intersection" of the symbolic and the real. Fantasy is just such an intersection.

In Lacan's first explanation of his use of the term *separation*, he points out that it resembles the verb *se parer* in French, which can mean *to get dressed* and *to protect oneself*. So, it should not be a surprise that separation involves taking on a role or position in order to defend oneself against something else. In separation, I take on a position as the object of the Other's desire, thereby separating myself from the signifying impasse that both the Other's desire and jouissance confront me with. Lacan also notes that etymologically, the French *se parer* comes from the Latin *se parere*, which means "to engender oneself" (XI, 239/214). This separation, which protects one from the abyssal encounters with the real, generates the structure of the subject as a junction and disjunction of language and jouissance.

But it still may not be clear why such an operation is called separation. Simply put, my question is this: What is being separated from in separation? Bruce Fink explains it the following way: "The child's unsuccessful attempt to perfectly complement its mother leads to an expulsion of the subject from the position of wanting-to-be and yet failing-to-be the Other's sole object of desire" (1995a, 51). This expulsion, spurred by an encounter with the Other's desire, can be seen as a separation from the Other. On this basis, it could be argued that what is separated from is twofold: in separation, the subject is expelled from "being" (an expulsion which is in fact already accounted for by alienation) and at the same time expelled from the Other, to the extent that the Other's desire precludes the possibility of being the complete object of the Other's desire, and settling down firmly in meaning. Separation implies a failure to be the complete object of the Other's desire, and the impossibility of becoming fully placed in symbolic terms.

But we have seen that the operation of separation is also about acquiring or constructing some kind of position for both jouissance and oneself in the Other in response to encounters with the real. Such a construction certainly implies that one is not the complete object of the Other's desire. As I argued in chapter 4, the Other's desire is something that is fundamentally ambiguous, and we do not experience it as something addressed to us. So even though separation seems to involve a "self-engendering" of a subject, a construction of a status for jouissance ("being") and myself, separation also presumes that jouissance is experienced as a disappearing, and that I am radically excluded from the Other.

So separation is, in one respect, a separation not only from jouissance or the real but also from the Other's desire in its radical impenetrability and alterity. Separation as an *operation* that produces the subject, however, describes what happens in the wake of this encounter with the Other's desire: the construction and assumption of a symbolic position supported by, guaranteed by, the Other's desire. Similarly, the fantasy that results from separation is a structure that presupposes an encounter with the Other's desire but also maintains a distance from that desire. Based on this reading, fantasy shows us how a subject is situated at both a junction and disjunction of language (the Other) and jouissance (or the real, or what Lacan calls "being" in his study of alienation). Fantasy not only joins the child to the Other (a junction that serves to give a place to the subject in the Other, and also serves to sustain a signification for jouissance), but it also presupposes and preserves a disjunction and an expulsion from the Other and "being."

CONCLUSION

I have been arguing that Lacan has two major theses on the subject. The subject is produced by an interaction of signifiers, and the subject is also produced by a resistance to signification. It is becoming increasingly clear that Lacan's subject cannot be reduced to language. For one thing, what I have been calling the subject-as-meaning, the symbolic place where a subject is represented, is indeed a critical factor in the subject's structure, but it is not identical to the subject. It is only when there are impasses in meaning, resistances to signification, that a subject, strictly speaking, comes about.

Fantasy shows us one way in which a subject comes about. Indeed, it seems to be a fundamental way, one without which there is no subject. But the conditions of fantasy are highly deterministic. That is, even though there is an operation called "separation" at work in fantasy, fantasy achieves nothing but the affirmation of a place for the subject in the Other. This place differs from what was discussed in chapter 3 as the subject-as-meaning, mainly because fantasy is something that comes after an impasse in signification has been encountered and confronted.

A theory of freedom is to be found in Lacan's work, but so far we have seen no sign of it other than in a few aspects of desire. For about half of Lacan's career, desire was always in part about refusing to be placed in the Other. Lacan's theory of fantasy, according to which fantasy is the support of desire, throws this aspect of desire out the window. Fantasy tells the story of how a child does something with his or her symbolic destiny: assuming it, or slightly modifying it. But it ultimately condemns the subject to desiring to be the object of the Other's desire. Lacan's theory of the act addresses this problem head on and provides him with a different way of describing freedom, one that is not about a wholesale refusal to be placed in the Other. In fact, his theory of the act also forces us to refine our understanding of the Other, as I will show in the next chapter.

CHAPTER 6

How Acts Use Signifiers

When we address ourselves to the other, we are not always going to express ourselves in witticisms. In a way, if we could we would be happier. (V, 150)

In his eleventh seminar, Lacan introduced the idea of a subject who has "traversed the radical fantasy" (XI, 273). This idea concerns the goal of a psychoanalytic cure, which suggests that Lacan saw fantasy as a sort of problem, and perhaps even an obstacle to analysis: something to be transformed on the way to a different organization of the subject. What would this entail? Bruce Fink writes the following about traversing fantasy, in connection with castration:

> The subject who refuses to "sacrifice his or her castration to the Other's jouissance" [...] is the subject who has not undergone the further separation known as traversing fantasy [. . .]. The subject must renounce his or her more or less comfortable, complacently miserable position as subjected by the Other—as castrated—in order to take the Other's desire as cause upon him or herself. The traversing of fantasy thus involves a going beyond of castration and a utopian moment beyond neurosis. (1998, 72)

Fantasy is portrayed here as an obstacle to analytic work, and Fink refers to the traversing of fantasy as a "utopian moment." Perhaps this is because such a traversal is never completely accomplished. Nevertheless, the important point is that traversing fantasy suggests that there is another way that a subject can be structured: "beyond neurosis."

Lacan does not actually say much about traversing fantasy. The only time the phrase is used explicitly is at the end of seminar eleven, when Lacan asks: "How can a subject who has traversed fantasy live the drive?" (XI, 273, translation modified). The idea arises again, in a slightly altered form, in the 1967 *Proposition sur l'analyste de l'école*, when Lacan writes of what happens "at the end of the transference relation" in terms of the subject "falling out of its fantasy" (Lacan 2001, 252). Nevertheless, I believe that the essential idea behind the traversal of fantasy mentioned in seminar eleven can be found in a topic that Lacan discussed in the seminars following seminar eleven: the act.

As Fink puts it, a traversal of fantasy transforms a subject's complacent "subjection" to the Other. Fink describes this in terms of taking on "the Other's desire as cause" upon oneself (1998, 72). If the Other's desire as such presents the subject with a signifying impasse, then traversing fantasy can be described as taking on this impasse as one's "cause." In fantasy itself (at least what Lacan calls the fundamental fantasy), the impasse of the Other's desire is given a meaning. This allows the subject to take a position with respect to that desire. Essentially fantasy involves getting desired by the Other. If traversing fantasy, in contrast, means taking on or assuming the Other's *desire* as one's cause (and not taking on a position as the meaning or object attributed to that desire), then perhaps the whole issue of having a position with respect to the Other is sidestepped by such a traversal. This leads me to suggest that assuming the Other's desire as one's cause means at least not primarily seeking to be desired or recognized by the Other.

If recognition is no longer the subject's primary aim after a traversal of fantasy, then such a traversal does not only imply a change in the subject's structure but a change in the status of the Other for the subject as well. Here I will consider how this change in the status of the Other is visible in the manner in which signifiers are used in acts. In other words, the major difference between fantasy and a traversal of fantasy—which I will henceforth refer to as an act—can be seen by looking at how each uses signifiers differently. Simply put, my claim will be that in an act, signifiers do not necessarily produce meanings that one wishes to have recognized by the Other. As a result, the subject position produced by an act is very different from the subject position produced in the fundamental fantasy. In an act, signifiers are used quasi-autonomously, and their use amounts to a repetition and an extension of a signifying impasse, converting an enigmatic tension into some kind of satisfaction.

This interpretation of Lacan's theory of the act is partly motivated by the interpretation that Slavoj Žižek has given recently in *The Ticklish Subject*, where he claims that "in Lacan, act is a purely *negative* category" (1999, 160, emphasis in original). Žižek makes this claim in the context of a discussion about the difference between the subject *tout court* and subjectivization. Subjectivization is to be seen as a moment of identification, a moment of subjection or subordination to a signifier, and can be understood as a moment that is productive of the subject. What Žižek wishes to emphasize is the distinction between the subject and any subjectivization, so that the subject, while always produced by a subjectivization, is still not to be conflated with the identity that subjectivization provides. This distinction between the subject and subjectivization is important to maintain, of course, but I do not think that maintaining it requires us to think of the act—or the subject, for that matter—as a "purely negative category" in contrast to the "positivity" that identification or subjectivization involves. Certainly, acts turn out to be saying "no" to something, as I will explain later. What I hope to show by studying how acts use signifiers, however, is that the notion that an act is purely, and perhaps exclusively, negative does not give us a full account of Lacan's theory of the act. Acts use signifiers in a way that is not limited to negation, and this is a use of signifiers that is also different from what occurs in subjectivization. I will expand on this point in chapter 7.

The view I will be advocating here, then, takes Lacan's theory of the act to be an illustration of how a subject's relation to signifiers may not be bound by identification and the desire for recognition. If Lacan's theory of the act is about a circumvention of identification and recognition, and if acts are still signifying, then what we find in acts is a subject produced by a signifying practice without a concomitant subjectivization. This is because the use of signifiers in an act is not oriented toward gaining recognition from the Other and does not depend upon the notion of a consistent Other, a subject-supposed-to-know, for its meaning and validity.

In explicating this view, I will begin with a discussion of the basics of a psychoanalytic act as Lacan discusses them in his fourteenth and fifteenth seminars. Then I will explore how Lacan's comments on the *Fort-Da* game in Freud's work shed light on how signifiers are used in an act. This will lead me to consider more closely the kind of signifying practice that an act is by comparing Lacan's comments on new signifiers and puns from his twenty-fourth seminar to what he says of them in seminar five. Finally, I will point out how puns, and perhaps acts, suggest a distinct type of linguistic operation, one that cannot be understood in terms of metaphor or metonymy.

THE BASICS OF AN ACT

The term *act* is found in two important psychoanalytic concepts—"acting out" and the *passage à l'acte*—but what Lacan calls an act is distinct from both. An "acting out" can be described as an impulsive action occurring in the framework of the analytic transference. Laplanche and Pontalis define acting out as

> a term used in psychoanalysis to designate actions usually of an impulsive character, relatively *en rupture* with the subject's usual motivations, relatively isolable in the course of his or her activities, often taking an auto- or hetero-aggressive form. In the appearance of acting out the psychoanalyst sees the mark of the repressed. When it appears in the course of an analysis (whether it is during a session or outside of one) acting out is to be understood in its connection with the transference, and often as an attempt to radically misrecognize the transference. (1967, 6)

An acting out is often addressed (unwittingly) to the analyst and may occur as a protest against a faulty interpretation, or a failure on the analyst's part to make an interpretation altogether. Acting out also can be considered a repetition of an unconscious and a fantasmatic scenario. A *passage à l'acte* is different. It too is usually a disruptive, precipitous act. But one thing that makes a *passage à l'acte* different from acting out is its relation to fantasy (X, 1/23/63). Whereas acting out is an enactment of a fantasy, a *passage à l'acte* seems to be a reaction to (and against) this fantasy, to this "scene" in which the subject maintains a desirable position for the Other. But a *passage à l'acte* is not yet an act *tout court*, because although it is a sort of protest against the fantasy, it does not yet leave the fantasmatic scenario behind altogether—it does not traverse fantasy.

Shoshana Felman discusses Lacan's theory of the act in her work *The Literary Speech Act* but does not point out that Lacan's theory of the act involves something other than what is found in actings out or *passages à l'acte*. Comparing Lacan to Austin, she writes: "Whereas Austin studies speech acts directly, psychoanalysis (in transference, for example) studies speech itself as an acting out or *passage into action*; and, of course, studies such 'passages into action' as speech effects or signifier effects" (1983, 93). While this is true, it should be kept in mind that what Lacan meant by an act is neither an acting out nor a *passage à l'acte*. What makes an act an act is not, according to Lacan, locomotion. One may be inclined to say, for example, that what makes a *passage à l'acte* or an acting out acts is that they bring out into the open what were previously only mental representations or scenarios (fantasies), conscious or not. But Lacan wants to get away from such an understanding of acts. For Lacan (and this should come as no surprise), an act is signifying: "*l'acte est signifiant*" (XIV, 2/22/67). So an act does not just involve doing something, it involves doing something with signifiers. Of course, we do many things with signifiers, but not all of these things—such as speaking, thinking, or daydreaming—qualify as acts either.

Lacan's notion of an act is indeed not far removed from what Austin called a performative speech act. Felman illustrates this quite well. A performative speech act gets something done with words by virtue of saying the right words in the right context. "I do" or "I hereby declare the meeting adjourned" will achieve marriages and closures by virtue of being said. Lacan shares with Austin the idea that such acts are transformative, and such acts are clearly "signifying," but Lacan's focus is not on acts that change the situation of the world or the set of facts within it. Instead he focuses on acts that change the structure of a subject. If Austinian speech acts change the state of affairs in the world—making meetings closed, bachelors married, and so on—then Lacanian speech acts change the subject.

Furthermore, an act for Lacan is essentially transgressive. "If I can walk to and fro here while talking to you this does not constitute an act," Lacan tells his listeners, again pointing out that locomotion is not what makes an act an act. He continues, "but if one day it amounts to crossing a certain threshold where I place myself outside of the law, my locomotion will have the value of an act" (XV, 11/15/67). Such threshold crossing would only be possible because of how the act signifies. Notice that Austinian speech acts, in contrast, are not at all transgressive but are in fact highly ritualized and codified. The conditions for the success of an Austinian speech act largely depend upon the existence of social guarantees and rituals. Marriages, for example, are only successfully accomplished when performed under very specific circumstances, and by the proper authorities. According to Lacan's conception, however, an act transforms a subject, and even though it occurs with signifiers, it does not happen by following a preestablished ritual or code. Also, of course, there is no authority that can ensure the legitimacy of such an act.

In the course of his fourteenth and fifteenth seminars, then, Lacan discusses these three aspects of an act: (1) it does something with words (it is signifying); (2) it changes the structure of the subject; and (3) it is transgressive. I would like to mention something about the second aspect before continuing.

Curiously, Lacan states that an act is both transformative of the structure of the subject and that it *inaugurates* the subject: "the subject is, as a subject, entirely transformed by the act" (XIV, 2/15/67). The use of the term *transformation* here implies that there was a subject before the act, and that after the act this subject is changed. But we can also find a different claim in seminar fourteen: an act is "the inauguration of the subject as such, that is to say, from a veritable act the subject arises differently [. . .] its structure is modified" (XIV, 2/22/67). For this reason, the idea of "transformation" does not quite do justice to what Lacan thinks goes on in an act. It is not the case that someone is simply changed by an act: he or she is reinaugurated as a subject. Where there was a certain structure or law operative for a subject prior to an act—imagine this to be an unconscious law, the kind of meaning and determination constructed by the fantasy—an act brings about a transformation in this structure and thereby inaugurates a new subject. In this way, an act situates one outside such a law, and for this reason it is appropriate to consider acts to be transgressive.

FORT-DA AS A MODEL FOR THE ACT

In seminar eleven, Lacan uses the *Fort-Da* game to expand on the difference between an act proper and mere locomotion, and along the way the key to how an act signifies is given. In the *Fort-Da* game, Freud's grandson threw an object away and reeled it back in, uttering a signifier with each gesture. Lacan claims that the game is "the first signifying thematization in the form of a phonemic opposition of certain situations that one can qualify as active" (XIV, 5/10/67). What activity is thematized by *Fort-Da*?

It should be kept in mind that what struck Freud about the game in the first place was the economic problem with which it presented him. In *Beyond the Pleasure Principle*, Freud studies instances in which the pleasure principle seems to be violated. Normally, according to the pleasure principle, an organism seeks to release excessive tensions, striving for the lowest possible amount of overall tension without dying. What is peculiar about the *Fort-Da* game is that in it there is an excessive, irresolvable tension coming from within the child himself. The child undergoes the trauma of his mother's departure, but then repeats this trauma in a game. This means that in the playing of the game an excessive tension keeps returning in the child, and not from an outside source. This led Freud to suggest that such phenomena give the impression that the child is "being pursued by a malignant fate or possessed by some 'daemonic' power," by some force that resists the tendency toward the lowest possible excitation (1955 [1920g], 21). This force was what Freud called the "death drive."

The pleasure principle is normally able to release tensions by binding them—Lacan would say by symbolizing what resists symbolization. What we see in the *Fort-Da* game is a repeatedly failed attempt to bind. An ineradicable libidinal tension is behind the game, and the repetitive nature of the game suggests that the game does not succeed in getting rid of that tension. Rather, the game is a part of the very tension that it is supposed to be resolving. *Fort* and *Da*, repeated, attempt to exorcise a traumatic event. Yet instead of leading to a simple release of libidinal tension, and perhaps a dissolution of the traumatic event, the *Fort-Da* game sublates that tension into a signifying activity—canceling the event out as an affective tension, yet preserving it as a signifying tension in the form of a compulsive linguistic repetition.

One of the striking features of this signifying activity, one that will allow me to explain how signifiers are used in acts, is that the *Fort-Da* game does not articulate a demand. It is not a cry to the Other. Also, the utterance of *Fort* and *Da* does not constitute an attempt to provide a meaning for the traumatic event of the mother's departure. Instead of being turned toward the Other in the articulation of a demand or a construction of meaning, it is more accurate to say that if this signifying practice is addressed to anything at all, it is to the event itself. Yet this is an odd sort of address, since it does not attempt to give the event meaning. Instead, the mother's departure is just repeated: this time, however, it is repeated in a signifying activity.

This distinction between an address to the Other and an "address to the event" mirrors an interesting distinction Lacan makes in his twelfth seminar between what he calls the "fundamental phrases" in language and the kind of language that is involved in identification:

> The subject is first of all at this root point of the event where it is said not that the subject is this or that person, but that there is something. "It's raining": such is the fundamental phrase in language [...]. It is in a second time that the subject identifies itself as the one who speaks. (XII, 3/3/65)

Lacan refers to two "times" of the subject here. At a "second time," a subject "identifies itself as the one who speaks." A subject who "identifies itself as the one who speaks" might be a subject who is able to say something like "I think that it is raining." In such an utterance, a speaking subject is represented by a signifier—I. Saying "I" makes it possible for one to conceive of oneself as a person with certain beliefs, a person who adheres to certain statements: in other words, "I" allows for a subject who has an identity, and, it might be added, it implies a distinction between "I" and "Thou."

If this subject at a "second time" is a subject who represents itself (to others as well as to itself), then what is the nature of the subject who is at that "first time"? Lacan associates this first time of the subject with what could be called a mere speaking of an event, a mere declaration of the fact that something *is*. Lacan refers to such declarations as the "fundamental phrases" of language. In other words, the function of signifiers in these fundamental phrases is not to signify in the sense of creating a meaning, which would amount to representing something or representing oneself. The fundamental phrases of language, according to Lacan, consist of saying merely that something is.

This is just the way signifiers are used in the *Fort-Da* game, where the traumatic event is also simply being said, or named, by being taken up into signifiers. Yet there is no production of meaning by these signifiers, and the game does not use signifiers as part of an attempt to obtain a recognition of the trauma from the Other.

How does this help us understand what is involved in an analytic act? The signifying activity involved in an act achieves something fundamentally different from what fantasy achieves. In an act, a subject does not constitute itself as a satisfying object of the Other's desire, and in it a subject is not demanding recognition of its own desire by the Other either. Rather, a subject is simply using signifiers autonomously, as it were, in a signifying repetition of a libidinal event. Perhaps this gives us a further hint as to why Lacan calls an act transgressive: an act uses the Other's language against, despite, and without, the Other, in what could be called a profound indifference to the Other. In a reference to the *Fort-Da* game in his eleventh seminar, Lacan even suggested this: "The activity as a whole symbolizes repetition, but not at all that of some need that might call for the return of the mother, and which would be expressed quite simply in a cry. It is the repetition of the mother's departure as cause of a *Spaltung* in the subject" (XI, 73, translation modified). In other words, the game is not making a demand on the mother to satisfy the child's needs. It merely repeats a trauma or signifying impasse that causes the subject and is an act in which the subject is disjoined from an Other who can bestow and guarantee recognition. This may be how Fink's idea of "taking on the Other's desire as cause" should be understood.

TOWARD A NEW SIGNIFIER

The idea that an act does not address the Other presents a problem, though, if we consider the way signifiers are used in the act.[1] If the Other is thought of as the receptacle of all signifiers, and an act uses signifiers, then does not an act have to bear some relation to the Other? If so, how could this relation be characterized as anything other than a pursuit of recognition? I think two notions addressed in Lacan's seminars try to address this: the notions of new signifiers and puns. I will discuss puns in the next section.

Acts that do something such as invent new signifiers would succeed in circumventing the articulation of a demand to the Other, if only for the reason that these new signifiers would not be the Other's signifiers. However, is anything like a new signifier possible in Lacanian terms? New signifiers come up for discussion in a few places in Lacan's work. In his third seminar, Lacan considers the presence of a signifier "in the real." This would mean, I believe, a signifier that is not bound up with the production of meanings already recognizable by the Other but one involved in the repetition of a resistance to signification:

> Let's flesh out the signifier's presence in the real, insofar as this is possible. The emergence of a new signifier, with all the consequences, down to one's most personal conduct and thoughts, that this may entail, the appearance of a register such as that of a new religion, for example, isn't something that is easily manipulated—experience proves it. Meanings shift, common sentiments and socially conditioned relations change, but there are also all sorts of so-called revelatory phenomena that can appear in a sufficiently disturbing mode for the terms we use in the psychoses not to be entirely inappropriate for them. The appearance of a new structure in the relations between basic signifiers and the creation of a new term in the order of the signifier are devastating in character. (III, 201)

Lacan is obviously talking about Christianity here. Christianity used some signifiers that were not necessarily entirely new to Roman society—Grace and Resurrection, to name two of the most salient—but

Christianity's use of these signifiers produced a shift in the meanings and "common sentiments" of the Roman world, as well as a change in "socially conditioned relations."

The theme of the act is not present in seminar three, and Lacan does not speak of this particular social movement in terms of an act. In his fifteenth seminar, *The Psychoanalytic Act*, he made similar points with respect to the Russian Revolution, and here he does use the term *act*:—"Is the act at the moment when Lenin gives such and such an order, or at the moment when signifiers were unleashed on the world?" (XV, 1/10/68). Giving an order could qualify as an act—it is signifying, it could be transgressive, and it could transform the structure of a subject. But here Lacan seems to be adding a new condition to the act, since Lacan's answer is clear: it is when signifiers are "unleashed on the world" that an act occurs. Lacan does not explicitly say here that these signifiers "unleashed on the world" are new. What may well have been new about the signifiers involved in the Russian Revolution, however, was the way in which they were used, just as was the case for Christianity.

In his twenty-fourth seminar, Lacan directly raises the question of whether the creation of new signifiers is possible, and the *Fort-Da* game happens to be in the background of this discussion. Lacan juxtaposes the invention of a new signifier to what he calls memory: "What I am stating, in any case, is that the invention of a signifier is something different from memory" (XXIV, *Ornicar?*, 17/18: 21). Memory here can be associated with an Other who is a subject-supposed-to-know, a site where signifiers are already laden with meaning. Inventing a new signifier introduces something that is not compatible with this treasury of linguistic "memory." But then Lacan retreats a bit and emphasizes that signifiers are always received and never really invented: "Our signifiers are always received. Why aren't new signifiers invented? A signifier, for example, that would not have any type of meaning, like the real?" (21). A signifier that would be "like the real" itself would do something other than produce a meaning for the real. This new signifier, then, would not directly produce new significations but would instead mark the presence, within language, of an essential impasse in and resistance to signification.

Lacan's line of thinking in his twenty-fourth seminar shifts from suggesting that inventing a new signifier is impossible to suggesting that it is just extremely difficult and rare. He goes on to mention a mundane signifying activity in which we see what the invention of a new signifier might be like—punning. While inventing a new signifier is hard, "It is not that one doesn't try. This is just what witticism is. It consists of making use of a word for another use than that for which it is made. One crumples it up a bit, and it is in this crumpling that its operative effect lies" (21). Puns distort words, crumpling them up and making them take on another function, thereby shaking up the linguistic meanings and values already present in the Other as a subject-supposed-to-know.

Should acts be seen in the same light? Perhaps they fail to invent totally new signifiers, signifiers that would not have any meaning at all ("like the real"), but they may at least distort a conventional use of signifiers, thereby marking the presence of the real in the symbolic. In this distortion acts would manifest a tendency toward non-meaning, and, because of the effect this has on the Other, acts might thus also go beyond fantasmatic attempts to get oneself recognized by the Other. Such a signifying distortion seems to be just what is found in the social movements Lacan mentions: Christianity and the Russian Revolution. Christianity did not seek recognition by what could be considered the Other of its time (Roman law), and the Russian Revolution of 1917 was not about seeking recognition for the Communist Party in the existing Russian state. Yet such social movements seem very unlike puns and witticisms. What do acts have to do with puns anyway? In what way, if at all, can puns be models for acts? Or are puns just to be seen as primitive acts, formally resembling them, without the resemblance going much farther?

PUNS: BEYOND METAPHOR AND METONYMY

Lacan's twenty-fourth seminar is not the first place he mentions puns. A lengthy study of them occurs in his fifth seminar, and there we find a slightly different account. Consider Lacan's lengthy discussion of the famous "famillionairely" pun from Freud's *Jokes and their Relation to the Unconscious*. In Heinrich Heine's *Reisbilder*, a character named Hirsch Hyacinth tells the author about his encounter with the famous millionaire Solomon Rothschild and claims that he was treated "as an equal," "quite famillionairely" by him (1960a [1905c], 16). The root word of this adverb, "famillionaire," is what Lacan refers to as a "new and paradoxical" signifier:

> What happens when "famillionaire" appears? We feel, first of all, something like an aim towards meaning, a meaning that is ironic, or satirical. Less apparent, developing in the after-effects of the phenomenon, spreading itself in the world in its

> wake, there also emerges an object, which, for its part, goes rather towards the comic, the absurd, non-meaning. (V, 29)

The signifier that a pun produces has a double tendency—it tends toward both a meaning and a non-meaning, and it produces a signified effect as well as what can be called a nonsense effect. By combining the signifiers "familiar" and "millionaire," the pun gives us a nonsensical word that still manages to make sense.

Lacan argues that this mechanism is not unlike what is found in metaphors (V, 30). Metaphors work by substituting one signifier for another (Lacan 1966, 515/Lacan 2002, 155–156). This substitution can be completely nonsensical. The two signifiers in a metaphor can be as unrelated to each other as can be; nevertheless, a signified effect that is not reducible to either signifier is created by this substitution. In the pun in question here, there is not really a substitution of one signifier for another but a combination of signifiers. True, the effect is in part the same as metaphor's, but an important difference is to be found in the fact that in a pun the new signifier first appears to be nonsensical. In metaphors, the signifiers involved are already recognizable members of a linguistic code. It is only their position or value that is strange and nonsensical, as in the famous example of a metaphor given by Lacan: "Love is a pebble laughing in the sun" (Lacan 1966, 508/Lacan 2002, 149). Puns, however, can use signifiers that do not appear to belong to the linguistic code at all, such as "famillionaire" (V, 24). While not every pun works this way, the important point is that punning allows for this type of signifying creation, while metaphor does not. Another way of putting this is just to say that puns tend to be neologisms, while metaphors are not.

Something Lacan says about metaphor later on in seminar five allows the difference between metaphors and puns to be made sharper. Speaking about his notion of the *point de caption*, the point where a signifier and a signified are pinned together, Lacan says the following:

> This pinning I'm talking about, the *point de capiton*, is only a mythical affair, because no one has ever been able to pin a signification to a signifier. On the other hand, what one can do is pin a signifier to a signifier and see what that brings about. In this case, something new is always produced, which is sometimes as unexpected as a chemical reaction: namely, the emergence of a new signification. (V, 196)

Pinning one signifier to another is the activity we find in metaphor, and it creates a new signification. Notice, however, that a pun does not pin one signifier to another. It garbles signifiers, it mixes them together. As Lacan said in his twenty-fourth seminar, it crumples them up. This garbling or crumpling of signifiers does not fit in to the two linguistic operations Lacan is most famous for studying—metaphor and metonymy. In his formulas for both of these operations, the relation between signifiers involved in each produces a little *s*, a signified. On Lacan's account in seminar five, a pun does produce a little *s*, but along with this a pun has to produce something else in relation to this *s*—call it an *x*, an enigma. I think the main difference between metaphor and metonymy, on the one hand, and puns, on the other hand, can be put this way: Whereas metaphor and metonymy can be said to respond to some initial *x*, to some enigmatic thing to be signified, precisely by putting a signified (a little *s*) in its place, puns do the reverse. In the place of an expectation of meaning, puns respond with an enigmatic *x*. This happens because of the fact that puns garble signifiers. Because of this garbling, some work has to be done with the new signifier first. It does not directly appear to have a meaning, as the signifiers in metonymies and metaphors always do. So a pun does not simply create a new signification, like metonymies and especially metaphors. It also makes something like a new, brute signifier, one that has signification subtracted from it, one that is, perhaps, like the real.

With this new signifier, a pun also involves a relation to the Other that is fundamentally different from the kind that is found in both metaphor and metonymy, two operations that are so crucial to the structure of desire. This difference between a pun, on the one hand, and metaphor and metonymy, on the other hand, has obvious parallels to the difference between an act and a fantasy. Consider Lacan's explanation of puns in seminar five:

> There is a signifying function proper to wit [insofar as it involves] a signifier escaping from the code, that is, from all the formations of the signifier that had up to that moment been accumulated, in its function of creating a signified. Something new appears which can be thought of as connected to the very source of what one can call the progress of language, or its transformation. (V, 28)

This passage gives puns an innovative role in language. Lacan tries to explain this role by means of two concepts: the *peu-de-sens* and the *pas-de-sens*. The former refers to a pun's most obvious effects. A pun is partly nonsensical. For this reason, Lacan clams that it makes a "lack of meaning" present (what I referred to earlier as an *x*), a lack that language has to catch up with. A pun is perhaps the biggest challenge an individual can make to language itself, short of an outright refusal to speak. It interrogates the Other about the Other's completeness by presenting the Other with a signifier that escapes from it. This signifier, then, questions the extensiveness and totality of the code. It is as if a pun is saying to the Other, alright, what do you make of this? In this way, puns emphasize a lack in the Other. For this reason, they can be put into a more direct relation to the enigma of the Other's desire as such (which presents us with a lack of meaning), whereas fantasy, indebted to the operations of metaphor and metonymy, comes up with an answer (an object or a meaning) to that enigmatic desire, again, by putting an object or a signification in the place of that *x* initially encountered in the Other's desire.

So from this I think it is clear how puns and acts are at least formally related. The problem with using Lacan's account of puns in seminar five as a model for what acts do is that he also claims there that a pun is "achieved" only when the Other gives it official papers, as it were. It is not clear that a similar authentication happens in an act. He speaks of this aspect of a pun as the *pas-de-sens*: not *pas* in the sense of "not" but *pas* in the sense of "step" (V, 98). The Other, by authenticating it, turns the pun's new signifier into a step toward meaning, we could say. So in a pun we see a movement from a lack of meaning to a step toward meaning. According to the account in seminar five, puns possess, then, a double tendency—they produce both a non-meaning and a meaning. The latter comes about when the signifier proffered by the pun ends up getting recognized by the Other, finding a place therein, and ultimately working to produce a meaning. This could be schematized as follows: First, a pun works with signifiers that have a signification; then, by garbling signifiers, it produces a signifier that is devoid of signification (an *x*); finally, the Other restores signification to this *x* by recognizing the pun, responding with laughter.

The complete lesson we learn from puns in seminar five, then, is this: The Other is capable of absorbing any and every signifying creation. In other words, it is always possible for a signifying practice, no matter how actlike, to become a truism. While there is something in the activity of punning that is not reducible to a pursuit of recognition from the Other for one's linguistic innovation, I will conclude that puns and acts are ultimately not isomorphic. Consider Lacan's reference to a "primitive pleasure" in signifying, which is central to punning:

> There is the subject and the Other. The subject is the one who speaks to the Other, and communicates to him or her the novelty as a witticism. After having traversed the segment of the

> metonymic dimension, the subject receives the lack-of-meaning [*peu-de-sens*] as such, the Other authenticates the step-towards-meaning [*pas-de-sens*] in it, and pleasure is achieved for the subject.
>
> It is to the extent that the subject is able to surprise the Other with its witticism that the subject is given some pleasure, and this is the same primitive pleasure that the infantile, mythical, archaic, primordial subject, which I evoked earlier, received from the first use of the signifier. (V, 99)

The "primitive pleasure" to which Lacan is referring sounds very much like the kind of pleasure found in the *Fort-Da* game: a pleasure in the repetition of an event in signifiers, a pleasure in the mere act of signifying. A pun is but a repetition of this pleasure because it relies upon the Other to receive this pleasure. The pleasure comes from surprising the Other, and the pun also asks permission from the Other to have such a pleasure. For this reason, I am not sure that punning can serve as an example of an act.

Yet there is something about punning that is similar to what Lacan described in his twelfth seminar: the subject described there at two distinct moments corresponds to the different uses of language we find in fantasy and acts. The first was a moment in which an event was simply said. This "simple saying" of an event is what I want to associate with the act, as well as with the challenge offered to the Other by a pun in the form of an enigmatic signifier. The second moment was one at which a subject identified itself as a speaker, a moment at which a subject can be identified. This could be characterized as a use of language that occurs within the scope of fantasy: absorbing the pun into the Other.

According to Lacan every act of speaking implies not only a speaker and an addressee but a third place, the Other, who guarantees the truth and meaning of what is being said. This Other, implied by the fact of speaking, always remains a structural necessity—that is, it is always a factor in any signifying practice. But acts evince a different relation to a different kind of Other: to an Other that is itself split, ruptured, and inconsistent, an Other incapable of acting as a guarantor or a site from which recognition can be bestowed. As a result, the subject of an act, in contrast to the subject of the fundamental fantasy, is no longer simply situated as the signified of the Other's desire. What is the status of this subject? As I have done for the notion of the act here, I would question whether the subject of an act is also a purely negative moment. Like an act, this subject would also have to be situated in between silence and making sense. These matters will be pursued in subsequent chapters.

CONCLUSION

It seems to me that Lacan tries to get at the notion of the act in different ways throughout his career. His ethic of "*bien dire*," especially as it is articulated in *Télévision*, seems quite close to how acts use signifiers (Lacan 1975b, 22, 30). I will discuss this more in the conclusion to this work. Also, apart from the social movements already mentioned, other social movements of which Lacan was fond—*les précieuses*, courtly love, surrealism—were also "signifying" movements that consisted of manipulating signifiers in a new way, forging a new way of speaking. These all call for further study as possible examples of acts. For now I would like to discuss a possible and somewhat distressing example of a Lacanian act from none other than Humpty Dumpty.

In Lewis Carroll's *Through the Looking-Glass*, Humpty Dumpty uttered a signifier whose use Alice did not recognize:

> "I don't know what you mean by 'glory,'" Alice said.
>
> Humpty Dumpty smiled contemptuously. "Of course you don't—till I tell you. I meant 'there's a nice knock-down argument for you!'"
>
> "But 'glory' doesn't mean 'a nice knock-down argument,'" Alice objected.
>
> "When *I* use a word," Humpty Dumpty said, in rather a scornful tone, "it means just what I choose it to mean—neither more nor less." (1998, 186, emphasis in original)

Lacan was structuralist enough to avoid fully endorsing Humpty Dumpty's position. Words do not mean whatever we want them to mean. Their meaning is determined by the linguistic system, by the Other. But as a psychoanalyst he certainly saw some kind of benefit in the possibility of a signifying practice in which some kind of unique signifier is invented (even if "glory" does not present us with that garbling characteristic of a pun). In the Rome Discourse, Lacan wrote the following:

> We analysts deal with slaves who think they are masters, and who find in a language—whose mission is universal—support for their servitude in the bonds of its ambiguity. So much so that one might humorously say that our goal is to restore in

> them the sovereign freedom displayed by Humpty Dumpty when he reminds Alice that he is, after all, master of the signifier, even if he is not master of the signified from which his being derived its shape. (Lacan 1966, 293/Lacan 2002, 79–80)

So we are not masters of the signified, but psychoanalysis may enable us to be masters of the signifier. In other words, we are always slaves to certain significations, yet despite this determination there is a possible use of signifiers that could be described as a "sovereign freedom" with signifiers, in the sense that such a use of signifiers is not bound up with our heavy destinies, with the Other as a site of meaning and recognition. In such signifying practices, a moment of "sovereign freedom" from the Other—yet not from signifiers themselves—would be manifested. Consider what Lacan says in another article in the *Écrits* about puns. What is the nature of the pleasure in punning? "Freud shows us that its proper joy comes from making us participate in the dominance of the signifier over the heaviest significations, bearers of our destiny" (Lacan 1966, 446). Again we see the idea here of a pleasure in signifying that goes beyond the production of meanings or the achievement of recognition in the Other. And here this use of signifiers goes against the "signified" that serves as a basis for our being for the Other. Lacan described this in his allusion to Humpty Dumpty, who was a master of the signifier, even if he was not master of the signified.

Does Humpty Dumpty give us an example of the kind of signifying involved in an act? Certainly not—he is still too concerned with being the master of the meaning of his signification. Humpty Dumpty certainly goes too far, then, when he claims that words *mean* whatever he wants them to mean. It does not look like this concern for meaning is part of an act.

We saw how the subject was situated at both a junction and disjunction of language and jouissance in fantasy. Can the subject of an act also be seen in terms of a junction and disjunction of language and jouissance? The disjunction in fantasy, I argued, was a disjunction from both the radical openness of the Other's desire and from the real's resistance to meaning. What is disjoined from in fantasy, in other words, is the Other as "barred" and the real as a resistance, and what is joined to is an unbarred, complete Other and a colonized real. In an act, what a subject is joined to and disjoined from would be very different. For example, in an act a subject is not disjoined from the barred Other but weds itself instead to this Other. So in an act, what one also has is less a colonization of the real, as we find in fantasy, than a possession by it. For in an act, disjunction infects language itself. The "junctive" aspect of a subject in an act can then be considered this way: in an act, a signifying resistance is brought to bear on, or is joined to, the Other. So a subject in an act disjoins from the Other as a site of knowledge, as a subject-supposed-to-know, and joins itself to that which resists this Other, which means that it joins itself to a fundamentally "barred" or "split" Other, an Other incapable of providing recognition for meaning or identity.

No wonder then that Lacan also discusses revolutionary acts in his fifteenth seminar, and that he referred to this seminar jokingly as his "Che Guevara" seminar. Unleashing new signifiers on the world, be it in an individual or a collective endeavor, is the stuff of which acts are made. An act maintains a disjunction in the Other by means of a signifying practice. So in an act we can see how the subject produced is also situated at both a junction and a disjunction of language and the real. In an act, joining to what resists signification within a signifying practice amounts to a disjunction from previous signifying configurations, from an Other who knows, and from previous identifications.

CHAPTER 7

Badiou and Žižek on Acts and Subjects

After the discussions in the last two chapters, it looks like Lacan's subject is in a Hokey Pokey with the Other: one foot in, one foot out, neither wholly outside nor inside. Furthermore, there are different ways in which this Hokey Pokey is danced. Lacan seems to have favored a certain kind of subject, one that is engaged in maintaining an inconsistency in the Other, one that signifies in such a way that the order of the Other itself gets scrambled. Instead of merely seeking a signification for an event in terms already available in the Other, an act puts a resistance to signification into words. This is why I explored the connections between acts and puns in the last chapter. A pun creates a new signifier that resists signification without being completely nonsensical. It is a signifier that is not simply "the Other's" but forces a new place for itself in the Other.

While it is fairly easy to see how acts use signifiers in a way that is different from other signifying practices, the position of the subject in an act, and whether this subject differs, structurally, from the subject as meaning, remains to be explored. One attractive aspect of the view of the subject-as-meaning was that such a subject seemed more or less thinglike and substantial: a knot of signifiers, if you will. This can be thought of as a "subject as substance": not the thinking substance that characterized the Cartesian cogito but substancelike nonetheless. The subject of fantasy fixed to object *a* captures this nicely too. This is a view of the subject as a thing, however, and not as an agent, although it does insist and repeat.

The act in Lacanian theory is not the result of a conscious decision, nor is it identical to a conscious deliberative process. Lacan's theory of the act requires us to conceive of a freedom that is not a metaphysical attribute of a subject but rather a phenomenon that may sometime occur to people. In this respect, Lacan breaks with humanism: Freedom is not an essential or a definitive attribute of "man." While such a theory can hardly answer in precise terms questions such as "What should we do?" or "How can we effect change?" it does offer a way to describe the structures and processes at work in individual and social changes. In this respect, it is doing something rather unique on the contemporary theoretical scene.

The status of the subject in an act remains imprecise, however. What would such a subject be like? One answer might be that the subject in an act is still a product of a signifying activity and thus still "thinglike" and not fundamentally different from the subject of fantasy. Another answer might be that the subject produced by an act is structurally unlike the subject of fantasy. Where the subject of fantasy is an insistent and a repetitive knot of signifiers, the subject of an act would be distinct from signifiers altogether. It would be negative, or a pure nothing. I will consider here two interpretations of Lacan that have taken up these readings, Alain Badiou's and Slavoj Žižek's. Neither reading is entirely correct. I will argue instead that the subject associated with Lacan's theory of the act is a subject that is negative yet nevertheless consists in some way. It consists in a sustained signifying activity or process that is still not like the signifying practice that characterizes the subject-as-meaning. Žižek is right to see the Lacanian subject in negative terms, but the subject in an act is negative with respect to a particular configuration of the Other, to the Other as a subject-supposed-to-know. In this way, it makes sense to speak of the subject in terms of a negative or destructive consistency or process.

"Destructive consistency" turns out to be exactly how Alain Badiou defines his own theory of the subject in his 1982 book of the same title, *Théorie du sujet*. Yet Badiou offers his definition as a contrast to Lacan's. To be a bit blunt about it, Badiou makes Lacan out to be a conservative Hegelian: The Lacanian subject, according to Badiou, is characterized by a "consistent repetition" (1982, 255). Such a phrase, I will argue, is an adequate description of the Lacanian subject of fantasy, which persists and insists in a colonization of the real. The subject of fantasy repeats a signifying destiny forged for the individual by the Other's discourse, ensuring some kind of recognition from the Other. However, the same cannot be said for the subject of an act.

What Žižek writes of the subject in Lacanian theory is helpful for my response to Badiou. Žižek argues that there is a sharp distinction in Lacan's work between the subject as such and any identification for and of that subject. This is certainly in line with Lacan's thinking. As we have seen, the subject is not equivalent to its identity, and the subject is never reducible to a signifier. Žižek goes farther—too far, I will argue—when he claims that some kind of identification is involved in *any* signifying practice. This suggests that any signifying practice always leads to an identified subject, a subject with a place in the Other—in other words, to the thinglike and insistent subject of fantasy. On Žižek's account, such a subject is always derivative of the purely negative moment that characterizes the subject as such. A pure subject, as Žižek conceives it, is one that is not bound to any signifying process at all, or even any signifier at all.

I will argue that what Žižek might be overlooking is the very kind of signifying practice that an act is all about: a practice in which, as it turns out, identification is not at stake. I argued in the last chapter that an act does not make any demand on the Other, and is thus not about getting recognition from the Other. In fact, an act maintains a split Other incapable of acting as a guarantee for any identification. An act is certainly using signifiers in some way (in a "new" way, Lacan was inclined to say) and is thus bound up with the Other as a site of signifiers in general. But the Other as a mere site of signifiers should not be confused with the Other as a site capable of granting recognition and guaranteeing identity and meaning. Acts, then, are ways of using signifiers in which identification is not at stake at all. The particular problem with Žižek's interpretation is that he does not allow for the subject of an act to consist of anything more than a "no!"—ultimately a "no" to signifiers as such. This makes the subject in Lacanian theory out to be more negative than it is.

While the subject of an act is still a product of signifiers, it is not a product of the kind found in the fundamental fantasy. If Badiou's interpretation of Lacan overlooks the role that the act plays in his theory, then Žižek's distorts the subject of an act into a pure nothing, opposed to any and every particular signifying process. My claim is that the subject of an act is a product of a particular type of signifying process, ironically very much like the one Badiou highlights in his work on Saint Paul, as we shall see—a process that is not simply saying "no" to something, but a more nuanced "no . . . but."

THE SUBJECT'S CONSISTENCY

Is there a grand unifying theory of the Lacanian subject? If fantasy offers us one version of the subject—a subject identified and recognized by the Other—then an act, by traversing fantasy, could be said to offer another view. But how different are they?

One thing we can say about Lacan's theory of the subject in general is that a subject is always a product or an effect of signifiers. But in what respect does the subject as a product of an act differ from the subject produced by a fantasy? I briefly addressed this matter in the last chapter when I considered the different kind of junction present in acts and fantasy. In fantasy, what is joined to is an Other capable of authenticating and guaranteeing a position or meaning for the subject and an event. That is, fantasy is all about identification and recognition. In an act, what is joined to is a different kind of Other—an Other itself split and inconsistent. In both cases, the subject is a product of signifiers. But in an act, the subject brings a resistance to signification into language.

It does not seem like the two types of subject have anything in common other than being produced by signifiers, and this does not seem to offer us enough ground for claiming that they are the same at some level. The subject in an act seems to be a total break with the subject of fantasy—its relations to the real, the Other, and language itself are different. The subject in an act can be characterized as a manifestation of freedom. The subject of fantasy looks more like a determined subject.

But the two types of subject do have something further in common—being produced by signifiers, they both consist in some way. "Consistency" is a word Lacan used quite a bit in his later seminars, and we can understand it to be a word that applies to the ontological nature of the subject. If act and fantasy describe two different structures for the subject, then consistency is a word that should apply to both ways, insofar as both are products of signifiers.

When Lacan used the term *consistency*, it was in the context of his study of Borromean knots as possible representatives of the structure of the psyche. A Borromean knot is a knot made up of three loops laced together in such a way that if one of the loops is cut, the other two are freed from each other. What is noteworthy about such knots, according to Lacan, is the fact that any two of the loops can only be joined by something outside or beyond them—a third loop. Lacan used these three loops to symbolize his three "orders"—the symbolic, imaginary, and real. As a whole, the Borromean knot is supposed to represent how the three orders hold together. A Borromean knot, then, can be used to give an image of how a psyche can be said to "hold together." Madness, presumably, would be represented by the three loops being disjoined from each other, as we might say that so-and-so has unraveled or fallen apart:

> The Borromean knot can only be made up of three. The imaginary and the symbolic do not suffice. There has to be a third element, which I call the real. This determining solidarity, of which there is a subject—a spoken subject, in any case—is necessary. The loss of any one of these three dimensions, [. . .] must lead to madness [*rendre folle*]. (XXI, 12/11/73)

Another way of considering the knot is to see it as a representation of something like a symptom structuring and determining an individual's destiny. This allows us to see more clearly why a word such as "consistency" is appropriate when speaking about the knot, and for speaking about the subject. A symptom, Lacan claims, is a "knot of signifiers" (Lacan 1975b, 22). The Borromean knot, tying together the symbolic, the real, and the imaginary, can be taken as a representation of a symptom understood in this way. The consistency of the knot, then, seems to be representing nothing other than what we already studied in terms of the unconscious signifying chain and the subject as a meaning for the Other: a consistency (of signifiers) making up a destiny.

But the consistency at work here is not only a consistency of signifiers. Although a symptom consists of a "knot of signifiers," this does not mean that a symptom is simply symbolic. The signifiers involved in a symptom also have real and imaginary traits, and these can be uncovered if we consider how a symptom also contains some relation to the Other (which could introduce us to the imaginary dimension), as well as a relation to an event (which would introduce us to the real).[1] Thus a symptom also produces a subject of signifiers with some sort of position with respect to both the Other and the event of sexuality (the real). Taken as a whole, a symptom can be said to be a way of enjoying. Because it consists of signifiers, Lacan referred to what a symptom ensures as a "jouis-sens," an enjoyment in or of meaning (1975b, 22). In fantasmatic terms, what is enjoyed is having a particular position for the Other and a particular way of enjoying. My question here is, if the Borromean knot shows us something like a symptom, and a symptom entails an identification as well as a way of enjoying, does the knot tell us anything about the subject? And which type of subject does it portray, the subject involved in fantasy, but not the subject in an act?

This question can be answered by considering how Lacan describes the position of the subject with respect to the Borromean knot. Lacan pointed out that the subject of such a knot is a "spoken subject." A subject is something that the knot determines:

> Representing [*Figurer*] the knot is not easy. I am not saying "imagining" [*se figurer*] the knot, because I am completely eliminating the subject. I begin, on the contrary, with the thesis that the subject is determined by the figure in question. Not that the subject is a double of the knot. But it is from these wedgings [*coincements*] of the knot, from what in the knot determines these triple points, it is from the grip of the knot that the subject is conditioned. (XXII, *Ornicar?*, 5: 30)

The subject of the knot, then, is something like the subject-as-meaning discussed earlier. As Lacan said, this subject is a spoken subject, a subject-effect of signifiers that can be said to have some sort of consistency because of the signifiers comprising it. In other words, the subject consists of its symptom, its particular "knot of signifiers" and its concomitant way of enjoying. The subject at stake in the knot, then, does seem to express something like the situation of the subject in fantasy. The subject of fantasy also consists insofar as there is a signifying chain, or a knot of signifiers, that supports it and its relation to the real, the Other, and language.

Lacan explicitly links the Borromean knot to the unconscious in his twenty-second seminar, and in doing so he also makes an interesting point about how the knot/unconscious comes to be in the first place: "The real is characterized by being knotted. Again, such a knot must be made. The notion of the unconscious is supported by the fact that not only is a knot found ready-made, but one finds oneself made—one is made, one is made by this act X by which a knot is already made" (XXII, *Ornicar?*, 5: 50). Is the use of the term *act* important here? The term is hardly used elsewhere in this seminar, but its use here evokes the question I asked earlier. Does the knot only present the subject of fantasy? And does the subject in an act have any consistency whatsoever?

My claim will be that some kind of consistency applies to both types of subject. If it is the case that any subject must be produced by signifiers, then any subject, whether it is a subject of fantasy or a subject of act, must also be said to have some consistency. The consistency a subject has is due to the knot of signifiers supporting it. But in order to determine whether a subject is "fantasmatic" or "actlike," one has to look at the structure of the knot of signifiers supporting that subject.

This would also involve considering the triple relation I have discussed in previous chapters: a relation to the real, the Other, and language.

We have seen that throughout Lacan's work a general description of the conditions of the subject can be found. Lacan studies the subject's structure, its genesis, and the dynamics at work in it. His basic methodological rule was to study the subject as a product of signifiers as well as an encounter with some sort of event. Ultimately, Lacan discerns two basic ways in which subjects can be. He considers the subject not only as something constituted but also at times as something in action. Clearly, even this latter subject is a product of signifiers. For this reason, a word such as "consistency" applies equally well to the subject found in an act as to the subject found in fantasy. No matter what, a subject is an effect of signifiers, and the consistency of these signifiers grants the subject some consistency too. So one way to consider the difference between the subject of fantasy and the subject of an act would be by looking again at the particular way in which signifiers consist in each.

BADIOU'S CRITIQUE OF LACAN

This discussion of the consistency of the subject is important for the interpretations of the Lacanian subject by Badiou and Žižek. But first a bit of background, because the following discussion refers to a periodization of Lacan's work, and whether the same theory of the subject is functioning or present in each period of Lacan's career. Attempts to divide Lacan's work up into discrete periods are common. There is widespread agreement that there is (at least) an early Lacan and a late Lacan, with a major transition occurring in seminar eleven. The reason there is seen to be a difference between the early and late Lacan does not only concern the fact that the eleventh seminar saw Lacan addressing a different audience—not the analysts-in-training he was used to but a broader and slightly more academic audience. The reason for the difference is usually attributed instead to the increasing importance given to the status of the real in Lacanian theory, as opposed to the predominance of the symbolic prior to seminar eleven (and the even earlier predominance of the imaginary in the pre-seminar Lacan).

Alain Badiou also claims that there are two Lacans, but his description of the two is at first sight unique, since it does not occur in terms of the symbolic, imaginary, or real. The early Lacan he calls an "algebraic" thinker, while the later Lacan is described as a "topological" thinker. What is meant by the use of "algebraic" and "topological" here? If we presume a given set of elements (such as signifiers), then algebra, according to Badiou, is concerned with the "systematic study of the 'interesting' relations between the elements of this set. Its most general concept is that of the law of composition" (1982, 226). Algebra is concerned with putting elements in a set together, linking them in a chain. Badiou cites as examples the laws of association and commutation: (a + b) + c = a + (b + c), and a + b = b + a. These are obviously "composition rules," and Badiou points out that the only thing that counts about the elements of the formulas is "their behavior according to the law [...]. An element is not algebraically distinguished by its localization in the set. It suffices that it belong to it" (ibid.). In other words, whether "a" comes first or second with respect to "b" has no effect on the result of the operation a + b. Thus Badiou concludes that in algebra "place is in a certain way universal," and what he calls "force" turns out to be lacking (ibid.). We will see the importance of force for Badiou's approach shortly. The important thing to note is that the "place" of an element in an algebraic operation does not have any bearing on the result of the operation. The formulas Lacan developed for metaphor and metonymy are similar to algebraic operations, according to Badiou. They describe ways in which signifiers interact with each other to produce a signified effect, without the position of any particular signifier really making a difference to the result. (This is a point I would not endorse, but it is Badiou's, not mine. It seems that the position of a signifier in a signifying chain should matter for the production of a signified effect.)

In contrast to the algebraic approach of the early Lacan, the later topological approach, Badiou claims, gives priority to what he calls "force" over place. Topology is further described as a study that requires a "grasp of movement" (ibid.). In contrast to algebra, for a topological study the place of the elements involved in a set is indeed important. Topology

> does not aim (like algebra) at what happens when two distinct and homogenous events come to be combined under (certain) constraints, but at the site of a term, its surroundings, what is more and more "close" to it, what diverges from it in continuous variations, its degree of isolation and adherence. If the master concept of algebra is that of law (of composition), topology is founded on the notion of neighborhood. (1982, 227)

A topologist is interested in what effects that changes in the shape of a knot, for example, might have on the relationships between different parts or points on the knot. Lacan's study of Borromean knots, according to Badiou, would qualify as topological. For example, what is important in a Borromean knot is the specific placement of each ring with respect to the other rings, and the manipulations that can occur to each string in the knot without changing the knot's "Borromean" structure.

Badiou emphasizes these differences between algebra and topology because he thinks that the position the real takes on in each approach differs as well. In other words, the difference between Lacan's algebraic early formulas, involving signifiers and their products, and Lacan's later topological figures, involving knots and bits of string, suggests two different ways of thinking about the real. And at this point, despite the unusual terms Badiou uses to distinguish between the two Lacans, we see that the real is still at stake in his periodization. Accordingly, Badiou argues that

> there are two concepts of the real in Lacan's work: the real of vanishing, which acts as a cause for the algebra of the subject; and the real of the knot, which acts as a consistency for its topology. (1982, 243)

In chapter 1 these two reals were dubbed $real_1$ and $real_2$. $Real_1$ was a presymbolic real, while $real_2$ was a real that was a name for an impasse in signification. Badiou gives the following passage from Lacan's "Seminar on the Purloined Letter" as a representative statement of the position of the real in what he calls Lacan's algebraic period:

> Originally, subjectivity is in no relation to the real, but to a syntax that engenders in the real a signifying mark. (Lacan 1966, 50)

In what Badiou is calling this algebraic period of Lacan's work, the subject is said not to be related to the real at all. A subject is born, rather, from "syntax." In other words, the subject is a product of a symbolic order that ends up having a certain effect on the real. Hence, the only kind of real a subject could have any relation to would be to a real that has been marked by the symbolic already. From this point of view, there is a real that is lost when an individual is symbolically marked and starts speaking the Other's language. This version of the real does resemble what $real_1$ was meant to describe. Furthermore, this lost real in turn has consequences on the shape the symbolic takes. So Badiou claims that what characterizes the real in this period of Lacan's thinking is the real as a lost or "vanishing" cause of the subject.

Badiou refers to the real in Lacan's Borromean knots as something that "acts as a consistency." This is a bit obscure, but it seems to be connected to the difference between $real_1$ and $real_2$. If $real_1$ is something like a lost and transcendent real acting on something outside of it (the symbolic and the imaginary), then $real_2$ is a real immanent to what it acts on or in. One could think of the distinction being addressed here as a distinction that mirrors the difference between desire, caused by a lost object, and drive, which has its object in itself, so to speak, and is aimed not at capture so much as at continuation and circulation.

For some reason, Badiou thinks it is important to consider how these two ideas of the real are brought together (1982, 244). This seems like a very Hegelian question to ask, as if to say, whenever a difference between two terms is posited, we must also ask a question about the hidden unity behind the difference. Badiou does think that there is a hidden unity of the two reals in Lacanian theory, and it is on this point that he thinks Lacanian theory errs. Thus the periodization of Lacan's work hides a more important continuity. According to Badiou, the unity of the two reals is thought by Lacan algebraically: thus the union of the two reals occurs in terms of $real_1$, not $real_2$. As a result, it is $real_1$ that is the true or dominant understanding of the real in Lacanian theory (1982, 247).

As evidence for this interpretation, Badiou presents the fact that Lacan considers the dissolution of a "Borromean knot" (the subject's very consistency) to be a kind of psychic collapse. To Badiou, this means that Lacan is "deriving consistency from cause" (1982, 248). That is, Lacan's whole topological vision of the real and the subject in his Borromean knot period is actually based on a fundamentally algebraic vision of the real, according to which the real functions as a fundamentally lost, absent cause. The Borromean knot is an organization that has already expelled a traumatic real and replaced it with a real subdued by a relation to the other orders. Insofar as the knot represents something like the subject's symptom, and the subject's very "consistency," the subject *is* then only to the extent that the traumatic real has vanished. This would strongly suggest that the real as a transcendent, lost real ($real_1$) does have some sort of priority in Lacan's theory, and that the real that is found as a signifying impasse or stumbling block only comes about after, or on the presupposition of, this first real's expulsion by an organization of signifiers, in an "act" that knots the three orders together and manages to keep the traumatic force of $real_1$ away.

Badiou thinks that this reading of Lacan has important consequences for the interpretation of Lacan's theory of the subject. If Badiou's reading is correct, whatever difference there might be between the subject of fantasy and the subject in an act would pale in comparison to their underlying similarity. Both subjects would be founded on an exclusion of a traumatic real, despite differences in the Other to which they relate, and despite any differences in how they might use signifiers. From this point of view, while an act may be using signifiers differently, it is ultimately doing the same thing with the real as the fundamental fantasy is, and thus the difference between the two is minimal.

As Badiou sets it out, both his and Lacan's definitions of the subject involve an idea of consistency. According to both, the subject consists of a knot of signifiers, produced by a signifying practice. But Badiou constructs his own theory of the subject in opposition to Lacan's by configuring consistency differently. Accordingly, Badiou defines Lacan's subject as "a consistent repetition, in which the real ex-sists," while his own definition of the subject is as follows: "The subject is a destructive consistency, in which the real ex-cedes" (1982, 255). The difference between a real that "ex-cedes" and one that "ex-sists" is the difference between a real that is transcendent to the subject's organization (ex-sistence) and a real that is immanent in it (ex-cedence).

Is there some justification for Badiou's point of view? Badiou's claim is that by thinking of the real as a transcendent, albeit an absent, cause of the subject, Lacan is led to see the subject as a signifying consistency whose purpose is to keep the brute, raw real away. The signifying practice or "knot of signifiers" that supports the subject is founded on a repression or repulsion of $real_1$. This is why Badiou uses the term *repetition* to characterize the consistency proper to Lacan's theory of the subject. The traumatic real must be kept outside of the signifying chain supporting the subject in order for the subject not to be "rendered mad," and thus this signifying chain must be constantly repeated in order to keep that primordial real away. If this chain or knot falls apart, then the traumatic real is no longer kept away, and a psychic breakdown occurs. On this interpretation, consistency, then, is conceived of by Lacan as a kind of repair work that defends the subject from an excessive irruption of the real. For this reason, Badiou reads the Lacanian theory of the subject as one in which the real is fundamentally ex-sistent. It stands outside of the system making up the subject. If there is a real that is immanent to this subject at all in Lacanian theory (and it should be kept in mind that one of the "rings" of the Borromean knot is precisely the real), then this is a tamed real, in contrast to the brutal real that must be excluded in order for the subject to come to be in the first place.

In this context, consider again Lacan's interpretation of the case of Little Hans. According to Lacan, the emergence of the real for Little

Hans resulted in a symbolic deconstitution—a traumatic loss of Hans's position or meaning with respect to his mother. This loss necessitated the invention of a new signifying constellation, which amounts to saying that signifiers act to colonize a real that is otherwise antithetical to signification. The real, then, can indeed be said to cause a signifying production, after which it becomes immediately "absent." If there is a real immanent in the subject, if some kind of enjoyment in signifiers does occur in Hans's case—that is, if there is finally the formation of a symptom—then this immanent real nevertheless seems to presuppose that a primordial, traumatic real has been expelled and replaced by a more manageable real. In other words, the immanent status of $real_2$ with respect to the symbolic in Lacan's theory of the subject only comes about on the basis of an exclusion of an earlier $real_1$, which is precisely Badiou's point.

Of course, it would be fair to wonder what the problem with this theory is. Does Badiou wish to say that there is something wrong with not flirting with psychic collapse? Is he after a slightly modified version of a Deleuzian schizo-analysis? Does keeping the traumatic real at bay amount to some kind of lack of courage? Badiou's dissatisfaction with his reading of Lacan's theory of the subject does seem to be coming from what are primarily political considerations. He claims that Lacan's theory is like one that would say that periods of social and political collapse inevitably meet with an emergence of something like a traumatic, chaotic real, a real that can be found, perhaps, in something like the "élan of the masses"—in violent, chaotic uprisings. As Badiou points out, the theory of the subject that Lacan endorses is then like a political theory that suggests that after such outbreaks "the imaginary will have its revenge [...] by assuring, under the sign of some communist or egalitarian utopia, the terroristic consistency of society" (1982, 261–262). In other words, because of the social danger inherent in revolutionary fervor—a revolutionary period leads to totalitarianism—according to Lacan's theory it would be better to advocate some kind of avoidance of "élan" for the well-being of society, just as some kind of repression of the "raw" real is absolutely necessary for the well-being and consistency of any subject. As I said earlier, Badiou makes Lacan out to be a conservative Hegelian, developing a theory to defend, in this case, the psychic status quo.

After putting Lacan's theory of the subject in these terms, Badiou is able to make sharper the contrast to his own position on the theory of the subject. He claims that what is missing from Lacan's work "is the thought of an effective destruction of the former law, and the acknowledgment that what is recomposed can no longer in any fashion be the same. This means that the real of the subject guarantees consistency without the mediation of the imaginary" (1982, 262). The "mediation of the imaginary" here refers to the primarily repressive function that a signifying chain seems to have with respect to the real. Because any and every signifying practice is founded on an exclusion of a traumatic real, the subject in Lacanian theory, according to Badiou, is profoundly repetitive—acts simply create new consistencies for the subject, and thus there are not two different types of subject in Lacanian theory.

And indeed, the implication is then that an act does nothing, really. It is simply a transitional moment between two signifying constellations, between two "knots of signifiers" giving consistency to the subject. Lacan argued that an act brings about a "different" subject, in the sense that it refounds the subject; but in another sense, there is only ever one type of subject going—the subject as a thing or consistency that insists in any signifying practice. What Badiou thinks is missing from Lacan's theory is the possibility that "what is recomposed" by, for example, the kind of signifying practice characteristic of an act, "can no longer in any fashion be the same" (1982, 262). This is why Badiou wrote that Lacan's theory of the subject cannot think of an "effective destruction of the former law" that was governing the subject (ibid.). There is always a return of the same law—in the sense that any constitution of the subject presupposes an exclusion of a traumatic real. This exclusion would be the primary, inevitable law for any subject. By seeing the subject as a "destructive consistency, in which the real excedes," Badiou claims that his theory can conceive of how nothing of a "former law" remains after an act. In Lacanian terms, the destruction at stake in Badiou's theory would be like a destruction of the Other itself. In this "destructive consistency" the real can be seen as something that exceeds in the subject. That is, the signifying practice that supports the subject can itself act as an event for the order of the "former law": whether this "former law" is thought of as a particular social arrangement, or, on an individual level, a particular idea of what it is that the Other wants. According to Badiou, Lacan fails to think destruction and the real *within* the subject, as positive components of the subject's consistency. Instead, Lacan conceives of the consistency of the subject as a consistency that altogether excludes the destructive aspect of the real.

How fair is this criticism of Lacan's theory? I have tried to establish that an act uses signifiers in a specific way. But using signifiers in a specific way does not necessarily mean doing anything different with the real. This is the point that I will address in what follows. An act is not just using signifiers in a certain way but is also doing something different with the real, only what is different about it must be looked for in the effects an act has on the Other.

The Other in Lacan's later theory is not just the field of any signifying practice whatsoever but is a name for a particular organization within which some signifying practices are recognized as legitimate and others are not. This can be thought of as the Other who is a "subject-supposed-to-know." Lacan's notion of an act leads to a theory of the subject in which the signifying practice supporting that subject acts like the real, in the sense that the signifying practice becomes an event for or within the Other. Although it is indeed the case that acts are signifying practices just as the fundamental fantasy is a signifying consistency, each uses signifiers in a different way, and it is in this use that one has to look for the difference. An act's use of signifiers, which is punlike insofar as the signifiers used are not immediately recognizable and able to be situated in the linguistic code, is not oriented toward obtaining recognition by the Other. An act creates new signifiers and new significations, ones that do not involve getting recognized by the Other. But since acts, like puns, are not entirely nonsensical either, and since they are using signifiers and creating sense, something of the Other is used in them, without that Other being posited as a subject-supposed-to-know. This is the point that is overlooked in Badiou's reading of Lacan. The very insistent or "ex-ceding" real that Badiou wishes to see taken into account in, and included in, a theory of the subject is present in Lacan's theory of the act—precisely in the form of the creation of new signifiers, which is not simply a symbolic activity but includes the real in the symbolic (in the kind of exceeding Badiou is after, I believe) insofar as it brings about a signifying "tension."

Another way to get at this same point is to consider the role of identification in an act—or rather, its lack of a role. I think it can be said that the subject in an act engages in a destruction of identification, and this would be another way of considering how the way an act uses signifiers is also a use of the real. Slavoj Žižek has called attention to this aspect of Lacan's work, and he gives us a good idea of how Lacan's theory of the act does not quite fit into what Badiou's critique is saying. But Žižek goes too far in another direction. Distinguishing between the subject and any possible identification for that subject, he tends to deny that the subject in an act has any consistency whatsoever—he construes it as a purely negative instance. He does not consider the possibility that a subject in an act may be sustained by a signifying practice that even though it is using signifiers is not bound up with a pursuit of identity and recognition. Thus Žižek's exaggeration of the negative dimension of the act in Lacanian theory leads him to make a nearly Sartrean interpretation of Lacan's theory of the subject.

AGAINST IDENTITY

Before I get to a more detailed discussion of Žižek's reading of Lacan, it is necessary to consider in more detail my claim that in Lacan's work there is a gesture, a tendency, toward thinking of a subject without an identity. Of course, it is difficult to imagine Lacan having such a view, given not only the importance of the theme of identification in his work but also the way in which he accounts for the production of the subject. A subject, as we know, is produced by signifiers. If identity involves signifiers (as Lacan puts it, "what we encounter in identification [...] is a signifying identification [*une identification de signifiant*]") then can there really be a subject without an identity (IX, 11/22/61)? On the one hand, no, since there will always be a proper name, and some kind of ego, and there will always be signifiers for any subject. But this is only a partial consideration, which overlooks the fact that not every relation of a subject to signifiers is a relation that can be described in terms of identification.

In the last session of his eleventh seminar—the same session in which Lacan mentions a traversal of fantasy—Lacan speaks of a "crossing of the plane of identification" (XI, 304/273). To describe this "crossing," he recalls the difference between psychoanalysis and hypnosis. In hypnosis what occurs is a "confusion" of an ideal signifier and object *a*: an "ideal signifier" becomes an incarnation of the object of desire. Hypnosis, then, is closely connected to love: indeed, when we fall in love with someone, something like hypnosis seems to be happening.

It is strange that Lacan speaks of an "ideal signifier" here. Is this supposed to be a person with a certain position (the hypnotist, or a certain special someone)? Yes, but it is the fact that such a person has such a position that is crucial. This position functions, then, as a signifier. So in hypnosis there is a double identification—an identification of a signifier with the object of desire and also, of course, the hypnotized person's identification with this signifier object. By means of such an identification, as we already know, a subject is able to believe that it has made itself desirable to the Other. By identifying with a signifier, and by identifying this signifier with what is desired by the Other (object *a*), a subject is able to configure itself as something that ultimately conforms to what he or she imagines that the Other wants.

As we know, such a process is at the heart of the production of any subject. A subject comes to be on the basis of a signifying chain that is taken to represent the Other's desire, which is otherwise inscrutable without the invention of some signifiers for it. Identification, then, has a fundamentally defensive function. It manages to keep the abyss of the Other's desire at bay, and it forges a place for the subject. Given this description, what could Lacan possibly have against identification? Identification seems to be necessary for the subject, and also for the well-being of any individual.

Lacan certainly has something against identification when the end of analysis is described in terms of an identification with the analyst:

> Any analysis that teaches that one has to end with an identification with the analyst reveals [. . .] that its true motive force is elided. There is a beyond of this identification, and this beyond is defined by the relation and the distance of object *a* to the idealizing capital "I" of identification. (XI, 302/271–272, translation modified)

The "idealizing capital I" here is the "ideal signifier" spoken of earlier. It can be taken to be a unary trait, or a signifier that represents the subject. Lacan's vision of the end of analysis has something to do with obtaining a distance between this signifier and object *a*, and perhaps with simply establishing that there is a difference between them. In fact, Lacan makes this point explicitly later on. The analyst "isolates the *a*, he or she puts it at the greatest distance possible from the 'I' that the analyst is called upon by the subject to incarnate" (XI, 304/273, translation modified). Here we get a bit more insight into what is going on in analysis for Lacan. As Lacan puts it here, the analysand expects the analyst to incarnate one of his or her ideal signifiers, what Lacan elsewhere called the "ego ideal," the point of view from which a subject can see itself as desirable. Expecting this incarnation at the same time amounts to conflating the ego ideal with object *a*, with what it is that the Other is supposed to want. By emphasizing the difference between object *a* and the ego ideal, the analyst that Lacan envisions recalls to the analysand the fundamental obscurity of the Other's desire, and perhaps also the fact that the object *a* put in the place of this desire is a semblance, an invention of what it is supposed to be that the Other wants. Later in the same paragraph, Lacan describes the analyst as "the support of a separating *a*" (XI, 304/273, translation modified). Such an analyst would separate the subject from an identification with the Other's desire, and presumably also from an attempt to get his or her own desire recognized and legitimated by the Other.

This, in fact, is the famous moment at which Lacan speaks of a traversing of fantasy. The question Lacan is struggling with here concerns bringing about the conditions for an act in an analysis. Despite the obscurities in the argument, what is clear is that one of the conditions for an act is the destruction of the conditions bringing about identification. According to Lacan, by keeping object *a* separate from the ideal ego, the analyst emphasizes the originally separating role of object *a* itself. I take this to mean that another dimension of object *a* is brought to the fore—not its dimension as something that the Other is supposed to desire, and that I must therefore desire or identify myself with in order to get recognized by the Other. Rather, what we see here is the dimension of object *a* as the Other's desire as such, in its very inscrutability. This means that object *a* refers one to the originally inscrutable and eventlike nature of the Other's desire:

> It is insofar as the analyst's desire, which remains an x, goes in a direction that is exactly contrary to that of identification, that the crossing of the plane of identification is possible, by the intermediary of the separation of the subject in the experience. (XI, 305/274, translation modified)

A subject can perhaps only be separated from its identity, from its ego ideal, as well as from object *a* as something that is desired by the Other, when the eventlike nature of the Other's desire is recalled. This shows that the other aspect of object *a*, its imaginary aspect as an object that the Other desires, is an invention. When object *a* as the Other's desire as such is recalled, the ego ideal loses its ground. The plane of identification would then be crossed. The subject would no longer have any motivation to identify with the analyst or with any particular signifier.

What is the point of all this? And to what does it lead? The point is that by doing this to the structure of identification, what Lacan refers to as an "absolute difference" arises: "The difference that intervenes when, confronted with the primordial signifier, the subject comes for the first time in the position of subjecting him or herself to it" (XI, 307/276, translation modified). What crossing the plane of identification, traversing the fantasy, or an act amounts to is a return to an original position, one in which a subject is first subjected to a signifier. Does this not also mean to the moment at which a subject is first produced by a signifier?

We know that an act is supposed to transform and also recreate the subject. I have interpreted Badiou's critique of Lacan as a critique that bears on the nature of the subject after an act. This detour through Lacan's arguments against identification helps make the following point clear: There is a fundamental difference between fantasy and act, and what happens during an act is perhaps not simply the continuation of a fantasy structure. My reason for saying this is that an act entails an entirely different relation to the Other's desire, and that, as a result, the relation to the Other entailed in an act is such that one cannot speak about an identification occurring in it. In an act, there is a relation to the Other's desire that does not consist of identifying with what that desire is supposed to be for—a quest for the signified of that desire. Rather, the signifying impasse characteristic of the Other's desire is preserved and handled in a new way in an act, instead of being merely avoided or covered up, which is what identification does, and this would be the "real" dimension of an act, the way in which the real "excedes" in an act, as Badiou would put it. If identification can still be spoken of here, then what we have is not an identification with a particular signifier that functions as an object of the Other's desire but an "identification" with desire as such. The end of analysis can then be seen not as a mere repetition of the subject's origin, but a repetition that recreates, bringing about a new way for the subject to be in relation to signifiers, the Other, and the real.

What can still be overlooked is how these relations are sustained through an act. This is why it is still important to see this reproduction of the subject as a signifying reproduction, something that is maintained in a signifying practice. In the next chapter, we will see how Badiou's theory gives an account of what such a signifying practice might look like on a social scale: It amounts to bringing an impasse to bear on the milieu of the Other. As I said before, a distinction needs to be made between the Other as a site that can function to guarantee meanings and grant recognitions and the Other's desire, which ruins any such site. Badiou's work shows us how the maintenance of a barred, desiring Other can only come about by means of a specific kind of signifying practice, one that is aimed at what could be called the blind spot of the Other as a subject-supposed-to-know. Lacan's theory of the act does not seem to be telling us anything different.

ŽIŽEK'S READING OF LACAN

The tendency in Lacan's work to argue against identification is something about which Slavoj Žižek is keenly aware, but Žižek takes it too far by making any kind of signifying process apparently impossible for the subject of an act. As Žižek would have it, an act is a negation of any relation to signifiers whatsoever, and not just a negation of a specific configuration of signifiers, characterized by the Other as a guarantee of meaning and recognition (the Other as a subject-supposed-to-know). In what follows, I hope to make these points clearer.

How does Žižek handle the question of the act? In *The Ticklish Subject*, he develops his theory of the act, as well as his theory of the subject, by developing a critique of Alain Badiou's theories. The critique of Lacan in Badiou's *Théorie du sujet* does not come into play here. Rather, Žižek takes Badiou's position on the subject in his more recent works as an example of a theory that conflates the subject with a moment of identification, with a moment of attachment to a signifier. The term Žižek uses for this attachment and identification is *subjectivization* (1999, 159). What Žižek wishes to emphasize, against Badiou, is the distinction between the subject as such and any of its subjectivizations. This allows the subject to be seen for what it is, according to him—a "negative gesture" that opens up a possible "space" for a future subjectivization (ibid.). The distinction Žižek is making here recalls a central distinction that Lacan made throughout his work: The subject is not the ego, and the subject is not reducible to signifiers. In short, a subject is never identical to its identity.

So what is the subject, according to Žižek? It is apparently negativity. But it is difficult to say that such a theory of a purely negative subject is strictly Lacanian (which Žižek wants to say), since it is clearly the case that Lacan also thought of the subject in terms of a consistency of signifiers. Žižek points this out when he considers the structure of the subject in more detail. The negativity of the subject is at one point described by Žižek as something that exists only because there are subjectivizations, leading him to argue that the subject is both a pure negativity "as well as the gesture of subjectivization" (ibid.). This is in line with Lacan's point about a subject always being produced by signifiers. If a subject is "negative," as Žižek would have it, then even this negative subject must be produced as a by-product of some kind of use of signifiers.

But Žižek persists in claiming that the subject proper or the subject as such in Lacan's work is a negative subject distinct from any subjectivization, and this raises a problem. The problem is at its sharpest in Žižek's reading of Badiou. Badiou's theory, according to Žižek, only theorizes subjectivization. Lacan, in contrast, teaches us that "the subject is the negative gesture of breaking out of the constraints of Being that opens up the space of possible subjectivization" (1999, 160). Here again a strong distinction is made between the subject as such and the "subjectivized" subject, the subject subjected to a signifier. Žižek admitted earlier that the two were actually part of the same whole. The subject as such is actually produced by the act of subjectivization, Žižek said, filled in by signifiers. But we are told now that it is this gap that is (really) the subject, whereas what is created by a subjectivization is not (really) the subject. This problem comes up again later, when Žižek discusses Lacan's notion of the act explicitly. According to Žižek, "in Lacan, act is a purely *negative* category" (1999, 160, emphasis in original).

Žižek's point about an act being negative allows for an interesting response to Badiou's critique of Lacan in 1982. By saying that acts are negative, Žižek might be able to respond to Badiou's claim that Lacan's theory could not conceptualize any real transformation of a symbolic order. Žižek is able to point out that an act is always in opposition to the symbolic or the Other, and thus, by implication, that Lacan is far from coming up with a conservative Hegelian theory of the subject. But this does not address the considerably trickier part of Badiou's critique. Badiou could well admit that Lacan thinks of an act as something negative. The real question for him is whether the act has any "positive" consequences. If not, we end up in the situation alluded to earlier, where moments of revolutionary élan merely end up solidifying the order to which they are opposed. If Lacan cannot theorize the positive consequences of an act without collapsing these consequences into merely another identification that seeks recognition from an established Other (a repetition or reinstatement of some primordial law—the exclusion of the traumatic real), then Lacan's theory is essentially conservative, and acts are basically similar to fundamental fantasies, despite their different use of signifiers, because both do the same thing with the real—they tame it. The question that needs to be asked then is whether there is a theory of a "negative" signifying practice in Lacan's work. Or are all signifying practices essentially conformist, necessarily seeking recognition from some big Other, thereby requiring us to say, with Žižek, that an act, and a subject, are only purely negative moments with no real consistency? My study of the act has shown that neither is the case. What Žižek does not consider is that an act must be, after all, a signifying process, and thus must produce some sort of consistency, even if it is a consistency that is primarily negative with respect to the Other as a "subject-supposed-to-know," a consistency that can be called "negative" because it brings an impasse into the Other.

It is interesting to consider an example Žižek uses to argue for the advantage of his conception of the act and the subject over Badiou's. If an act is primordially, and apparently exclusively, a negative gesture, then the rejection of Communism in the former Soviet Union and Eastern Bloc countries can be seen as acts in the Lacanian sense:

> If we accept the Lacanian distinction between the act as a negative gesture of saying "No!," and its positive aftermath, locating the key dimension in the primordial negative gesture, then the process of disintegration did none the less produce a true act in the guise of the enthusiastic mass movement of saying "No!" to the Communist regime on behalf of authentic solidarity; this negative gesture counted more than its later failed positivization. (1994, 169-170n28, emphasis in original)

Žižek employs this example to point out how Badiou is excessively strict about what qualifies as an act (and, of course, an event).[2] If a political act leads to a "failed positivization," then for Badiou it was never really based on an event, and was thus never really an act. It is sympathetic on Žižek's part to want to say that there are more acts and more events than Badiou's theory might allow for. But what if we reconsider one of the conditions for an act that I discussed in the previous chapter? According to Lacan, one of the conditions for an act is that it must transform the subject. Badiou's theory certainly includes this dimension. This may be why Badiou emphasizes the importance of some sort of positivization and "subjectivization": without such things, no subject can be constituted, and acts would just peter out. Žižek himself emphasized this transformative aspect of Lacan's theory of the act in an earlier work, *Enjoy Your Symptom*!:

> The act differs from an active intervention (action) in that it radically transforms its bearer (agent): the act is not simply something I "accomplish"—after an act, I'm literally "not the same as before." In this sense, we could say that the subject "undergoes" the act ("passes through" it) rather than "accomplishes" it: in it, the subject is annihilated and subsequently reborn (or not), i.e., the act involves a kind of temporary eclipse, *aphanisis*, of the subject. (1992, 44)

What if we add this criterion to the example Žižek gives in *The Ticklish Subject*? Did the events in the Eastern Bloc radically transform any subjects? I would not rule it out, but how could they have done so on the basis of a mere "saying no"? In other words, I want to suggest that saying "no" is not enough for a transformation of the subject to come about. It may well bring about the kind of eclipsing Žižek spoke of earlier, but for a transformation to occur, some kind of further signifying production would be necessary. Such an idea is worked out quite well in Badiou's *Théorie du sujet*, as well as in his later work, *Saint Paul*, a work that plays a central role in Žižek's critique of Badiou. In these works, Badiou shows us how an act does more than say "no," even though saying "no" is a crucial element of any act. As Badiou describes it, an act articulates a "no . . . but" (1997, 67–68). In his reading of Paul's letters, Badiou looks at how Paul effectively managed to operate a negation of the world of Roman law by proffering new signifiers. Referring to St. Paul's famous phrase, "You are no longer under the law, but under grace," Badiou claims the following:

> We maintain in fact that a rupture on the basis of an event always constitutes its subject in the divided form of a "no . . . but," and that *it is precisely this form that bears the universal*, because the "no" is the potential dissolution of closed particularities (whose name is the "law"), whereas the "but" indicates the task, the faithful labor, of which the subjects of the process opened by the event (whose name is "grace") are the co-workers. (1997, 67–68, emphasis in original)

If we conceive of an act in terms of a "no . . . but" structure, then it is easier to account for how an act would transform a subject. The transformation occurs not so much through the negation produced by an act but by the articulation of something else—by the production of a new signifier that negates. According to Badiou's argument, this new signifier in Paul's works is "grace," a signifier that implied an entirely different subject-position from the ones recognized by the "Roman Other." In fact, maybe the negation can only be sustained as a negation if it is supplemented by a "but" supporting an alternative signifying practice. This is the point that needs to be retained, and it is a point made by both Badiou and Lacan.

Again, this reading of an act illustrates how a subject's relation to signifiers is not always about identification. For there to be an identification, one has to add the further idea of an Other capable of bestowing recognition. If this idea is excluded from Badiou's theory of the subject, as well as from Lacan's theory of the subject in an act, then what we find in both is a subject produced by a signifying practice, a subject "attached" to signifiers, without this attachment involving an identification, or what Žižek called a "subjectivization." This is because the signifiers used rule out any recognition by the Other and do not depend upon a consistent Other for their meaning and validity. They are rather something like puns, challenging the code that organizes a particular, supposedly consistent Other—an Other who does not desire but is a subject-supposed-to-know.

CONCLUSION

My reading of Lacan's theory of the subject places his view somewhere between Badiou's critique of Lacan and Žižek's critique of Badiou. In contrast to Badiou's critique, according to which Lacan's theory is too "conformist" or conservative-Hegelian, and in contrast to Žižek's response to Badiou, according to which Lacan's theory is eminently "negative," I am inclined to portray Lacan's subject in terms of a positive or incarnate negativity, or as a negativity with a positive insistence. This is precisely what the notion of the act calls our attention to, and I will expand on this view in the next chapter.

It is worth noting that Lacan is sometimes vague about exactly what an actlike signifying process looks like, even though he does give us a variety of conditions for an act. In those last pages from his eleventh seminar that I discussed earlier, Lacan describes a crossing of the plane of identification, and in his usual jargon he discusses what goes on in it. But what does it actually look like? Just when he is on the verge of having to describe what an act looks like, Lacan often avoids any detailed description. Instead, he says something like the following: "This crossing of the plane of identification is possible. Anyone who has lived through the analytic experience with me to the end of the training analysis knows that what I am saying is true" (XI, 304/273). He usually does not say more.

Yet examples are not lacking. In the last chapter, I studied puns and the *Fort-Da* game as examples. A signifying act also may be said to occur in the case of Xénophon from chapter 3, insofar as Xénophon was involved in a signifying practice that transformed the way in which the signifier "cross" had determined him (arriving at the new signifier "star-crosses" and a different mode of being in relation to it). Indeed, the signifying process that occurs during the analytic cure in general ought to be taken as the major paradigm for the Lacanian act. I also am inclined to see Badiou's work as a project that fills in what is sometimes obscure in Lacan, and I will be using an example from his work in the next chapter to further illustrate the nature of a Lacanian act.

CHAPTER 8

An Act beyond Recognition

In Lacan's theory of the act, the plane of identification is supposed to be crossed and the fantasy traversed. I argued in the last chapter, against Žižek, that this does not produce what could be called a purely negative subject. True, an act does not produce a subject who is identified with any particular signifier, but it does not produce a subject separate from signifiers altogether either. How can signifiers be used such that they avoid making a demand on the Other for recognition? If an act uses signifiers in a punlike way, and if it does not make a demand on the Other, then what does it do? Is it simply incomprehensible? A meaningless blah blah blah?

Signifiers must be employed in some way in an act, but this does not mean that an act has to fall on either side of an unsatisfactory division: on the one hand, a meaningless, onanistic blah blah blah, in which what is enjoyed is nothing but the sound of one's own voice; or, on the other hand, an either latent or manifest attempt to get recognized by the Other by means of what is being said. As Lacan puts it in one of his late seminars, what he is aiming at is a kind of signifying activity that can be found in "some artistic practices," one that could be said to be "beyond the symbolic" (XXIV, *Ornicar?*, 15: 12).[1] This does not mean it would be preverbal or nonverbal, however. Lacan says instead that it should be seen as "hyper-verbal," "a verbal to the second power" (XXIV, *Ornicar?*, 15: 12). Lacan was inclined to speak about this kind of signifying practice in such terms—describing a signifying act as "beyond the symbolic" may come as a surprise to some familiar with Lacan—since within the symbolic every signifying practice is either part of an "idiotic jouissance" (a blah blah blah) or a demand for recognition.

Since one of the important features of an act is its difference from a performance of identity, I will here discuss how Lacan's theory of the subject differs from Judith Butler's. According to both Butler and Lacan, identity as such is a frustrating swindle. Even attempts to avoid alienation by coming up with our own identities (say, in a project of aesthetic self-creation, or, as we shall see, in a Butlerian politics that affirms the openness of identity) are still always going to be geared toward getting recognition from the Other. If we are interested in identity, in determining or asserting what we are (or even what we want to be), then we are interested in being objects of the Other's desire. This interest relies upon an Other construed as a subject-supposed-to-know. No pursuit of the self, no matter how apparently subversive it may be, can avoid making an implicit appeal to this kind of Other. Both Butler and Lacan pursue the implications of this impasse, yet despite these similarities, there is an important difference in their results. This chapter will explore the way in which Lacan's theory of the act opens up horizons for thinking about the limitations of an approach to the subject that focuses primarily on the subject's relation to identity.

Identity has become an important term in contemporary political discussions, and what is said of identity here has some bearing on those discussions. Žižek (1999) describes the impasses of identity politics quite well in *The Ticklish Subject*. An identity politics usually makes a demand for recognition by appealing to notions of justice and equality, but there is often something more in its demands. For this reason, the recognition and victories obtained may be unsatisfying, because for many in the movement the movement was not just about the recognition of specific demands. This can lead to fragmentations in the movement, splits between those not happy with the new status and compromises that recognition brings with it, and others satisfied, stopping the struggle altogether. On Žižek's account such scissions happen in political movements because there is always a desire lurking behind the demands that a group makes: a desire that cannot be satisfied the way a demand can be (1999, 266–268). This desire is, as Žižek describes it, essentially negative. A movement that would respect the negative desire that constitutes it is one that might demand nothing in particular, yet would still protest. In fact, Žižek describes how some very effective political movements have done just this, and his reading of the fall of Communism in Eastern Europe seems to go in this direction. As I will show later on in this chapter, Badiou (1985) makes a similar point about political movements in *Peut-on penser la politique*? For Žižek and Badiou, a movement's inability to articulate a specific demand, in contrast to movements that are quite specific and goal oriented, is an important marker of its political status.

In a collaborative work with Judith Butler and Ernesto Laclau, Žižek points out that the dimension of act is missing from Butler's work (Butler, Laclau, and Žižek 2000; 124). I will argue here that this is indeed the case, and that this is a real flaw in Butler's work on the subject. While Butler argues that the subject has no core, unchangeable identity, she does argue that the subject has an unchangeable fixation to identity as such. Her characterization of this fixation leads me to claim that despite her attempts to include a notion of agency in her work, her theory possesses a deterministic streak. The inclusion of a consideration of how acts use signifiers in a way that is not bound up with identification and recognition would remedy this.

BUTLER'S IMMANENT SUBJECT

When Butler discusses the subject, it tends to be in the context of a discussion of agency. Butler is against a metaphysical approach to the subject, according to which the subject would be a "doer" preceding its "deed" (1990, 25). For this reason, she describes agency as follows: "All signification takes place within the orbit of the compulsion to repeat; 'agency,' then, is to be located within the possibility of a variation on that repetition" (1990, 145). In other words, agency is not prior to signification but enabled by it. Describing Foucault's conception of power as a matrix of intelligibility that imposes certain identities on people, Butler gives us a more specific understanding of the situation of the subject implied in this view of agency:

> The coexistence or convergence of such discursive injunctions produces the possibility of a complex reconfiguration and redeployment; it is not a transcendental subject who enables action in the midst of such a convergence. There is no self that is prior to the convergence or who maintains "integrity" prior to its entrance into this conflicted cultural field. (1990, 145)

When Butler says that there is no transcendental subject, I take her to be saying that there is no subject transcendental to or preceding the "coexistence or convergence of [...] discursive injunctions." Quite clearly, then, the subject depends upon the activity of signification. But what is the nature of this dependence? As she puts it in the passage just quoted, the subject does not enable this signification. Could the criticisms that were directed toward Lacan's theory by Borch-Jacobsen, and Lacoue-Labarthe and Nancy be more appropriately directed toward Butler? For Butler, is the subject anything other than language?

Butler does not, as far as I am aware, ever say anything like "the subject is language," and I do not believe her theory ever suggests such an equation. In fact, at some points Butler seems to suggest that a subject is not identical to its identity. If identity is discursively constructed, then this might lead one to think that the subject is also something other than discourse. One could have an identity constituted by language and a subject who is not entirely absorbed by this identity.

But it is important to recall that there are two kinds of identity operative in Butler's work. She argues that the subject is not identical to its identity only when this identity is taken to be a prediscursive substance or core. But what about when identity is understood correctly, when identity is seen as nothing other than a convergence of discursive injunctions? From this point of view, the passage I already cited about "the convergence of various discourses" could be taken to be saying that the subject reduces to language somehow. The subject is not transcendental to the "conflicted cultural field" constituted by the injunctions that bring it into being—the subject would be a network of various discourses, and nothing apart from them.[2]

I have been arguing that when Lacan makes the subject something separate from identity, he also means that the subject is not reducible to language or discourse. This is because he also takes the event of sexuality into account when describing the subject's genesis. Lacan's theory is an example of a nontranscendental view of the subject that does not reduce the subject to language or any other of its elements (the real, or jouissance). Neither transcendental to the field that constitutes it, nor immanent in that field, the subject according to Lacan is a function that results from language's effects on the body. Instead of understanding the subject in terms of a function or effect, Butler opts for an immanent view of the subject. In *Bodies That Matter*, this immanent view is plainly visible. In a discussion of the converging power relations that constitute the subject, Butler claims: "There is no self-identical subject who houses or bears these relations, no site at which such relations converge. This converging and interarticulation is the contemporary fate of the subject. In other words, the subject as a self-identical entity is no more" (1993, 230, emphasis in original). Consider also a caveat running through Butler's work—the idea that agency is not to be located outside of discourse: "There is no possibility of agency outside of the discursive practices that give those terms the intelligibility that they have" (1990, 148). Much of what Butler says here would also hold for Lacan's view. But equally essential to Lacan's theory is the idea that the subject is neither reducible to nor immanent in language. This means that an outside of discourse, an outside found in the body, the real, or jouissance, is a necessary component of Lacan's theory of the subject.

In terms of the controversy I discussed in chapter 1, Butler seems closer to reducing the subject to language than Lacan. In their readings of Lacan, Borch-Jacobsen and Lacoue-Labarthe and Nancy argued that for Lacan language is the subject: Language is endowed with the powers and abilities that the classical subject always had. Language constitutes, it acts, it represents, and it creates.

I have already shown that this is not Lacan's position. I do not think that this is exactly Butler's position either. Making the subject immanent in language, or reducing the subject to language—which Butler does, on my reading—is not the same as making language into the subject. The former involves the idea that all the powers that are supposed to be possessed by a subject are really nothing but the powers of language. The latter view holds that language as such is actually the subject. According to this latter view, language would be some kind of structure that lords it over individuals, determining which kinds of actions are possible and which kinds of actions are actually done, something like Hegelian Spirit perhaps. The former view, however, still allows some aspects of language to function as a nonsubject and thus allows individuals a bit of free space with respect to the categories enabled by language. In other words, all this view is saying is that language has many effects, and among them happen to be those that we mythologize or reify into a "subject." Agency on this view, in fact, consists of the exploitation of discursive possibilities not already given a place in what Butler calls the "matrix of intelligibility." The other view actually claims that everything that language does is the action of a subject: Language is a power that is the subject. This is the view that Borch-Jacobsen and Lacoue-Labarthe and Nancy wanted to attribute to Lacan. In its ability to construct meanings and representations, in its ability to bestow recognition and determine behavior, language is, on this view, doing everything the subject was supposed to be doing.

So if there are problems with Butler's reduction of the subject to language, they are not the same problems that Borch-Jacobsen and Lacoue-Labarthe and Nancy pointed out with respect to the idea of making language into the subject. One of the problems with this position, according to them, was that in it the classical portrayal of the subject is merely transferred onto something else: All of the properties that the subject was endowed with were merely transferred onto language itself. It is not a subject who represents, creates, and acts, but language that does all of this. Hence, language was in fact "the subject" on their reading of Lacan. I suspect that Butler would want to avoid merely transferring a traditional notion of the subject from one locality (consciousness) to another (language). She calls most of the qualities of the classical subject into question. Witness her criticism of the idea of a doer behind the deed, as well as her claim that the subject is not self-identical. Yet Butler does transfer the subject into the field of language and seems to attribute, at least partially, some notion of the subject to language in her view of agency.

I suggest that by reducing the subject to language, Butler is trying to work out a compromise position. Without wanting to grant language the full powers of the classical subject, she does find some linguistic operations to be subject-phenomena, yet in a way very different from Lacan's. I will elaborate on this compromise position in the next section.

THE STATUS OF THE REAL

Butler's accounts of agency and the subject do not require any notion of something external to or other than discourse. She can account for subjects and agents as well as transformations within the "matrix of intelligibility" from a perspective that only considers the discursively constructed nature of identity. Nevertheless, Butler wants to avoid giving the impression that she adheres to an extreme "linguisticisim." The work that followed *Gender Trouble* was *Bodies That Matter*, and in the preface Butler asks herself a question she was often asked: "What about the materiality of the body?" (1993, ix). Butler wants to include some notion of the body in her account of identification while avoiding two things. On the one hand, she wants to avoid making the body into a purely linguistic construct. On the other hand, she also wants to avoid making the body into something simply outside of discourse. What she arrives at is a notion of the body as a limit point to identification and language:

> The linguistic categories that are understood to "denote" the materiality of the body are themselves troubled by a referent that is never fully or permanently resolved or contained by any given signified. Indeed, that referent persists only as a kind of absence or loss, that which language does not capture,

> but, instead, that which impels language repeatedly to attempt that capture, that circumscription—and to fail. This loss takes its place in language as an insistent call or demand that, while *in* language, is never fully *of* language. (1993, 67, emphasis in original)

As she describes it, the body presents language with a problem and is certainly not reducible to language, but the body is also not radically distinct from language, otherwise we would never be able to account for the body as a resistance to signification. Butler is trying to think of the materiality of the body as something experienced *within* language, and this actually sounds very much like the Lacanian understanding of the real as an impasse in signification ($real_2$). Only whenever Butler comes across the term *real* she systematically understands it to be a domain radically distinct from language and does not seem willing to acknowledge that there is another approach to the real in Lacan's work, one where the real is just an "impasse in formalization."

While Butler is, in *Bodies That Matter*, trying to remedy her overemphasis on discourse, her inclusion of a notion of the body that is very close to the Lacanian real does not lead her to consider that there may be a subject produced in a relation to this real that has nothing to do with performing identity. *The Psychic Life of Power* does contain a revision to her theory of the subject, but not the right one. She introduces the term *psyche* in order to discuss notions—such as libidinal attachment—that seem to be kept out of her earlier theory of the subject, but she continues to use the term *subject* for the more restricted domain of identities included within the matrix of intelligibility. On this view, then, "subject" is always something subjected to a particular configuration of power, knowledge, and discourse, while the "psyche" is described as the source of possible resistances to this configuration, even though it also assents to subjection. Butler writes: "The psyche [...] is very different from the subject: the psyche is precisely what exceeds the imprisoning effects of the discursive demand to inhabit a coherent identity, to become a coherent subject. The psyche is what resists the regularization that Foucault ascribes to normalizing discourses" (1997, 86).[3] This revision does not lead Butler to consider what is going on in an act, since even the psyche is deeply committed to identification—even if it is to the multiple, conflicted kind of identity that Butler wishes to affirm.

Despite her attempt to include something like the real in her work, then, Butler does not draw the same consequences from it as Lacan does. In Lacan's work, the real is an "impasse in formalization" that can be handled in two different ways—it can be covered up by creating a signified for it, or it can be preserved in a particular type of signifying practice. Badiou argued that Lacan's theory embraced a covering up of, or a distancing of the subject from, the real, and I countered with the claim that Lacan actually embraced the alternative position in his theory of the act. Butler's notions of the body and passionate attachments to identity do not lead her to develop a theory of the act, which would be in part about renewing and rewriting our very attachment to identity itself. In other words, Butler does not seem to consider the possibility that certain signifying practices may be entirely outside the domain of identification. According to Butler, we remain committed to subjection, and thus identification, at the psychic or unconscious level. In fact, this is the very condition for us to be subjects at all.

Butler does claim that "the capacity of desire to be withdrawn and to reattach will constitute something like the vulnerability of every strategy of subjection" (1997, 62). A particular configuration of power is always vulnerable because desire is malleable. It can be invested in its own subjection to an identity, and this investment is for Butler necessary for there to be a subject, even if the subject can somehow pull back from such investment. Yet the subject's very ability to pull back is rendered problematic by her calls to resist the "lure" of identity, but not identity itself.

Butler envisions a turning away from what she calls "the law," a turning that resists the law's "lure of identity" (1997, 130). In *Bodies That Matter*, where identity is described as a "necessary error," she calls for an affirmation of the disidentification latent in any identification (1993, 230). Critical of a politics and ethics that strive for full recognition, Butler writes:

> Does politicization always need to overcome disidentification? What are the possibilities of politicizing *dis*identification, this experience of *misrecognition*, this uneasy sense of standing under a sign to which one does and does not belong? [...] If the term [a signifier like "women," for example] cannot offer ultimate recognition—and here Žižek is very right to claim that all such terms rest on a necessary *méconnaissance*—it may be that the affirmation of that slippage, that failure of identification, is itself the point of departure for a more democratizing affirmation of internal difference. (1993, 219, emphasis in original)

What Butler means by "disidentification" here is what she revealed in *Gender Trouble* to be the truth of identity: Identity is a repeated performance, it is discursively constructed, and for that very reason it is never fixed and never pure. The truth of identity, one could say, is that it also always implies a disidentification: We are attached to it but frustrated by it at the same time. Consider the alienating experience Butler refers to in the passage just cited, the experience of "standing under a sign to which one does and does not belong." Identity in Butler's work entails this alienating experience of belonging and not belonging, of being recognized and misrecognized in one's identity, of needing a signifier in order to exist and be recognized as a subject but also of not being reducible to a signifier.

In *The Psychic Life of Power*, the paradox of having to be subjected to power in order to be a subject comes under further scrutiny: "If the terms by which we gain social recognition for ourselves are those by which we are regulated *and* gain social existence then to affirm one's existence is to capitulate to one's subordination—a sorry bind" (1997, 79, emphasis in original). Butler reiterates here that it is only by being subjected to a signifier that identifies us that we can be subjects capable of resisting that identification, resisting a reduction to that signifier, and acting as agents. Once again, the preservation of some kind of relation to identity is absolutely crucial for Butler. Without a relation to an alienating identification, the kind of subversive activity she wants to affirm would not be possible. In fact, there would be no "subject" at all, and thus no chance for agency, without both an identity and the preservation of a frustrated *relationship* to this identity.

Although she does not believe that anything like the achievement of a "full recognition" of an identity is possible, it can still be argued that Butler hangs on to a Hegelian understanding of desire, according to which human desire is essentially a desire for recognition. And, giving this a Kojèvian spin, we cannot not seek recognition without ceasing to be human. This view that we are condemned to seek recognition is what leads me to wonder what possibilities for an act beyond recognition remain in Butler's theory. While she always points out that any particular identity is fluid, conflicted, and changeable, our commitment to identity itself bears none of these characteristics. It is a commitment that can be considered the core of what we are. It is something so important to us that we cannot, according to Butler, give it up. Ethically, Butler thinks that it is important to maintain the desire lurking behind our identifications, a desire that is ultimately a desire for recognition that can never be satisfied.

From a Lacanian point of view, as we have seen, identification is also a moment in the production of the subject. The relation between a unary trait and a signifier for the Other's desire is a relation that precipitates the subject as a meaning and a being for the Other. However, this covers only one aspect of the subject in Lacan's work: fantasy. Lacan's theory of the subject differs in an important way from Butler's when he discusses the act. Because of being wed to the real in a different fashion, an act involves the realization that there is no Other of the Other, nothing behind the Other, as it were, acting as a ground. Consequently, an act transforms the subject (of fantasy) and consists of a signifying practice that does not rely on the Other as a guarantee of meaning and recognition. As my discussion of the *Fort-Da* game in chapter 6 showed, an act is not for the Other.

But is not Lacan's idea of a desiring Other just like Butler's idea of identity as a conflicted cultural field? They sound alike insofar as both involve a rejection of the fiction of an Other who is a subject-supposed-to-know. But the resemblance does not go much farther. Butler's "matrix of intelligibility," out of which identity is forged, contains a multiplicity of signifiers whose interrelations can lead to unpredictable possibilities for identity. But in Lacan's work, an encounter with the Other's desire is not an encounter with a multiplicity of signifiers offering various possibilities for identity. Rather, an encounter with the Other's desire is an encounter with the absence of any signifier offering a support, guarantee, and recognition point for identity. It is such an absence that makes an encounter with the Other's desire into an encounter with an impasse in symbolization, which is the mode in which the real appears in an act. Thus the encounter with the Other's desire can be thought of as an encounter with the real.

The difference between Lacan's notion of a split, desiring Other and Butler's notion of a multiple, conflicted social order is the difference between not having a signifier and having a cornucopia of signifiers, which is one way to figure the difference between a theory that includes the real in the symbolic, and a theory that overemphasizes the symbolic (although Butler would not use this term to describe her theory). While her discussion of the body as an impasse is an attempt to resolve this issue, it does not lead Butler to focus on how the subject may have a relation to something other than identity, and how the subject may be doing something other than performing an identity—at least sometimes.

BADIOU ON POLITICS

There is more to the subject than identity, and I have been discussing how Judith Butler's theory of identity and the subject does not a describe a subject who does anything other than perform its identity. Lacan's theory of the act, I am arguing, gives us a portrait of a subject doing something other than this. My study of the *Fort-Da* game in chapter 6 already showed this. My concern now is to show that the notion of an act in Lacanian theory need not be so "solipsistic" (for lack of a better term) as that. In the last chapter I portrayed Badiou, somewhat provocatively, as someone who is closer to Lacan's theory of the subject than the most prominent of Lacanian advocates, Slavoj Žižek. Badiou's description of politics in his 1985 *Peut-on penser la politique?* contrasts well with Butler's description of an ethic of (dis)identification and is also useful for demonstrating what a Lacanian act beyond identification and recognition might look like when it is something other than a private affair, as the child's *Fort-Da* game and Xénophon's cross were. Many things about Badiou's political theory have changed since 1985, and I refer the reader to Peter Hallward's *Badiou: A Subject to Truth* (2003) for a discussion of these changes and a relevant bibliography. For my purposes, Badiou's 1985 essay is useful because it discusses a specific example of a signifying act in politics.

Badiou's goal in *Peut-on penser la politique?* is to rehabilitate a notion of *la politique* (politics), which, he argues, is dwarfed in contemporary liberal democracies by the concerns of *le politique* (the political). The political is characterized by consensus building and the achievement of an adequate representation of the will of the people: "The political is philosophically designated as the concept of the communitarian link, and of its representation in an authority" (1985, 15). The association of the political with the process of obtaining representation for different constituencies leads Badiou to make the occurrence of an impasse in political representation into one of the key characteristics of politics. "In order to portray the political as a fiction and orient oneself towards politics, the first task is to disengage the latter from the prescription of connection. A de-fixation of politics as a communitarian connection or relation must be theoretically and practically brought about" (1985, 18). Politics, then, brings forth something that does not fit into the kinds of social connections (representations) sought after by the political. What this means is that politics is illegitimate from the point of view of the political.

Peut-on penser la politique? works out a concept of politics by asking what is living and what is dead in Marxist thought. Badiou's contention is that politics is almost nonexistent, because much in Marxism—which offered the vocabulary for thinking about politics—is dead. The kinds of social and political movements Marxism predicted no longer take place, while the movements that were actually occurring (in 1985, when the work was published) tended to go against the tenets of classical Marxism. For example, Badiou argues that "neither the socialist states, nor the battles for national liberation, nor the worker's movement constitute historical referents capable of guaranteeing the concrete universality of Marxism" (1985, 48). According to Badiou, these movements do not fit within a classical Marxist theory. For example, even though it based itself on Marxist theory, "really existing socialism" did not take place in industrialized countries; nationalist movements in the twentieth century tended not to be internationalist, as communism was supposed to be; and the Solidarity movement in Poland, which could not have resembled more the kind of workers' movement classical Marxism was talking about, actually did not make any use of or reference to Marxist theory at all. And to top it off, it took place in a country that was, at least officially, Communist.

Yet in 1985 Badiou did not wish to add his voice to anti-Marxism. If there were still any life to be found in Marxism, he argued that the original theoretical and practical situation out of which Marx's work grew needed to be updated and rethought. Lenin claimed that there were three key sources of Marxist thought: German Idealism, the revolutionary French workers' movement, and English political economy (1985, 62). Marx's originality consisted of using these three sources to elaborate on what Badiou calls a fundamental declaration of a social fact: "There is a revolutionary worker's movement" (1985, 57). Badiou characterizes this declaration as follows: "It is not a matter of separating out and structuring a part of the existing phenomenon. It is a matter of a 'there is,' of an act of thought cutting across a real [en coupure d'un réel]" (1985, 58). The declaration in the nineteenth century, that "there is a revolutionary workers' movement," is read by Badiou as a signifying act, as an attempt on Marx's part to signify something that had not yet received signification in his time, thus its association with an act "cutting across a real." In what follows, I will consider how such a political signifying act resembles the Lacanian act's creation of a new signifier.

If much in Marx is effectively dead, then Badiou argues that this is because the original force of the founding declaration of Marxism has been exhausted. The existence of a revolutionary workers' movement is no longer so evident, and, more importantly, it is no longer "traumatic" for us: The status of such a declaration in contemporary culture no longer has the effect of bringing a signifying impasse to bear on contemporary political discourse. That is, the existence of such a movement would no longer press upon us, forcing us into a new signifying production in order to make sense of it. In fact, we have an entire history of Marxist theory and practice in terms of which such a movement could be interpreted. But even the contemporary explanatory power of classical Marxist theory is exhausted, according to Badiou, because it has lost its real historical power. The historical referents upon which Marxism was founded—German philosophy, French politics, and English economic theory—are no longer major referents for contemporary culture, to say the least!

Obviously, what Badiou suggests is that the emergence of politics now would have to occur from a different type of declaration, one that formally or structurally resembles Marx's: that is, it would have to bring into signifiers something that has no representation in the political, or the state. With such a signifying act, Badiou believes that one would be more faithful to Marxism than a classical Marxist is, for one would then be developing a politics on the basis of a declaration that would, again, cut across the real, which is precisely the kind of relationship between signifiers and the real described in Lacan's theory of the act.

Peut-on penser la politique? is one of the first works in which Badiou makes use of the concept of the "event," which would end up playing a central role in his later work. In his destruction and recomposition of Marxism, he claims that

> the determination of the essence of politics, which cannot be provided by structure (because of the inconsistency of sets, of dis-connection) nor from meaning (History is not whole), has no other reference point but the event. The evental [*événementiel*] "there is," taken according to its chance appearance, is precisely the site where the essence of politics is circumscribed. (1985, 67)

Marxism applied a theoretical framework to what was at the time a new event. Badiou argues that the way to revive Marxism today is to apply a contemporary theoretical framework to what, for us, has the status of an event.

The example that Badiou uses for a contemporary event is surprising for its lack of apparent grandeur. The notion of a historical or political event would tend to suggest something large scale, like October 1917 or May 1968. The event Badiou chooses to focus on is the much less well-known Talbot 1983-1984. This requires some explanation, no doubt, but it will be clear why Badiou thinks that what happened in this particular place in France occurred at an "evental" social site, even if it was already, by Badiou's own admission, largely forgotten by the time he published *Peut-on penser la politique?* A perceptive political historian, however, would bring the long period of rioting in France in 2005 into a connection with these events that took place twenty years earlier.

Between November 1983 and February 1984, an automobile factory in Talbot, France, was occupied by striking workers. Clashes occurred among the strikers themselves, as well as with the police. An attack happened on one of the shop floors by what the press called "non-strikers"—a group composed of predominantly North African migrant laborers, in fact. The attack was condemned by one of the largest unions in France, which, under some pressure, soon decided to encourage the acceptance of one of management's earlier offers. Another major union called for an end to the occupation of the factory shortly thereafter.

As Badiou points out, the objective facts surrounding this event are quite simple and not all that unusual or unimaginable. What makes it an event in Badiou's particular sense is what he calls the subjective break that followed from it. In the next elections, the Socialist Party, which was in power at the time, plummeted in the polls, the Communist Party became a nonentity, and the extreme Right of Le Pen gained ground. Badiou attributes these post-Talbot election results to several factors. The socialist government's policy of industrial "restructuring" had been a manifest failure. The other left-wing parties had no ability to control the migrant workers, as Talbot showed. And finally, the Right was successfully able to rally the French public against the migrant workers at Talbot. The right wing was in fact doubly successful, because it did not only win votes with its racist appeals. Its attractiveness to the electorate even forced the Socialist Party to start talking about toughening up on immigration (1985, 72). In other words, after Talbot the right wing was controlling the political debate within France, with everyone focusing on the "immigrant problem."

These are some of the repercussions Talbot had in the political domain in France, but they do not tell us why Talbot was something that could be the source of a contemporary politics. What Badiou focuses on is an apparently straightforward statement the migrant workers were making at the time: "We want our rights" (1985, 73). Yet this statement, Badiou claims, had no resonance at all in the French electorate, and he argues that structurally it could not have any resonance within France. This is what makes Talbot so interesting for Badiou. "This statement, which does however bear on rights, is intrinsically unrepresentable, and it is in this unrepresentability that the politics of this statement consists" (1985, 74). Why this should be the case is not so clear. The statement had no place in the political discourse in

France, according to Badiou, since a parliamentary democracy is about obtaining representation for different constituent groups in the state. One of the things at stake in the claims made by the Talbot workers is precisely which groups are officially in the state and which are not. While many of the workers had been living and working in France for over twenty years, they were still not citizens and had an illegal status. The problem, then, was that "as the government and unions said in chorus: the rights in question do not exist" (1985, 75). As I will argue in the next section, the status of the statement in this particular example, and this particular context—"We want our rights"—can be compared to a Lacanian act.

HOW AN ACT AVOIDS MAKING DEMANDS

I have been claiming that the Lacanian act uses signifiers in a way that is not bound up with the pursuit of recognition for one's identity. Can Talbot be taken as an example of what such an act might look like socially and politically? The obvious problem here is that it is difficult to claim that the migrant workers were not actually seeking recognition from the state. It may have been nonsensical for them to demand recognition of their rights in the French state, yet recognition of their rights may well have been something they actually expected from the "French Other." Badiou suggests that even if this is what they expected, this is not what made the claim "We want our rights" into the stuff of politics: "Politics begins when one proposes not to represent victims [. . .] but to be faithful to the events upon which the victims declare themselves" (1985, 75). And so politics would involve taking the claim seriously despite its nonsensical political status. Badiou also refers to the fact that the workers did not succeed in articulating a program, even though they tried. It is as if the statement "We want our rights" intrinsically could not lead to the creation of any legitimate demand. For this reason, what Badiou thinks is significant about the statement is that with it the workers were simply asserting their "impossible" existence within French society. And this is, according to Badiou, reflected in how their statement was treated by French society: The rights in question simply did not exist, and there was thus no political basis on which the workers could make such claims within France.

It is conceivable, however, that their statement could have been treated like a legitimate demand. It could have been taken up by a political party and could have led to the formation of programs and legislation. To shed further light on what politics is about, then, Badiou claims that politics, unlike "the political," entails the mere assertion of an impossible existence, and is actually not concerned with achieving an adequate representation of that impossible existence in "the political." In politics, "It is not the case that something that exists can be represented. It is a matter of that by means of which something comes to exist that nothing represents, and that purely and simply presents its existence" (1985, 87). Politics is about a presentation that causes an impasse in representation. Such a presentation occurs, Badiou argues, when migrant workers say, "We want our rights."

But is not politics about seeking a correction to this impasse in representation? Badiou seems to acknowledge this when he describes politics as something that seeks to make the impossible possible (1985, 78). But it can only do this because the signifying act in politics calls into question the very domain within which programs and demands can be made. Politics calls into question the very organizing principle of the political (in this case, the limiting principle that the "people" to be represented in the state are "citizens of France"). The reason politics remains distinct from "the political" and its concern with representing is that politics forces a realization of the inadequacy of any programmatic solution to the problem the event poses. In other words, Talbot brought out the structural inability of "the political" to take into account demands from non-French workers in France. As evidence for this, Badiou cites the various failed attempts workers made to articulate their fundamental statement in terms with which political discourse would have been familiar, such as demands for lump sums of cash, a reimbursement of social costs, and an extra month's salary for every year of a workers' seniority. Badiou takes the extravagance of these demands to be a measure of their impossibility, and, indeed, a measure of the fact that they could not be recognized as serious political demands at all.

I have been discussing this account of politics in Badiou's work for two reasons. First, it sheds more light on some of the dimensions of the Lacanian act that I have discussed already, insofar as the statement Badiou focuses on brings an impasse—in this case, a social impasse—into signification. Second, I have dwelled on it because politics for Badiou is not about the assertion of identity and the procuring of representation, and in this respect I see it as a continuation of Lacan's project and a contrast to Butler's work. With a theory of politics that includes a notion like the real as an impasse in signification, Badiou is able to highlight the kinds of effects politics has outside of calls for the recognition of identity.

The resemblance between Lacan's theory of the act and what Badiou calls politics should, then, be clear. Although the term *Other* is not used by Badiou in this context, the places where it would fit are obvious. The domain of the political—the state—resembles the Lacanian Other as a subject-supposed-to-know. Politics sustains an impasse in this Other, just as a Lacanian act emphasizes the Other's lack of consistency, coherence, and totality. Signifiers also play an important role in Badiou's theory, even though he does not refer to them directly. The statement he focuses on in the wake of Talbot is a signifying act, and he even works in a place for an idea of the subject as an effect in his political theory. Writing about how politics propagates an event, he claims that "this propagation is never a repetition. It is a subject-effect, a consistency" (1985, 77). Politics does not consist of repeating the circumstances of an event, of, for example, trying to bring about again what happened at Talbot. Instead, politics as a signifying act preserves the impasse in signification caused by the event. Politics does not let this event stop being an event for the social. In other words, it does not let an event get fully absorbed or placed in the Other. Politics, then, is a signifying practice that remains faithful to the subjective rupture an event brings about. Politics' reminder to the Other that all cannot be represented is what Badiou calls the subject-effect of politics. Thus the political subject for Badiou is essentially linked to rupture. The consistency of a political subject, oddly, is nothing other than a consistency of rupture. As Badiou (1982) described it in *Théorie du sujet*, the subject is a destructive consistency.

I argued in chapter 7 that in Lacanian theory the subject of an act is not something from which the real is excluded or repressed. While a signifying act does not present us with the real in the raw, it is not a completely tame real that it presents either. It is precisely the real's status as an impasse in formalization and signification that is presented in an act. I opened this chapter by asking what the signifying practice of an act does if it does not make demands. If it does not make demands, if it does not seek recognition by the Other, then is it just a meaningless blah blah blah? Badiou's discussion of politics shows us how an act is not like this. Politics, as Badiou conceives it, does something to the social without articulating a demand to the social Other. While such an act, strictly speaking, has no place, no meaning, in the Other, and while Badiou does not refrain from calling such an act "nonsensical," such acts are not simply meaningless and are reminiscent of the way Lacan described puns. As Lacan described it, a pun contains a *pas-de-sens*, a step toward meaning that never gives a full incarnation of meaning in one signifier. This step, far from simply negating the Other, engages in something like a reinvention of the Other. Certainly, since an act avoids making demands it does not engage with the Other as a subject-supposed-to-know, and it can be said to be in a negative relation to such an Other. But by preserving some kind of relation to the creation of a new meaning, it manages to go toward the establishment of a different Other in the place of this Other-who-knows: an Other whose inconsistency and incoherence are laid bare.

Once again, we can see how an act is not like the production of meaning in a metaphor. In chapter 2, I claimed that a metaphor succeeds in creating the illusion that there is an incarnation of an absent signified in one particular signifier (latent or manifest) in a signifying chain. This signifier then appears as an enigma, containing within it the keys to its own interpretation, an interpretation that only succeeds in giving more signifiers and never a final signified. Is the signifying production of an act doing something like this? A distinction between creating a new signifier in an act and creating a new signified in metaphor ought to be maintained. A metaphor exploits signifiers that are already recognizable by the Other. It just deploys them in an unusual way. An act (like a pun) creates a signifier whose place in the Other itself is not assured, a signifier without well-established links to other signifiers that might be able to provide it with meaning. The signifier used in an act (and the phrase "We want our rights," in Badiou's discussion, can be taken as a signifier) is something less than an enigma, because it does not appear to be pregnant with any sense at all. It appears to be nonsensical, and yet it could make sense. So this is why I am saying that an act seems to bear more resemblance to the punning *pas-de-sens* than to metaphor.[4]

Conclusion

An act entails the demolition of the Other as a subject-supposed-to-know, the Other as a support of identification, capable of providing that treasure of treasures, recognition. Erik Porge wrote that an act performs a "désêtre" on the subject-supposed-to-know—a dismantling of its being, which raises the question of what remains of the Other after the act (2000, 273). Many of the themes Lacan proposed for thinking about the end of analysis in the 1970s can be understood as attempts to think about the end of analysis in the wake of the act's voiding of the Other. These themes tend to involve the possibility of using signifiers beyond recognition and meaning, using signifiers "without" the Other, if you will; signifiers that would, Lacan felt, "be like the real" insofar as the production of sense is not a factor for them (XXIV, *Ornicar?*, 17/18: 21). Hence Lacan's interest in Joyce in this period, which I think is representative of his long-standing interest in what could be called a quasi-asocial use of signifiers.

Yet there are some important questions concerning the relationship between the notion of the act and some of the other ways in which Lacan thought about the end of a psychoanalytic cure, and in particular I would like to address how the notions of "*bien dire*" ("saying it well") and "*savoir y fair avec le symptome*" (a "know-how with the symptom") relate to what I have been saying about the act. In his 1997-1998 seminar *Le partenaire-symptome*, Jacques-Alain Miller claimed that the act is a negative counterpart to the fantasy in Lacanian theory—the psychoanalytic act is an act against the fundamental fantasy, in the form of a traversal (1997–1998, 3/4/98). Understood this way, the act suggests a crossing, a going beyond, a stepping out and into a previously inaccessible and nonsubjectified region (which we can quickly abbreviate here as the real). This suggests that fantasy is a barrier against the real, or a talisman against jouissance, while an act risks an encounter with the real. In seminar seven, Lacan had struggled with what it is that analysis is to do with the real, if anything at all—should distance be kept from it or not? Miller claims that after seminar seven, Lacan became interested in how psychoanalysis does something to the real with words, how it is able to affect this inaccessible region by means of signifiers (3/4/98). But by seminar twenty, from 1973 to 1974, Lacan is addressing another problem, in which it is no longer the opposition between fantasy and the real or jouissance that is central but an opposition between jouissance and the Other. The notion of the fundamental fantasy seems to drop out of the picture, and the notion of the sinthome emerges in its place.

The sinthome is a symptom that is a joining together of jouissance and the Other—the Other this time not as a subject-supposed-to-know but as the split, desiring Other.[1] The sinthome is thus an articulation of signifiers that is invested in libidinally, and it thus brings together two things that are usually separated by an abyss in Lacanian theory: language and jouissance. This means that in the sinthome something of the Other is enjoyed; the Other of the sinthome is not simply the Other who recognizes meanings and identity. This is the basis for Miller's idea of the partner-symptom, according to which the sinthome is seen as our life partner, as a supplement that allows us to live. The Other in Lacanian theory had always been construed as the treasure trove of signifiers and was often portrayed as a barrier to jouissance. In the sinthome, the Other is an Other possessed by or infused with enjoyment, such that signifiers themselves can be said to deliver enjoyment.

I want to consider the implications that this shift in Lacanian theory has for the notion of the act as a signifying process. When signifiers are themselves portrayed as "modes of enjoying," when language itself is perceived to be an "apparatus of jouissance," as is clearly the case by seminar twenty, Miller claims that the framework that had been used since seminar seven for thinking about the end of analysis had to be revised. The problem presented by the sinthome is not that of a disturbance caused by an inaccessible jouissance on its "other side," so to speak. The sinthome is already a way of enjoying—a way of enjoying with and through signifiers. Thus traversing the fantasy may not be the appropriate way of understanding what is at stake in the analytic cure. While one might expect that there is something to be met with on the other side of fantasy—namely, an encounter with the drives—on the other side of the sinthome, Miller argues, lies something more like a structural impossibility, having to do with the signifying impasse presented by sexuality as such. In other words, where a fantasy possesses and establishes a relationship to the Other's desire, the sinthome is the mark of a permanent nonrelation to the Other, yet it uses the Other, in the form of signifiers, to address the impasse that sexuality poses. The problem presented by the sinthome then is not about whether a relation to language has rendered the real inaccessible, or whether the real is too near or too far, so to speak. Instead, the problem presented by the sinthome is a problem of the articulation of a signifying impossibility (3/4/98). This is why "crossing" the sinthome in a psychoanalysis would be senseless, for there is nothing to meet on the other side of it but an abyss. Dissolving the sinthome would amount to an unraveling of the Borromean consistency that holds the subject "together," as it were.

The famous question Lacan asks at the end of seminar eleven—How can one live the drive after traversing fantasy?—is accordingly revised by Miller into a question about how one can live the drive without the sinthome. Miller takes Lacan's final answer to be that one cannot (12/10/97). And, according to Miller, this is why Lacan starts thinking about the analytic cure as a "savoir y faire" with the sinthome (XXIV, *Ornicar?*, 12/13: 7; 14: 5). Promoting a know-how, or, "knowing how to manage," with the sinthome as the end of analysis does suggest that the sinthome's presence is ineradicable, and rather than doing something to the sinthome itself (dissolving it, adjusting it), what is aimed at is a different subjective orientation toward the sinthome.

Miller takes Lacan's later approaches to the end of analysis to be attempts to illuminate the ways in which analysis can do something to or at the level of the real, which configures analysis as something other than an activity geared around a mere manipulation and production of signifiers, via free association and interpretation. Yet it seems that these later approaches can still be linked back to the older notion of the act. Miller tries to contrast the act to a "savoir faire" because of what happens with libidinal investment in each; he reads the act as a disinvestment of fantasy and reads a "savoir faire" with the sinthome as a reinvestment in the sinthome. From this perspective, the act suffers for being too symbolic an approach to the end of analysis, an approach that is appropriate perhaps if fantasy is the central issue or obstacle in analysis but not enough when the sinthome, and the different problems the sinthome presents, is seen as the central issue.

MILLER ON *BIEN DIRE*

This difference between the act as a disinvestment in fantasy and the later versions of the end of analysis as reinvestments in strange, de-Othered signifiers is also addressed in Miller's discussion of another way Lacan described the analytic cure in the 1970s—that of "*bien dire*," or speaking/saying [it] well. Miller proposes two understandings of the cure as a bien dire. One consists of taking *bien dire* to mean that something relatively simple is to be said in as elaborate and artsy a fashion as possible. This is the "classicist" approach to *bien dire* and is something that Lacan seems to have adhered to in his writings. One way to see how this could be an analytic ethic is to take it to mean "keep talking," keep symbolizing. The other, more relevant way of understanding *bien dire*, Miller claims, is to take it not as an attempt to provide a series of skillful variations on the same theme (making a multiplicity out of one, if you will) but as a crystallization or condensation of many disparate signifying strands into one theme (*e pluribus unum*). The idea here is that what emerges in the course of an analysis is at some point able to be reduced into something like a formula, a succinct signifying chain, and thus, effectively, "well put."

This latter understanding of *bien dire* makes the end of analysis sound not unlike a formation of the unconscious: it is a result, or product, generated in response to some libidinal difficulty, that can be understood to contain some level of libidinal investment and provide some new satisfaction for the analysand. Indeed, Miller compares his understanding of *bien dire* to one of the classical Freudian formations of the unconscious—the witticism. A pun, as we have seen, is a condensation of several signifiers into one new signifier. The end of analysis can be seen, similarly, as a condensation of a series of familiar, repeated signifiers into a new one. In an analysis, the analysand brings forth the "elements of his history" and condenses all of it into what Miller calls "*le bien dire d'un Witz*" ("the well-said of a witticism") (4/29/98). This account of *bien dire* as a formation of the unconscious is obviously very close to the way I have described the act and would be an accurate way of considering Xénophon's production of the new signifier "star-crosses" in chapter 3 as well as the production of the signifier "We want our rights" studied in chapter 8.

Yet it is true that Lacan associates the act with a traversal of fantasy, and these examples have little to do with a traversal of fantasy. Miller's contention is that the analytic act in Lacanian theory was thought primarily as traversal, and thus as negation, as disinvestment. As we have seen, this is also how Žižek describes the act. If the fantasy is something in which one makes oneself subject, in which there is some procurement of enjoyment that comes along with a position recognized by the Other, then the disinvestment in question in an act is a separation from this position. Thus an act would entail a dissolution of the subject of fantasy and its replacement by a new subject. But what, if anything, does an act do to something like a sinthome?

Nothing at all, according to Miller. The sinthome does not budge after the libidinal disinvestment in fantasy that characterizes an act. What the act, thought of as a libidinal disinvestment in the fundamental fantasy, does not affect is the sinthome as a kernel of enjoyed meaning. The act may traverse fantasy and decompose both the subject of fantasy and the Other, but, Miller contends, it would not touch the sinthome. Nor should it, as far as he is concerned. Miller promotes the practice of *bien dire*, then, since it takes what was going on in the act yet addresses what is at stake in the sinthome—the union of a signifying articulation and a libidinal investment in signifiers, in contrast to what he sees as the act's mere disarticulation of the fundamental fantasy.

This is a helpful correction, but I do not think it requires a complete abandonment of the notion of the analytic act. One important thing about the act as Lacan portrays it is that the subject is an effect of it and does not produce it. I still think that it is important to keep this in mind, lest something fundamental be misunderstood about what happens during a psychoanalytic cure—as well as elsewhere, in those moments when we humans, now and then, find ourselves in the process of an act. I have been arguing that an act offers a way of thinking about manifestations of freedom without the usual presupposition of a sovereign, conscious subject exercising the freedom, or a structure of some type exercising its freedom in the subject's place. An act is a production of the unconscious, which is, of course, not an irrational thing but a calculating, thoughtful thing—if it can be called a thing at all.

It should be kept in mind that the thinking that is done consciously is not without relation to the work of the unconscious. Recall Freud's claim that what is said about a dream when awake, when communicating it to someone or thinking about it, still needs to be taken as part of the dream itself, part of the same production of the unconscious![2] While an act is signifying, and very much an affair of signifiers, it is not the result of a decision or an act of will or any conscious deliberation but should be seen as a production of the unconscious, a production whose conditions for emergence can be enhanced by certain things (such as what goes on in analytic discourse). Despite being an "affair of signifiers," an act is of course not without its libidinal components as well. Lacan's notions of *bien dire* and *savoir faire* may be better suited for addressing this libidinal aspect of the analytic cure, as Miller claims, but both notions still rely on a production of signifiers that is similar to the act as it has been studied here.

I would like to present two more instances that will highlight how signifiers and a libidinal jouissance come together in an act. In a discussion of repetition in analysis, from "Remembering, Repeating, and Working-Through," Freud mentions how repetition takes the place of remembering at times, such that a patient may not remember how, for example, he came to "a helpless and hopeless deadlock in his infantile sexual researches" (1958 [1914g], 150). Instead of remembering this failed research, the patient has "a mass of confused dreams and associations" that are just repetitions of the earlier deadlock (ibid.). This is an interesting and a rather tangential way of getting at the meaning of these dreams. Freud tells us that the meaning of these dreams is not to be found by plumbing the depths of their confused content. Rather, it is to be found in the simple, superficial fact that the dreams themselves are confused. They are enigmas, and the suggestion that there is a deeper, hidden meaning to the dream that has yet to be revealed is the very point of the dream. This creation of an aura of inaccessible meaning is where the dream can be read as a repetition of an original deadlock or impossibility—namely, the patient's failure in childhood to find an answer in his or her researches into the enigma of sexual reality. The confused and enigmatic dream repeats the enigma that was sexuality itself for the child.

In the Geneva Conference on the symptom, from 1975, Lacan makes a similar point about symptom formation. Psychoanalytic theory generally approaches the symptom as a solution to a libidinal impasse, a solution that consists of constructing a meaning where there was an abyssal lack of meaning. Lacan's account of symptom formation at the Geneva Conference differs from this typical account when it indicates that prior to such a construction of meaning there needs to be an investment and satisfaction in a use of signifiers as such. In this particular discussion of the origin of symptoms, Lacan refers us to early childhood and the way in which children use signifiers such as "perhaps" and "not yet" before they are able to use them properly, or before, one assumes, they know what they mean (Lacan 1988, 14). What is noteworthy about the use of such signifiers by children is that this use is not about meaning. That is, it seems to be a highly imitative use of language, a use of signifiers precisely as enigmas received from the Other and then offered back to the Other by the child. As Lacan describes it, signifiers such as "perhaps" and "not yet" are good examples of the "detritus" that the ocean of language throws up at the child—strange signifiers that end up in a child's hands, like those strange, unidentifiable, and sometimes intimidating objects that wash up on the seashore. A child's use of such signifiers ought to be seen more as a mere wielding of signifiers and less as an attempt to probe the meaning of the signifiers themselves.

Of course, these enigmatic signifiers are not the only enigmas confronted in childhood. Lacan points out that along with the detritus of language itself comes something that "terrifies" the child, an enigma that Lacan calls at this conference "sexual reality" (ibid.). The circumstances surrounding this confluence of two enigmas, language and sexuality, were studied in chapter 4. Lacan seems to think that a child's major achievement is the construction of an answer to these two enigmas that consists of fusing the two enigmas, making one enigma answer the other. This is the kind of signifying articulation combined with a libidinal investment, quite apart from the pursuit of meaning and recognition of identity, that is exactly what the notion of the sinthome is trying to get at, as well as, in part, the notion of the act.

This description of symptom formation sounds very structuralist, and it evokes the way in which Lévi-Strauss describes the function of myths in his famous essay on the Oedipus cycle in "The Structural Study of Myth." According to Lévi-Strauss, myths should not be seen as proto-scientific attempts to explain the natural world. The purpose of mythologizing, according to Lévi-Strauss, is more symbolic or cultural than that. In myths, one social or cultural problem is solved with another social or cultural problem or, rather, by simply putting two problems together a myth creates the effect of a solution, when it is really just a matter of bringing an impasse into articulation (1963, 229). This seems to be the very thing Lacan was trying to get at with his later approaches to the end of analysis—when, as Miller puts it, he was interested in bringing the articulation of signifiers together with a libidinal investment.

One of the problems explored in my closing chapters was the question of what remains of the Other after the act, and what can be done with what could be considered a de-Othered symbolic. Miller claims that in the sinthome one forms a partnership with something of the Other at the level of enjoyment—one enjoys the Other through one's sinthome, and this enjoyed Other, which seems to occur in the form of an "enjoyed meaning" or sens-jouis, is contrasted to the Other as a site that guarantees meaning and confers recognition. What happens after the voiding of the Other is that rather than an investment in fantasy, which is mediated by the Other, there is a direct investment in signifiers as such; and it is on this basis that a partnership with the Other, on the level of enjoyment, is forged. Although Miller arrives at these conclusions through his study of the role of the sinthome in Lacanian theory, they also describe very well the space of freedom posited by the act in Lacanian theory.

Notes

CHAPTER 1

1. In his article "Subversion of the Subject," Lacan describes the Other as the "signifying battery," but, as we will see, this is not all that is to be understood by the Other (Lacan 1966, 806/Lacan 2002, 293).

CHAPTER 2

1. I should mention that it is nearly impossible to maintain a rigorous distinction among these concepts, and that Lacan did not have such a goal in mind when discussing them. Of course, a trace is never entirely self-sufficient. It is dependent in a certain sense upon what caused it, and it at least depends upon its surroundings in order to be noticed as a trace distinct from anything else. The concept "trace" that is being used in this chapter is simply heuristic. I am using it, as Lacan did, to explain what signs and signifiers are. If one simply abstracts from a trace's dependence upon its context or environment, then one has what can be considered a self-sufficient entity. This is, admittedly, only an abstraction. Similarly, a radical distinction between the sign and the signifier is difficult to maintain. As a matter of fact, the primary concept here is "signifier," and "sign" and "trace" have to be seen as derivations of this concept. However, for the purposes of explaining what a signifier is, it is better to start out with concepts such as "trace" and "sign," which are more easily understood.

2. The same definition can be found in Peirce's work. Lacan credits his source in seminar seven: "The sign, as Peirce put it, is that which is in the place of something else for someone" (VII, 110/91).

3. Derrida's essay "La différance" reminds us that whatever kind of presence a signifier could be said to have, it could not be a simple presence. What is a presentation of pure difference if not a presence that perpetually cancels itself out, and is thus no more present than it is absent (1982, 3–27)? This is exactly the condition of the Lacanian signifier. In his fourteenth seminar, in fact, Lacan argues that "it is of the nature of any and every signifier not to be able to signify itself" (XIV, 11/16/66). All of this leads me to wonder whether the signifier has any manner of presentation at all, other than a self-effacing or vanishing presence.

4. As I will go on to argue, Lacan is clearly using a Saussurean idea of language here. But there are also some Heideggerian echoes to this theory. Heidegger says the following about signs: "Signs are not things which stand in an indicating relationship to another thing but are *useful things which explicitly bring a totality of useful things to circumspection so that the worldly character of what is at hand makes itself known at the same time*" (1996 [1927], 80/74, emphasis in original). Every sign actually makes present an entire "referential totality." This applies more to Lacan's understanding of the signifier than to his understanding of the sign of course.

5. Lacan himself uses this term in his fifth seminar and in "The Signification of the Phallus." Lacan said of the phallus there: "C'est le signifiant destiné à designer dans leur ensemble les effets de signifié, en tant que le signifiant les conditionne par sa présence signifiante" (Lacan 1966, 690). Sheridan translates this as "It [the phallus] is the signifier intended to designate as a whole the effects of the signified, in that the signifier conditions them by its presence as a signifier" (Lacan 2002, 285). Rose gives this passage as "For it is to this signified [*sic*] that it is given to designate as a whole the effect of there being a signified, inasmuch as it conditions any such effect by its presence as signifier" (Lacan 1985, 80). Despite the typo in Rose's translation, making what should be "signifier" into "signified," I believe that her rendering of this passage—"the effect of there being a signified"—is better than Sheridan's "the effects of the signified." The latter is misleading, since it gives the impression that there is a signified that has effects proper to it. It is rather the case that the signified is nothing other than the effect of there being a signified, somewhere. For "les effets de signifié" I would propose the awkward but I hope clear translation "signified effects." Fink uses "meaning effects" in this passage: "It is the signifier that is destined to designate meaning effects as a whole, insofar as the signifier conditions them by its presence as signifier" (Lacan 2002, 275).

6. Thus I cannot follow Marc Darmon, who tries to make Saussure closer to Lacan than he really is. Saussure, Darmon writes, "is opposed to a conception of language as nomenclature" (1990, 17). This is true. For Saussure, the primary function of language is not simply to name or designate objects. But Darmon cannot justify his next point, I believe: "Lacan is thus toeing the line of [*c'est dans le droit fil de*] Saussure's discovery when he writes the algorithm S/*s*, signifier over the signified [. . .]. Lacan posits that this separation of two distinct orders by a bar is the only thing that allows for a study of

the connections proper to the signifier and the function of these connections in the genesis of the signified" (1990, 18). It is this idea of a "genesis of the signified" that Saussure would not have allowed for, making Lacan's position something other than a toeing of the Saussurean line. Lacoue-Labarthe and Nancy are right here: The Lacanian signifier entails the destruction of the Saussurean sign (1992, 34).

7. In his later work, Lacan makes an important distinction between the letter and the signifier that modifies this position a bit. It is indeed the case that no particular signified is necessarily attached to a signifier, but it is also the case that a signifier seems to be always in fact caught up in the production of some signified effect. Signifiers are essentially differential units. As such, they are what they are only in their relation to other signifiers. This means that a signifier is always in fact included in an, at least, implicit chain of signifiers (a reference of one signifier to another, and so on). Thus it seems that the signifier is never able to be removed from the production of meanings and signified effects. Lacan uses the idea of a "letter" to speak of a unit that would be outside of the production of meaning, "outside" in a way that a signifier never really can be, even if it is as such meaningless. Thus he explains that a letter is "in the real, and the signifier, in the symbolic" (XVIII, 5/12/71). The symbolic is an order of signifiers and signifying productions, and the real at this point in Lacan's work is $real_2$, an impasse for signification, or an impasse of formalization (XX, 85/93). According to this view, the letter would be something like a signifier's return to the state of a trace. It would be a signifier beyond any possible production of a signification. For further discussion of this issue, see Hoens and Pluth (2002, 19).

8. *Synecdoche* is usually the term given for a figure of speech in which a part replaces a whole. *Metonymy* is usually described as being closely related to but different from synecdoche. Metonymy applies more often to cases involving proper names or place names: "Washington" serves as a name for the federal government, "Shakespeare" for an entire oeuvre.

9. The resemblance of this example to the famous joke from Freud's *Jokes and Their Relation to the Unconscious* is not coincidental: "Two Jews met in a train at a Galician railway station. 'Where are you traveling?' asked one. 'To Cracow,' was the reply. 'Now see here, what a liar you are!' said the first one, bristling. 'When you say that you are traveling to Cracow, you really wish me to believe you are traveling to Lemberg. Well, but I am sure that you are really traveling to Cracow, so why lie about it?'" (1960a [1905c], 115).

10. It could just as well be said that what distinguishes a signifier from a sign is the fact that the former brings a "signified effect" with it. A sign does something else: it has a referent, even though a sign is ultimately subject to the same conditions as the signifier.

11. See François Raffoul's article on this topic, "Lacan and the Event of the Subject" (1998). In the third part of the article he argues for a reading of the unconscious, according to which the subject of the unconscious cannot be

taken to be a substance or hypokeimenon and does not preexist signifiers. Thus the idea that the Lacanian subject is a mere reversal of the classical subject of consciousness, or a mere replacing of this subject, is argued against. Bruce Fink's (1995a) *The Lacanian Subject* also describes the subject as something that does not have a substantial consistency but the consistency of a flash between two signifiers. In chapter 7, I will be discussing in more detail what kind of consistency the subject might have.

12. See Colette Soler's discussion of Freud's forgetting the name Signorelli: "What Freud designates as unconscious, the forgotten name 'Signorelli,' while but a very minor example, is clearly not something that intends to express itself. The Freudian unconscious is not expression, and is only present in some failure of activity: speech, memory, or bodily action" (1996a, 44).

CHAPTER 3

1. I am saying that a subject is a particular kind of effect of signifiers on a real individual because it is possible for signifiers to have effects on an individual that do not bring about a subject. According to Lacan, psychosis is an example of such a phenomenon. One of the limitations of my study is that what is being said about the subject does not hold for the psychoses, and probably not for perversions either. This study is restricted to neuroses. For an informative, clear summary of Lacan's changing theories of psychosis, and how his theory is being applied and expanded on today, see Maleval's *La forclusion du nom-du-père* (2000).

2. Mathelin herself expresses some doubt about this diagnosis, and the end result of the cure leads one to wonder whether the child was ever really autistic in the strict sense.

3. Lacan calls the subject a barred subject, written "$," in order, among other things, to indicate the split condition of the subject as a product of the signifying chain. An explanation of in what sense, precisely, the subject is split is one of the goals of this chapter.

CHAPTER 4

1. It is often not clear whether one should write other with a lower-case "o" or Other with an upper-case "O" in a discussion of this aspect of Lacan's theory. I am following the practice of using other with the former when talking about a concrete other, another person, and Other with the latter when talking about the third-party position posited by making a demand, an Other beyond the other, if you will. Lacan, in fact, suggested the following English translation for "l'Autre": "the Otherness" (XIV, 1/25/67). During his trip to the United

States in 1966, Lacan found that there was some problem with the translation of "l'Autre" by "the Other." The definite article, he felt, led English speakers to believe that the term still referred to a particular other. Using "the Otherness" to translate "l'Autre" would remind us that Lacan's notion of "the Other" is a kind of reification of a property belonging to concrete others. In other words, it is an attribute of others that possesses a kind of independence, in much the way that language, in order to be studied as a system, needs to be abstracted from all particular language speakers. Lacan abstracts what is other about others when he speaks about "the Otherness."

Maybe there is some advantage to using "the Otherness" instead of "the Other." However, years of translations of Lacan's work into English make the introduction of such a term a bit senseless.

2. For a good reflection on this story, see Darian Leader's *Why Do Women Write More Letters Than They Post?* (1996, 102–103, 107–113).

3. See Lacan's similar discussion of this point in "D'une question préliminaire" (Lacan 1966, 579/Lacan 2002, 208).

4. Psychic structure is for Freud and Lacan governed by the pleasure principle. In Freudian terms, the aim of this principle is to keep excitation in the organism to a minimum, at an amount that is just enough for life to be sustained. In Lacan's terms, the pleasure principle is not a biological function but the rule of the psychic economy insofar as it is subjected to the signifying order: "The function of the pleasure principle is in fact to carry the subject from signifier to signifier, while putting as many signifiers as necessary to maintain the level of tension that rules over the entire functioning of the psychic apparatus at the lowest level" (VII, 143/119).

5. There is still much ambiguity about the relation between desire and drive in Lacanian theory. Often the two are conflated, or, even worse, the drive is seen to be something that derives from a more original desire. The latter error is committed by Richard Boothby in his work *Death and Desire.* For example, he claims that "the emergence of desire in the signifying chain brings with it a promise of jouissance" (1991, 109). I would point out that jouissance is far from being what desire hopes for, and it is certainly not something that desire even promises. Boothby motivates his union of desire and jouissance on the basis of the concept of the death drive, because Lacan at times links desire with death (1991, 17). On this basis, desire and jouissance can be associated with each other, since Boothby rightly sees that jouissance has something to do with the death drive. Yet it is surely not right to see the death drive as "a mythical expression of pure desire." Furthermore, Boothby sees the drive as merely "a specification or determination of desire in terms of selected organ functions [...] as such, no drive can exhaust the potentialities of desire" (1991, 57). This makes it sound like desire is a reservoir out of which the drives are constituted, or that a drive is the continuation of desire by other, lesser, more restricted means. Yet Lacan portrays desire as a defense against jouissance, which is the satisfaction of a drive (Lacan 1966, 825/Lacan 2002, 309). Bernard Baas also

refers to jouissance as the promise of desire's satisfaction, so Boothby is not alone. In fact, this misreading is quite common, and it is not a slight matter. Such a reading might lead one to think that Lacan is some sort of high priest of lack, which would overlook his emphasis on the "positivity" of the drives and jouissance—which would have little, if anything, to do with lack—in the constitution of every subject.

6. The reason for all the scare quotes here is that I am using energetic terms where they do not really apply. Lacan referred to Freud's energetics as Freud's mythology, which Lacan spoke of instead in terms of the real. The problem is that speaking in terms of the real at this point would only make matters less clear.

CHAPTER 5

1. The *Petit Robert* dictionary defines "Gribouille" as follows: It is the name of a naive and foolish character in French literature, who "stupidly throws himself into the very troubles, the very evils, that he wanted to avoid."

CHAPTER 6

1. "Toward a New Signifier" is a subtitle given by Jacques-Alain Miller to the May 17, 1977, session of Lacan's twenty-fourth seminar (XXIV, *Ornicar?*, 17/18: 19-23).

CHAPTER 7

1. A relation to the Other is obviously symbolic, insofar as it is a relation based on signifiers. But this relation can also be imaginary to the extent that these signifiers are "imaginarized" by being made into signifieds, for example, signifieds of what it is that the Other is supposed to desire.

2. It should be noted that Badiou does not tend to use the term *act* in his works but rather the phrase "truth-process."

CHAPTER 8

1. For a commentary on this and similar passages in Lacan's work, see Declercq and Verhaeghe's essay "Lacan's Analytic Goal: *Le sinthome* or the Feminine Way" (2002).

2. The position I am describing here is somewhat like the position Fred Evans is working out with his theory of the multivoiced body. Although Evans (2003) usually uses this idea to discuss societies and cultures, he does attempt to apply it to individuals. His theory is also against a transcendental approach to the subject, and I believe that it too tends to identify the subject with a multiple field of discourses, both possible and actual. While I can only agree with the desire to avoid transcendentalism, I am not sure that embracing radical immanence is without problems of its own, and here I am trying to explain why.

3. In this respect, the unconscious is now included in Butler's theory. Oddly, Butler refuses to admit that there is a subject of the unconscious: "It is important to distinguish between the notion of the psyche, which includes the notion of the unconscious, and that of the subject, whose formation is conditioned by the exclusion of the unconscious" (1997, 206n4).

4. This may sound odd, since Lacan often spoke of the connections between metaphor and the subject, for example, in the second appendix to his *Écrits*, entitled "La metaphore du sujet" (Lacan 1966, 889–892). This appendix explores the production of a subject as a meaning, an operation that is much more "metaphoric" than "metonymic." But my argument all along has been that with the ideas of traversing fantasy and act, Lacan adds a new dimension to the subject, more properly approached through the notion of the pun.

CONCLUSION

1. See Hoens and Pluth (2002) for a discussion of how the sinthome relates to other notions in Lacanian theory.

2. In "What If the Other Is Stupid?" Dominiek Hoens and I make a similar point about the prisoners in Lacan's essay on "Logical Time." It is not the case that the "moment of concluding" the interminable line of reasoning, during which the prisoners are trying to figure out, silently, whether a white or black disk has been placed on their backs by the sadistic game warden who will release the first prisoner to conclude correctly, emerges "ex nihilo," we say (2004, 187). We point out instead that the line of reasoning, although, strictly speaking, fruitless in the sense that it does not generate the right conclusion, is "not without" a relation to the conclusion, the point being that the moment of concluding would be entirely irrational without the line of reasoning that, nevertheless, does not lead up to it.

Bibliography

WORKS BY LACAN

The Seminars

Seminar I — *Le Séminaire, livre I: Les écrits techniques de Freud. 1953-1954*. Texte établi par Jacques-Alain Miller. Paris: Seuil, 1975. (English translation: *The Seminar of Jacques Lacan, Book I: Freud's Papers on Technique: 1953–1954*. Translated by John Forrester. New York: Norton, 1988.)

Seminar II — *Le Séminaire, livre II: Le moi dans la théorie de Freud et dans la technique de la psychanalyse*. 1954-1955. Texte établi par Jacques-Alain Miller. Paris: Seuil, 1978. (English translation: *The Seminar of Jacques Lacan, Book II: The Ego in Freud's Theory and in the Technique of Psychoanalysis: 1954–1955*. Translated by Sylvana Tomaselli. Notes by John Forrester. New York: Norton, 1991.)

Seminar III — *Le Séminaire, livre III: Les Psychoses*. 1955–1956. Texte établi par Jacques-Alain Miller. Paris: Seuil, 1981. (English translation: *The Seminar of Jacques Lacan, Book III: The Psychoses: 1955–1956*. Translated by Russell Grigg. New York: Norton, 1993.)

Seminar IV *Le Séminaire, livre IV: La relation d'objet*. 1956–1957. Texte établi par Jacques-Alain Miller. Paris: Seuil, 1994.

Seminar V *Le Séminaire, livre V: Les formations de l'inconscient*. 1957–1958. Texte établi par Jacques-Alain Miller. Paris: Seuil, 1998.

Seminar VI *Le désir et son interprétation*. (1958-1959). Unpublished.

Seminar VII *Le Séminaire, livre VII: L'Ethique de la psychanalyse*. 1959–1960. Texte établi par Jacques-Alain Miller. Paris: Seuil, 1986. (English translation: *The Seminar of Jacques Lacan, Book VII: The Ethics of Psychoanalysis: 1959–1960*. Translated by Dennis Porter. New York: Norton, 1992.)

Seminar VIII *Le Séminaire, livre VIII: Le transfert*. 1960–1961. Texte établi par Jacques-Alain Miller. Paris: Seuil, 1991.

Seminar IX *L'identification*. 1961–1962. Unpublished.

Seminar X *Le Séminaire, livre X: L'angoisse*. 1962–1963. Texte établi par Jacques-Alain Miller. Paris: Seuil, 2004.

Seminar XI *Le Séminaire, livre XI: Les quatre concepts fondamentaux de la psychanalyse*. 1964. Texte établi par Jacques-Alain Miller. Paris: Seuil, 1973. (English translation: *The Four Fundamental Concepts of Psychoanalysis*. Translated by Alan Sheridan. New York: Norton, 1978.)

Seminar XII *Problèmes cruciaux pour la psychanalyse*. 1964–1965. Unpublished.

Seminar XIII *L'objet de la psychanalyse*. 1965–1966. Unpublished.

Seminar XIV *La logique du fantasme*. 1966–1967. Unpublished.

Seminar XV *L'acte psychanalytique*. 1967–1968. Unpublished.

Seminar XVI *D'un Autre à l'autre*. 1968–1969. Unpublished.

Seminar XVII *Le Séminaire, livre XVII: L'envers de la psychanalyse*. 1969–1970. Texte établi par Jacques-Alain Miller. Paris: Seuil, 1991.

Seminar XVIII *D'un discours qui ne serait pas du semblant*. 1970–1971. Unpublished.

Seminar XIX . . . *ou pire*. 1971–1972. Unpublished.

Seminar XX *Le Séminaire, livre XX: Encore*. 1972–1973. Texte établi par Jacques-Alain Miller. Paris: Seuil, 1975. (English translation: *The Seminar of Jacques Lacan, Book XX: Encore: 1972–1973*. Translated by Bruce Fink. New York: Norton, 1998.)

Seminar XXI *Les non-dupes errent*. 1973–1974. Unpublished.

Seminar XXII *R.S.I.* Texte établi par Jacques-Alain Miller. *Ornicar?* 2 (1975): 87–105; 3 (1975): 95–110; 4 (1975): 91–106; 5 (1975): 15–66.

Seminar XXIII *Le Séminaire, livre XXIII: Le sinthome*. 1975–1976. Texte établi par Jacques-Alain Miller. Paris: Seuil, 2005.

Seminar XXIV *L'insu que sait de l'une-bévue, s'aile a mourre*. 1976–1977. Texte établi par Jacques-Alain Miller. Ornicar? 12/13 (1977): 4-16 ; 14 (1978): 4-9; 15 (1978): 5-9; 16 (1978): 7-13; 17/18 (1979): 7-23.

Seminar XXV *Le moment de conclure*. 1977–1978. Unpublished.

Seminar XXVI *La topologie et le temps*. 1978–1979. Unpublished.

Seminar XXVII *Dissolution*. 1979–1980. Unpublished.

ADDITIONAL WORKS BY LACAN

Lacan, Jacques. 1966. *Écrits*. Paris: Seuil (English translation: *Écrits: A Selection*. Translated by Bruce Fink. New York: Norton, 2002. Alternate translation: *Écrits: A Selection*. Translated by Alan Sheridan: Norton, 1977. Unless otherwise indicated, references are to Fink's translation.)

———. 1966b. "Réponses aux étudiantes en philosophie." *Cahiers pour l'analyse* 3: 5–13.

———. 1972. *Jacques Lacan. Conférence de Louvain suivie d'un entretien avec Françoise Wolff*. Videotape.

———. 1975a. "La troisième." *Lettres de l'École freudienne* 16: 177–203.

———. 1975b. *Télévision*. Paris: Seuil.

———. 1976. "Kanzer Seminar," in "Conférences et Entretiens dans des universités nord-américaines." Scilicet 6/7: 7–31.

———. 1985. *Feminine Sexuality*. Edited by Juliet Mitchell and Jacqueline Rose. New York: Norton.

———. 1986. "Conférence de Bruxelles sur l'éthique de la psychanalyse." *Psychanalyse: Revue de l'école belge de psychanalyse* 4: 163-187. (Conference delivered on March 9, 1960.)

———. 1988. "Conférence à Genève sur la symptôme. Geneva Lecture on the Symptom." *Le Bloc-notes de la psychanalyse* 5: 5–23 (Translated by Russell Grigg. *Analysis* 1/7: 1989: 7–26.)

———. 1996. "Position of the Unconscious." Translated by Bruce Fink. *Reading Seminar XI*. Edited by Richard Feldstein, Bruce Fink, and Maire Jaanus. Albany: State University of New York Press.

———. 2001. *Autres écrits*. Paris: Seuil.

ADDITIONAL REFERENCES

André, Serge. 1995. *Que veut une femme?* Paris: Seuil.

Althusser, Louis. 1971. *Lenin and Philosophy and Other Essays*. Translated by Ben Brewster. London: NLB.

———. 1993. *Écrits sur la psychanalyse: Freud et Lacan*. Paris: Stock/IMEC.

Baas, Bernard. 1992. *Le désir pur*. Louvain: Peeters.

———. 1998. *De la chose à l'objet*. Louvain: Peeters.

Baas, Bernard, and Armand Zaloszyc. 1988. *Descartes et les fondements de la psychanalyse*. Paris: Navarin Osiris.

Badiou, Alain. 1968. "La subversion infinitésimale." *Cahiers pour l'analyse* 9: 118–37.

———. 1969a. *Le concept de modèle*. Paris: François Maspero.

———. 1969b. "Marque et manque." *Cahier pour l'analyse* 10: 150–73.

———. 1975. *Théorie de la contradiction*. Paris: François Maspero.

———. 1982. *Théorie du sujet*. Paris: Seuil.

———. 1985. *Peut-on penser la politique?* Paris: Seuil.

———. 1988. *L'être et l'événement*. Paris: Seuil.

———. 1989. *Manifeste pour la philosophie*. Paris: Seuil.

———. 1991. "On a Finally Objectless Subject." Translated by Bruce Fink. In *Who Comes After the Subject?*, ed. Peter Connor et al., 24–32. New York: Routledge.

———. 1993. *L'éthique: Essai sur la conscience du Mal.* Paris: Hatier.

———. 1996a. "Descartes/Lacan." Translated by Sigi Jöttkandt and Daniel Collins. *Umbra* 1: 3–17.

———. 1996b. "Psychoanalysis and Philosophy." Translated by Raphael Comprone and Marcus Coelen. *Umbra* 1: 19–26.

———. 1997. *Saint Paul: La fondation de l'universalisme.* Paris, PUF.

———. 1998. *Court traité d'ontologie transitoire.* Paris: Seuil.

Badiou, Alain, and François Balmès. 1976. *De l'idéologie.* Paris: François Maspero.

Badiou, Alain, Joël Bellassen, and Louis Mossot. 1978. *Le noyau rationnel de la dialectique Hégélienne: Traductions, introductions, et commentaires autour d'un texte de Zhang Shiying (Pékin, 1972).* Paris: François Maspero.

Barnard, Suzanne, and Bruce Fink, eds. 2002. *Reading Seminar XX.* Albany: State University of New York Press.

Bernard-DeSoria, Odile. 1992. *Autisme et psychoses d'enfants.* Paris: Soleil Carré.

Bernet, Rudolf. 1993. "Imagination et fantasme." In *L'homme et ses destins*, ed. Antone Vergote. Louvain. Peeters. 191–208.

———. 1994. *La vie du sujet.* Paris: Presses Universities de France.

Boothby, Richard. 1991. *Death and Desire.* New York: Routledge.

Borch-Jacobsen, Mikkel. 1991. *Lacan: The Absolute Master.* Stanford, CA: Stanford University Press.

Braunstein, Nestor. 1992. *La jouissance: Un concept lacanien.* Cahors France: Point Hors Ligne.

Brousse, Marie-Hélène. 1995a. "The Drive (I)." In *Reading Seminar XI*, ed. Richard Feldstein, Bruce Fink, and Maire Jaanus. Albany: State University of New York Press. 99–108.

———. 1995b. "The Drive (II)." In *Reading Seminar XI*, ed. Richard Feldstein, Bruce Fink, and Maire Jaanus. Albany: State University of New York Press. 109–118.

Butler, Judith. 1990. *Gender Trouble.* New York: Routledge.

———. 1993. *Bodies That Matter.* New York: Routledge.

———. 1997. *The Psychic Life of Power*. Stanford, CA: Stanford University Press.

Butler, Judith, Ernesto Laclau, and Slavoj Žižek. 2000. *Contingency, Hegemony, Universality*. London: Verso.

Cadava, Eduardo, Peter Connor, and Jean-Luc Nancy Eds. 1991. *Who Comes After the Subject*? New York: Routledge.

Carroll, Lewis. 1998. *Alice's Adventures in Wonderland and Through the Looking-Glass*. Edited and Introduction by Hugh Haughton. London: Penguin.

Charraud, Nathalie. 1997. *Lacan et les mathématiques*. Paris: Anthropos.

Copjec, Joan. 1994. *Read My Desire*. Cambridge: MIT Press.

———. 1999, "The Tomb of Perseverance: On *Antigone*." In *The Politics of Propinquity*, ed. Joan Copjec. New York: Verso. 233–266.

Critchley, Simon. 1999. *Ethics, Politics, Subjectivity*. London: Verso.

———. 2000. "On Alain Badiou." *Theory and Event*. 3:4: 43 pars. http://www. muse.jhu.edu/journals/theory_&_event/v003/3.4_ critchley.html

Darmon, Marc. 1990. *Essais sur la topologie lacanienne*. Paris: Editions de l'Association Freudienne.

Declercq, Frédérique. 2000. *Het reële bij Lacan*. Gent: Idesça.

Declercq, Frédérique, and Paul Verhaeghe. 2002. "Lacan's Analytic Goal: *Le Sinthome* or the Feminine Way." In *Re-inventing the Symptom*, ed. Luke Thurston. New York: The Other Press. 59–83.

De Kesel, Marc. 2002. *Eros en ethiek: Een lectuur van Jacques Lacans Séminaire VII*. Leuven: Acco.

Deleuze, Gilles. 1993. *The Deleuze Reader*. Edited and Introduction by Constantin Boundas. New York: Columbia University Press.

Derrida, Jacques. 1976. *Of Grammatology*. Translated by Gayatri Chakravorty Spivak. Baltimore, MD: Johns Hopkins University Press.

———. 1981. Positions. Translated by Alan Bass. Chicago: University of Chicago Press.

———. 1982. *Margins of Philosophy*. Translated by Alan Bass. Chicago: University of Chicago Press.

———. 1991. "'Eating Well,'" or the Calculation of the Subject: An Interview with Jacques Derrida." In *Who Comes After the Subject?*, ed. Eduardo Cadava, Peter Connor, and Jean-Luc Nancy. (Interview translated by Peter Connor and Avital Ronell). New York: Routledge. 95–119.

———. 1998. *Resistances of Psychoanalysis*. Translated by Peggy Kamuf, Pascale-Anne Brault, and Michael Naas. Stanford, CA: Stanford University Press.

Derrida, Jacques, and Elisabeth Roudinesco. 2001. *De quoi demain . . . : Dialogue*. Paris: Fayard/Galilée.

Dufour, Dany-Robert. 1998. *Lacan et le miroir sophianique de Boehme*. Paris: Les Éditions et Publications de l'École Lacanienne.

Dunand, Anne. 1995a. "The End of Analysis (I)." In *Reading Seminar XI*, ed. Richard Feldstein, Bruce Fink, and Maire Jaanus. Albany: State University of New York Press, 243–250.

———. 1995b. "The End of Analysis (II)." In *Reading Seminar XI*, ed. Richard Feldstein, Bruce Fink, and Maire Jaanus. Albany: State University of New York Press, 251–258.

Evans, Fred. 2003. "Witnessing and the Social Unconscious." *Studies in Practical Philosophy: A Journal of Ethical and Political Philosophy* 3:2: 57–83.

Feldstein, Richard, Bruce Fink, and Maire Jaanus. 1995. *Reading Seminar XI*. Albany: State University of New York Press.

———. 1996. *Reading Seminars I and II*. Albany: State University of New York Press.

Felman, Shoshana. 1983. *The Literary Speech Act*. Translated by Catherine Porter. Ithaca, NY: Cornell University Press.

Fink, Bruce. 1995a. *The Lacanian Subject*. Princeton, NJ: Princeton University Press.

———. 1995b. "The Real Cause of Repetition." In *Reading Seminar XI*, ed. Richard Feldstein, Bruce Fink, and Maire Jaanus, Albany: State University of New York Press, 223–232.

———. 1996a. "Alain Badiou." *Umbra* 1: 11–12.

———. 1996b. "Logical Time and the Precipitation of Subjectivity." *Reading Seminars I and II*, ed. Richard Feldstein, Bruce Fink, and Maire Jaanus, Albany: State University of New York Press, 356–386.

———. 1996c. "The Subject and the Other's Desire." In *Reading Seminars I and II*, ed. Richard Feldstein, Bruce Fink, and Maire Jaanus, Albany: State University of New York Press, 76–97.

———. 1998. *A Clinical Introduction to Lacanian Psychoanalysis*. Cambridge, MA: Harvard University Press.

———. 2004. *Lacan to the Letter*. Minneapolis: University of Minnesota Press.

Foucault, Michel. 1972. *The Archaeology of Knowledge*. Translated by Alan Sheridan. New York: Harper.

———. 2001. "Espace, savoir, et pouvoir." (Entretien avec P. Rabinow. Trad. F. Durand-Bogaert). *Skyline* (March 1982): 16–20. In *Dits et Ecrits II: 1976–1988*. Manchecourt: Gallimard.

Freud, Sigmund. 1955 [1920g]. *Beyond the Pleasure Principle. The Standard Edition. Volume XVIII*. Translated and edited by James Strachey. London: Hogarth Press, 3–64.

———. 1955b [1921c]. *Group Psychology and the Analysis of the Ego. The Standard Edition. Volume XVIII*. Translated and edited by James Strachey. London: Hogarth Press, 69–143.

———. 1958 [1914g]. "Remembering, Repeating, and Working-Through." *The Standard Edition. Volume XII*. Translated and edited by James Strachey. London: Hogarth Press, 145–56.

———. 1960a [1905c]. *Jokes and Their Relation to the Unconscious. The Standard Edition. Volume VIII*. Translated and edited by James Strachey. London: Hogarth Press.

———. 1960b [1901b]. *The Psychopathology of Everyday Life. The Standard Edition. Volume VI*. Translated and edited by James Strachey. London: Hogarth Press.

———. 1961a [1919e]. "A Child Is Being Beaten: A Contribution to the Study of the Origin of Sexual Perversions." *The Standard Edition. Volume XVII*. Translated and edited by James Strachey. London: Hogarth Press, 179–204.

———. 1961b [1925h]. "Negation." *The Standard Edition. Volume XIX*. Translated and edited by James Strachey. London: Hogarth Press, 235–39.

———. 1961c [1915d]. "Repression." *The Standard Edition. Volume XIV*. Translated and edited by James Strachey. London: Hogarth Press, 146–58.

———. 1961d [1915e]. "The Unconscious." *The Standard Edition. Volume XIV*. Translated and edited by James Strachey. London: Hogarth Press, 166–215.

Freud, Sigmund, and Wilhelm Fliess. 1985. *The Complete Letters of Sigmund Freud and Wilhelm Fliess*. Translated and edited by Jeffrey Mousaieff Masson. Cambridge, MA: Harvard University Press.

Gilson, Jean-Paul. 1994. *La topologie de Lacan*. Montréal: Editions Balzac.

———. (n.d.). *La topologie Lacanienne: une présentation du sujet*. Ecole lacanienne de Montréal. http://www.elm.qc.ca/Topologie/topologie_lacanienne.html

Granon-Lafont, Jeanne. 1997. *La topologie ordinarie de Jacques Lacan*. Cahors, France: Points Hors Ligne.

Green, André. 1983. *Narcissisme de vie, narcissisme de mort*. Paris: Les Editions de Minuit.

Grigg, Russell. 1991. "Signifier, Object, and the Transference." In *Lacan and the Subject of Language*, ed. Ellie Ragland-Sullivan and Mark Bracher. New York: Routledge, 100–115.

Hallward, Peter. 2003. *Badiou: A Subject to Truth*. Minneapolis: University of Minnesota Press.

———. 2004. *Think Again: Alain Badiou and the Future of Philosophy*. London: Continuum.

Harasym, Sarah, ed. 1998. *Lévinas and Lacan: The Missed Encounter*. Albany: State University of New York Press.

Heidegger, Martin. 1996 [1927]. *Being and Time*. Translated by Joan Stambaugh. Albany: State University of New York Press.

Hoens, Dominiek, and Ed Pluth. 2002. "Sinthome: A New Way of Writing an Old Problem?" In *Re-inventing the Symptom*, ed. Luke Thurston. New York: The Other Press, 1–18.

———. 2004. "Working Through as a Truth Procedure." *Miracles Do Happen. Communication and Cognition*. 37:4, 279–292.

Julien, Philippe. 1990. *Le retour à Freud de Jacques Lacan*. Paris: Les Éditions et Publications de l'École Lacanienne.

Kant, Immanuel. 1965 [1787]. *Critique of Pure Reason*. Translated by Norman Kemp Smith. New York: St. Martin's Press.

Kristeva, Julia. 1996. *Sens et non-sens de la révolte: Pouvoirs et limites de la psychanalyse I*. Paris: Fayard (Livres de poche).

———. 1997. *La révolte intime: Pouvoirs et limites de la psychanalyse II*. Paris: Fayard (Livres de poche).

1991. *Lacan avec les philosophes*. Paris: Albin Michel.

Lacoue-Labarthe, Philippe, and Jean-Luc Nancy. 1992. *The Title of the Letter*. Translated by François Raffoul and David Pettigrew. Albany: State University of New York Press.

Laplanche, Jean. 1970. *Vie et mort en psychanalyse*. Manchecourt: Champs/Flammarion.

Laplanche, Jean, and J.-B. Pontalis. 1967. *Vocabulaire de la psychanalyse*. Paris: Presses Universitaires de France.

Laurent, Eric. 1995a. "Alienation and Separation (I)." In *Reading Seminar XI*, ed. Richard Feldstein, Bruce Fink, and Maire Jaanus. Albany: State University of New York Press.

———. 1995b. "Alienation and Separation (II)." In *Reading Seminar XI*, ed. Richard Feldstein, Bruce Fink, and Maire Jaanus. Albany: State University of New York Press.

Lavendhomme, René. 2001. *Lieux du sujet*. Paris: Seuil.

Leader, Darian. 1996. *Why Do Women Write More Letters Than They Post?* London: Faber and Faber.

Leclaire, Serge. 1971. *Démasquer le réel*. Paris: Seuil.

———. 1975. *On tue un enfant*. Paris: Seuil.

Le Gaufey, Guy. 1994. *L'éviction de l'origine*. Paris: Les Éditions et Publications de l'École Lacanienne.

———. 1998. *Anatomie de la troisième personne*. Paris: Les Éditions et Publications de l'École Lacanienne.

Lévi-Strauss, Claude. 1963. *Structural Anthropology*. Translated by Claire Jacobson and Brooke Grundfest Schoepf. New York: Basic Books.

Maleval, Jean-Claude. 2000. *La forclusion du nom-du-père*. Paris: Seuil.

Marx, Karl. 1978. *The Marx-Engels Reader*. 2nd ed. Edited by Robert C. Tucker. New York: Norton.

Mathelin, Catherine. 1999. *Lacanian Psychotherapy with Children.* Translated by Susan Fairfield. New York: The Other Press.

May, Todd. 1997. *Reconsidering Difference.* University Park: Pennsylvania State University Press.

Miller, Jacques-Alain. 1966. "La suture." *Les cahiers pour l'analyse.* 1: 37–51.

———. 1968. "Action de la structure." *Cahiers pour l'analyse* 9: 93–105.

———. 1984. "D'une autre Lacan." *Ornicar?* 28: 49–57.

———. 1986-1987. *Extimité.* Unpublished seminar.

———. 1987. "La topologie dans l'ensemble de l'enseignement de Lacan." *Quarto.* 2: 13–29.

———. 1991a. "The Analytic Experience: Means, Ends, and Results." In *Lacan and The Subject of Language*, ed. Ellie Ragland-Sullivan and Mark Bracher. New York: Routledge, 83-99.

———. 1991b. "Language: Much Ado About What?" In *Lacan and the Subject of Language*, ed. Ellie Ragland-Sullivan and Mark Bracher. New York: Routledge, 21-35.

———. 1993-1994. *Donc.* Unpublished seminar.

———. 1996a. "Commentary on Lacan's Text." In *Reading Seminars I and II: Lacan's Return to Freud*, ed. Richard Feldstein, Bruce Fink, and Maire Jaanus. Albany: State University of New York Press, 422–428.

———. 1996b. "The Flirtatious Remark." Translated by Andres Zlotsky. *Umbra* 1: 87–102.

———. 1997-1998. *Le partenaire-symptome.* Unpublished.

———. 1998-1999. *L'expérience du réel dans la cure psychanalytique.* Unpublished.

———. 2001. *La tendresse des terroristes et autres letters ecrits par Jacques-Alain Miller à l'opinion éclairée.* Paris: Atelier de psychanalyse appliquée.

Milner, Jean-Claude. 1983. *Les noms indistincts.* Paris: Seuil.

Moyaert, Paul. 1994. *Ethiek en sublimatie.* Nijmegen: Sun.

Peirce, C. S. 1960. *Collected Papers: Volume II.* Cambridge, MA: Harvard University Press.

Pluth, Ed. 1999. "The Pauline Event?" Review of *Saint Paul: La fondation del'universalisme*, by Alain Badiou. *Theory and Event* 3.3: 11 pars. http://www.muse.jhu.edu/journals/theory_&_event/v003/3.3r_pluth.html

Pluth, Ed, and Dominiek Hoens. 2004. "What If the Other Is Stupid? Badiou and Lacan on Logical Time." In *Think Again: Alain Badiou and the Future of Philosophy*, ed. Peter Hallward. London: Continuum, 182–190.

Porge, Erik. 1988. "Une forme du sujet: la subjectivation. D'après *Le temps logique*." Littoral 25: 49–59.

———. 1997. *Les noms du père chez Jacques Lacan*. Ramonville Saint-Agne: Erès (Point Hors Ligne).

———. 2000. *Jacques Lacan: Un psychanalyste, Parcours d'un enseignment*. Toulouse: Points Hors Ligne.

Rabinovich, Diana. 1986-1987. Presentation in Jacques-Alain Miller, *Extimité* (1986–1987). Unpublished.

Raffoul, François. 1998. "Lacan and the Event of the Subject." *Cultural Semiosis: Tracing the Signifier*, ed. Hugh J. Silverman. New York: Routledge, 63–82.

Ragland-Sullivan, Ellie, and Mark Bracher, eds. 1991. *Lacan and the Subject of Language*. New York: Routledge.

Roudinesco, Elisabeth. 1993. *Jacques Lacan*. Paris: Fayard.

Salecl, Renata. 2000. *(Per)versions of Love and Hate*. London: Verso.

Sartre, Jean-Paul. 1956. *Being and Nothingness: A Phenomenological Essay on Ontology*. Translated by Hazel E. Barnes. New York: Washington Square Press.

Saussure, Ferdinand de. 1986. *Course in General Linguistics*. Edited by Charles Bally and Albert Sechehaye, with Albert Riedlinger. Translated by Roy Harris. La Salle, IL: Open Court Press.

Soler, Colette. 1995a. "The Subject and the Other (I)." In *Reading Seminar XI*, ed. Richard Feldstein, Bruce Fink, and Maire Jaanus. Albany: State University of New York Press, 39–44.

———. 1995b. "The Subject and the Other (II)." In *Reading Seminar XI*, ed. Richard Feldstein, Bruce Fink, and Maire Jaanus. Albany: State University of New York Press, 45–54.

———. 1996a. "The Symbolic Order (I)." In *Reading Seminars I and II*, eds. Richard Feldstein, Bruce Fink, and Maire Jaanus. Albany: State University of New York Press, 39–46.

———. 1996b. "The Symbolic Order (II)." In *Reading Seminars I and II*, eds. Richard Feldstein, Bruce Fink, and Maire Jaanus, Albany: State University of New York Press, 47–55.

———. 2001. *L'aventure litteraire*. Paris: Editions du Champ Lacanien.

Spinoza, Baruch. 1982 [1677]. *The Ethics and Selected Letters*. Translated by Samuel Shirley. Indianapolis, IN: Hackett.

Stavrakakis, Yannis. 1999. *Lacan and the Political*. New York: Routledge.

Védrine, Hélène. 2000. *Le sujet éclaté*. Paris: Le livre du poche.

Verhaeghe, Paul. 1994. *Klinische psychodiagnostiek vanuit Lacans discourstheorie*. Gent: Idesça.

———. 1996a. "The Desire of Freud in His Correspondence with Fliess: From Knowledge to Truth." *Umbra* 1: 103–108.

———. 1996b. *Tussen hysterie en vrouw*. 2d ed. Leuven: Acco.

———. 1999. "Subject and Body: Lacan's Struggle with the Real." *The Letter: Lacanian Perspectives on Psychoanalysis* 17: 79–119.

———. 2001. *Beyond Gender: From Subject to Drive*. New York: The Other Press.

Weber, Samuel. 1991. *Return to Freud: Jacques Lacan's Dislocation of Psychoanalysis*. Translated by Michael Levine. Cambridge, MA: Cambridge University Press.

Žižek, Slavoj. 1989. *The Sublime Object of Ideology*. London: Verso.

———. 1992. *Enjoy Your Symptom*! New York: Routledge.

———. 1993. *Tarrying with the Negative*. Durham, NC: Duke University Press.

———. 1999. *The Ticklish Subject*. London: Verso.

———. 2001. *On Belief*. London: Routledge.

Index